Piss Off!

How Drug Testing and Other Privacy Violations Are Alienating America's Youth

Laura L. Finley

Peter S. Finley

Common Courage Press   Monroe, Maine

Copyright © 2005 by Laura Finley and Peter S. Finley
All rights reserved.
Cover design by Matt Wuerker and Erica Bjerning
Cover photo Randy Allbritton Getty Images

ISBN 1-56751-296-8 paper
ISBN 1-56751- 297-6 cloth

**Library of Congress Cataloging-in-Publication Data is
available on request from the publisher**

Common Courage Press
121 Red Barn Road
Monroe, ME 04951
800-497-3207

FAX (207) 525-3068
orders-info@commoncouragepress.com

See our website for e versions of this book.
www.commoncouragepress.com

Printed in Canada
First Printing

We dedicate this book to our daughter Anya, in the womb at it's beginning and a year at it's completion. We know you will make the world a more peaceful place.

Acknowledgements

<u>Peter Finley</u>

I must thank my parents, Doug and Marilyn, for their endless support in my every endeavor, for encouraging critical thinking, and for instilling the belief that a job worth doing is worth doing well. I thank my brother Doug for our years of lively, thought provoking conversations on countless subjects and, most importantly, for consistently demonstrating that happiness can be rooted in risk taking. Finally, I owe my lovely wife (and co-author) Laura thanks for being the motivating force in my life.

<u>Laura Finley</u>

First, our utmost thanks goes to the kind folks who gave us feedback on drafts of the book. Professors Sue Caulfield and Hal Pepinsky offered much appreciated comments, as did friends and educators Alicia and Tom Greig. I wish to extend more specific gratitude to my mentors at Western Michigan University, who introduced me to a critical perspective. In particular I thank Dr. Caulfield for helping me balance this critical perspective with a desire for more humanistic interventions in all arms of criminal justice. I also thank my parents and my twin Sarah for their love and interest in my pursuits. To my husband and co-author Peter, let us always enjoy collaborating as we did on this project. Many more to come?!!

Contents

Preface
Why Kids Are Telling Adults to Piss Off!

The Mission Of This Book

> Uncontrolled search and seizure is one of the first and most effective weapons in the arsenal of every arbitrary government.
> —*Benninger v. U.S.* 330 U.S. 160

It is our hope to convince the reader that the search policies used in many schools are not only asinine, they are destructive. They are ineffective, not cost-efficient, and deny teens constitutionally guaranteed rights. They further the disintegration of human relationships and generally serve to alienate and piss off the next generation. Yet these policies persist and, under the Bush regime, have been expanded. Part of the explanation, as many of the chapters point out, is that schools merely reflect broader societal trends. Our war-making climate has certainly reduced civil liberties for all in the name of "safety." But there's more to it than simply the fact we are in an era of expanded governmental surveillance and diminished public rights, although this topic will receive ample attention. We propose five primary reasons for the persistence and expansion of school searches, all inter-related.

First, now that we've whipped up a nice moral panic about youth, there is a need to appear as though something is being done about the hyper violent thugs and pothead reprobates running rampant in our educational institutions. Second, reacting to the perceived problems in ways that demonize youth as a category allows adults off the hook for a) their role in creating the problem in the first place; b) not looking deeper for sources of the problems and implementing useful interventions; and c) for their own violence and addictions, much more egregious than those of most teens. Third, the teen-bashing, search and punishment business serves a number of functions in our society and is quite lucrative to the defenders of the status quo. Fourth, privacy-violating searches persist in schools because they are easier than the alternatives. Finally, the Republican agenda has been to consistently destroy public schooling. While the President felt comfortable asking for an additional $87 billion to "liberate" Iraqis, education remains woefully under-funded. The desired result apparently is to have better, i.e., private, schools for the children of the wealthy and table scraps for the rest. Of course, many Democrats also support this agenda; the distinction between the two parties is often in name only. President Bush's No Child Left Behind legislation is one extension of that effort. To the extent that schools spend scarce resources on surveillance and punishment instead of education, public schools become even less functional, and less palatable to those forced to reside there. What better way to support the end of public education than by turning it into a prison?

Lest the reader dismiss us as idealistic fools who are out of touch with the reality in high school, we rebut that this is precisely **why** we felt this book is necessary. We were both high school teachers for a number of years and know that kids are not as bad as they are often presented. We experienced first-hand many of the over-reactions to the hype about dangerous and/or wasted kids and their negative impact on both the individual and macro level. While certainly there are good people involved in schools who truly care for kids, we contend that a militaristic ideology has pervaded education and made it seem logical to wage war against kids, a war manifested in outrageous searches and severe punishments.

Piss Off explores the culture of meanness as it has manifested in our continued assault on students' privacy rights. It is divided into three parts: Part One provides the framework; Part Two describes the logistics of specific types of searches in schools; and Part Three addresses impact. Each chapter ends with questions designed for critical thinking and review, as well as topics for further inquiry. The Epilogue provides five ways teens can defend themselves in this assault.

Part One of the book contains the Prologue, an Introduction, and Chapter One, and is intended to lay a foundation for understanding current search policies in schools. The Prologue elaborates on the five points made above, demonstrating that being a teen alone is enough to be suspect; attendance in a public school compounds the problem. The Introduction addresses the "big picture": How is it we've come down this far down the surveillance highway? Chapter One shows how the groundwork for the assault on student privacy rights has been laid via Supreme Court decisions. Three cases, 1985's *T.L.O v. New Jersey*; 1995's *Vernonia School District v. Acton*; and 2002's *Earls v. Pottawatomie School District*, are detailed in order to describe the legal precedents to the atrocities schools commit in the name of safety and being drug free.

Part Two describes five types of searches conducted at schools across America. For each selected cases are discussed and critiqued. In Chapter Two we address the following questions: Under what conditions can school officials search student lockers? What about vehicle, or personal items within lockers or vehicles? What happens if police are involved? Are anonymous tips enough cause to search students? From whom and under what circumstances? Chapter Three describes metal detector and canine searches. In this chapter we question the cost, effectiveness, prevalence, and impact of such searches. Chapter Four includes examples of sensory-based searches as well as the use of snitches in schools. Can smell, dress, or a student's location on campus be enough cause to search them? Who is involved in school snitching? What impact does the snitch culture have on the school climate? The primary question addressed in Chapter Five is how can such an atrocity as the strip-searching of students **ever** be justified? Chapter Six addresses the case of school drug testing, both for athletes as well as for those in other extra-curricular activities. The chapter explores briefly how we came to collect urine in schools. It also raises questions about the cost, accuracy, potential for error, and effectiveness of drug testing programs.

Part Three takes a more detailed look at the impact of school searches. Chapter Seven questions the effectiveness of searches as a whole! Are they deterrents, as many suggest? Chapter Eight is focused on micro-level impact. It describes how we continue to erode student's due process rights, addressing who is most likely harmed by our search and punishment policies and in what ways they are hurt. How are search policies connected to repressive punishments, like Zero Tolerance laws? Chapter Nine begins with a sociological exploration of why we have turned to invasive and repressive school search and punishment policies. The focus is on how the militarization of all U.S institutions, especially schools, precludes the use of more empathic approaches.

Prologue

The Crime—
Living While Adolescent

Did you know America ranks the lowest in education but the highest in drug use? It's nice to be number one, but we can fix that. All we need to do is start the war on education. If it's anywhere near as successful as our war on drugs, in no time we'll all be hooked on phonics.

—Leighann Lord

And on the seventh day, God stepped back and said 'There is my creation, perfect in every way...oh, damn it, I left pot all over the place. Now they'll think I want them to smoke it...Now I have to create republicans.

—Bill Hicks

Reason One: We Gotta Do SOMETHING!

The first and most simple reason why school officials often crap all over their students' privacy rights is that they, like politicians, feel the need to do something about the perceived problems of school violence and drug use by teens. As we will outline, the problems are really much more minor than the public is told. But, as every sociologist knows, perception is more important than reality. After the two minutes of hatred of teens (Orwell had it wrong-it's usually more like a steady diet than two minutes), everyone's in an emotional frenzy and feels the pressure to react. In a vicious cycle of teen repression, the media convince the public teens are evil and destined to shoot up their schools and hook your baby on drugs. Concurrent with the increase in crime coverage has been more prolific use of opinion polling. Opinion polls show the government the public does indeed feel there's a problem and is demanding a solution. The government and/or school officials use these opinion polls to justify their repressive actions, claiming they are only giving the people what they want. And they feed the stories of these isolated incidents to the media, who continue to cover the issues and reinforce the perception of a problem.

Since we are a militarized society, this ideology frames the responses that the public advocates and that politicians suggest. Most importantly, these responses treat teens as the enemy and ignore structural roots of the problem. As Victor Kappeler, Mark Blumberg and Gary Potter explain in *The Mythology of Crime and Criminal Justice*, it is common for politicians to advocate use of the most severe sanctions at the pinnacle of sensationalism over an issue and to promote the notion that existing solutions will work if we simply do more of them.[1] Criminologist Matthew Robinson argues similarly, saying that crime is framed as a failure of criminal justice (this part is true), so if we allow criminal justice broader influence, they'll be able to catch the baddies and prevent crime (this part is false).[2] So if schools still have kids who toke on the occasional wacky tobaccy despite drug-testing the athletes, widen the scope of your search and test **everyone** involved in extracurriculars. Hell, just test the entire student body, then we're bound to catch us some druggies. Don't let those pesky civil liberties stop you from doing what it takes to **claim** you are drug and violence free!

Administrators have indeed reported feeling a need to do something about school shootings, despite their rarity. A nationwide survey found that the number one reason for updating security, cited by 56% of the respondents, was in response to publicity in the news. Only six percent reported updating or changing security due to an **actual** incident or threat at their school.[3] The authors' experience is consistent with these findings; we both worked at schools that followed the post-Columbine paranoia with a variety of technological and punitive strategies, despite there being no evidence of a direct threat at either location.

Defocusing Tactics

The second reason why invasive school searches persist is because they divert attention from issues with adults. They do this in three primary ways; by shifting attention from adult's role in creating the problems; by absolving adults of responsibility for addressing the problems appropriately; and by deflecting scrutiny from the fact that adults have bigger problems than do kids. First, adults are, at least in part, responsible for the genesis of violent and/or drug using kids. Kids do what they see adults doing. As Mike Males, author of *Scapegoat Generation* and *Framing Youth: Ten Myths About the Next Generation*, succinctly states, "Adults' behaviors set the standards for society."[4] In fact, teen violence and adult violence (or drug use) are "so interrelated with adult violence that analyzing it separately obscures more than it illuminates."[5] According to Kirk Astroth, extension specialist in the state 4-H office at Montana State University in Bozeman, today's teens generally lead healthier lives than adults. They have lower rates of suicide, violent death, unwed pregnancy, drug abuse, smoking, and drunk driving.[6] Most teens that drink or use drugs do so with their parents.[7] Additionally, some of the worst drug problems among youth are those born of their parents' addictions. The primary reason for foster placements is parental neglect as a result of drug or alcohol addiction.[8] One of the strongest predictors of adult violence is whether an individual suffered from abuse as a child. Even worse is when that abuse was at the hands of a parent, who is supposed to love and protect, not demean and harm.[9]

Further, simply saying one thing and doing another doesn't fly. Teens have pretty well developed shit-detectors. Further evidence that they are rational critters able to understand consequences is they know that the slick ad campaigns created by adults are so-much-crap. One ad campaign, part of a $1 billion, five-year effort to "send a signal to young people" and to "break the back of the drug culture" featured a pretty young lady busting up the kitchen with a frying pan in order to allegedly show how drugs wreck families. Yet more families are certainly wrecked by adult drug addiction, starting with those who poison their children in womb, than are by out-of-control teens.[10] Teens are unlikely to believe that they're putting the nation at risk of terrorism by smoking a joint. In fact, such complete lunacy may only convince them to disregard all anti-drug messages, regardless of their validity. In a boy-who-cries-wolf phenomenon, few will believe a government that repeatedly issues bold-faced prevarications. Teens see the hypocrisy of adults (especially those in authority positions) who advocate harsh punishments for small-time drug offenders when they themselves were once small-time drug offenders lucky enough to avoid sanction (Presidents Clinton and Bush II, for example).[11] As Richard DeGrandpre explains in *Ritalin Nation*, "the widespread use of Ritalin has a normalizing effect on kids' overall views of drugs and drug taking. Despite all the 'just say no" slogans, the 'just do it' manner in which children are now prescribed psychotropic drugs, from Prozac to Ritalin, greatly undermines the anitdrug rhetoric of saying no."[12] Yet ad campaigns and political rhetoric are predicated on the assumption of a problem and reify for the public the need to do something, hence school searches.

By ignoring the fact that adults shape what kids do we can place the blame solely at the individual level. That way we can justify dropping the hammer on kids, arguing, "they're old enough to know better" and "they chose to act like animals." Males offers a solution: "If adults don't like the way teenagers act, the solution is not to turn a generation over to the professional treaters and imprisoners who have markedly worsened matters over the last decade, but to change our behaviors and the conditions in which youth are raised."[13] Lest the reader be confused, when we discuss blame at the individual level, we're not referring to individual teens. Teens are generally categorized as a group of demon seeds waiting to reek carnage. Rather, by placing the blame at the individual level we ignore structural causes, chalking any and all teen deviance up to some form of innate pathology rather than the fact that we have abandoned them fiscally, emotionally, and in virtually every conceivable way. "If every kid was bad, parents by definition were not to blame."[14] Kids today are so bad they apparently don't deserve our money, time, love, etc. What they apparently need, however, is our moralizing contempt that results in constant suspicion and perpetual surveillance.

Adults should also bear some responsibility for failing to address the causes of these so-called teen social problems and for failing to devise appropriate interventions. "Today's mythology that most or all youths are 'at risk' scatters valuable resources and dilutes efforts to help the minority of youths who are genuinely troubled."[15] Adults are in control of all our major institutions, including schools. Teens generally have no voice whatsoever (although they can demand one-see the Epilogue). Invasive school searches are **their** doing. It's difficult to imagine, were we to ever actually allow teens input into school policies in any sort of meaningful way, a group of them suggesting the best way to deal with student drug experimentation is to assess the girth of their crotches or demand their urine in a Dixie cup. School search policies that alienate and piss off youth persist because adults want tighter control over the kids they fear.

It follows that adults also dream up the punishments that hammer kids while going lightly on their own demographic. Mike Males provides an example in *Scapegoat Generation*. In 1987 a school district in Montana stripped a varsity letter from an athlete accused of having a party in which underage drinking occurred, yet the same district felt it unnecessary to take any action when a 31-year old coach pleaded guilty to a drunken assault against a 19-year-old woman.[16] One of the authors of this book taught at a midwestern high school where a faculty member was not only arrested and charged with drunken driving, but was found in possession of marijuana. Although initially he was fired, the district reinstated him when they had difficulty finding another teacher qualified to fill his slot. We like the fact that he was given a second chance, but feel pretty confident that no students would be offered similar chances. It's all about protecting your own, it seems. And, despite the fact that this teacher is a documented drug user, no one is rallying to demand he be drug-tested before work each day.

Adults should be wise enough that, when they think teens

might be suffering from some legitimate (not mediated) problem, they thoroughly assess what might be the root of the problem before jumping willy-nilly into implementing repressive policies and purchasing technological pseudo-safety devices. As Social Psychologist Elliot Aronson points out in *Nobody Left To Hate*,

> Young mass murderers don't mow down their neighbors or shoot up the local video arcade. They kill their classmates and teachers, and sometimes themselves, in or around the school building itself. Looking for root causes in individual pathology is an approach that seems sensible on the surface, but it does not get to the root of the problem. What is it about the atmosphere in schools themselves that makes these young people so desperate, diabolical and callous?[17]

We are definitely **not** arguing that all educators are dumb. Our case is simply that adults are so immersed in a militaristic, blame-the-victim culture that they often cannot see the bigger picture. There are also some who simply do not **want** to see it. To see it would be to acknowledge that we have full-scale abandoned kids in this country. "Today's young people are scapegoated by an adult generation that is abandoning them," said Lori Nelson, youth and education director for Los Angeles's National Conference on Communities and Justice.[18] By failing to see the bigger picture, we continue the tendency to do more of the same; more money on metal detectors, more cops on campus, more students drug tested, more, more, more.

Demonizing teens in the media, and using those flawed images to justify flawed discipline policy, also serves to divert attention from the group with the true problems: adults. It is always comforting to demonize others, as it allows us to clarify that we're OK. If "they" are the bad guys, if "they" have the problem, and I'm not one of "them," then I must be one of the good guys. And we need to nail those bad guys with the most severe punishments in order to "deter" them and make them more wholesome, like us. In regard to crime-related issues, this is a bunch of hooey. Research has shown that 90% of all Americans have committed some crime for which they could be incarcerated.[19] In other words, we're not so different from "them."

Adults are more violent and use (and abuse) drugs at much greater rates than do teens. Just as the government now uses 9/11 to justify **everything** (as in, "we need to look at what you checked out at the library, you know, because of 9/11), school shootings (or the fear of them) have been the catalyst for many of our search and discipline policies.[20] Columbine provided many examples of the unquestioning support for military-style government interventions. For instance, in the summer following the shooting police agencies across the country decided to train their SWAT teams (which we have more of than ever, due to our increased militarization) to assault local schools. They conducted mock raids that were not only reported but applauded in the media. "CBS News discovered that a patchwork strategy is starting to evolve and many have one thing in common: the grownups are starting to take control of the schools again, and they're imposing strict grownup controls," stated the reporter solemnly, amidst a backdrop of heavily-armed and garbed SWAT members "deploying" down a school hallway.[21] More recently, a South Carolina High School was raided by police, SWAT style, who were searching for drugs and weapons. Armed officers ordered students to hit the ground while dogs sniffed their backpacks. No contraband was uncovered. Responding to the lawsuit about the atrocity of armed officers hovering menacingly above cowering students while dogs root through their belongings, the Berkeley County School District has argued the raid was justified and reasonable in scope. Compared to what?

The shootings in Pearl, West Paducah, Jonesboro, Edinboro, and Springfield resulted in eleven deaths over eight months, the same as the average number of kids killed by their own parents in **two days** in the United States.[22] On the same day as the Jonesboro shooting, a mother used duct tape to suffocate her three children. Aside from those involved in the criminal case and the immediate parties involved, who knows about this? But virtually every American who hasn't lived in a cave has heard of Andrew Golden and Mitchell Johnson, the Jonesboro shooters. While we're certainly not minimizing the fact that people died in these school shootings, the inordinate amount of attention paid to them in comparison to the very little given to adults who murder their own offspring is unsettling. Between 1980 and 1997, the era of the "superpredator" teen, the amount of felonies committed by those over 30 increased a whopping 148%, far greater than the increases for any other age group, especially youth.[23] "Headlining 'children killing children' is the latest official ploy to pretend to care for America's young while advancing political anti-youth agendas."[24] We say that our concern is about gun violence, but is it really? Or is it simply fear of teenagers? Because if we were truly concerned about gun violence, we'd worry about the fact that more than half of all the young people who die from gun shots are not killed by their peers, but by adults who have the legal right to own a gun. We already have legislation barring adolescents from arming themselves so clearly when kids shoot up their schools some adult, be it their parents, gun manufacturers or wholesalers, or educators, failed. The point is that when we treat kids as criminals, as our school search policies often do, we help to maintain the perception that they **are** criminals and continue the cycle of repression.

Likewise, adults today have far greater problems with drugs than do teens. Since 1980, the number of adults in their 30s to 40s taken to hospitals for cocaine or heroin overdoses rose an appalling 2500%.[25] The adult drug death rate in the mid 1990s was nearly ten times that of adolescents.[26] New research announced in July 2003 indicates that drug addiction is the hidden scourge among seniors. Yep, that's right, researchers found that at least 17% of all Americans age 55 or older have either alcohol or drug problems or both.[27] So where are the calls for drug testing before they pick up their Bingo cards? How about random searches of their sewing baskets and denture cases? The 2002 Drug Abuse Warning Network (DAWN) survey found a 20 percent increase in emergency room visits involving narcotic pain medications.[28] Despite claims to "put children first," the Clinton administration was virulently anti-teen. Drug-policy chief Lee Brown and Health and Human

Services leader Donna Shalala ignored evidence of skyrocketing heroin and cocaine deaths among middle-agers in order to go after the casual marijuana using teen.[29]

It's All About the Status Quo

We should know better, but we don't. The third reason for the persistence of school search policies is they serve a number of functions for the maintenance of the status quo. As Robinson states, whether intended or not, the war on crime, and all it's ideological counterparts, benefit those in power. And those people have absolutely no incentive to change. Filmmaker and author Michael Moore asserts that, "it is my firm belief that Bush and his cronies (especially Attorney General John Ashcroft) have only one goal in mind; to scare the bejesus out of us so that whatever bill they want passed, whatever power they want Congress to give them, we will happily hand it over."[30] The quest for more power always involves neutralizing threats to that power; what better way than to so diminish the privacy rights of children that they cannot even remember they **have** such rights?

The premier function of our war on teens is that it lines the pockets for many people quite nicely. That certain agencies and industries might foster the panic about teen violence and drug abuse is not surprising. The "discovery" of a teen drinking problem in the mid-1970s was largely a concoction of the newly founded National Institute on Alcohol Abuse and Alcoholism.[31] By telling people that teens have a problem but, by George, our metal detector-drug dog-video-camera etc. will fix it for you, technocrats feed the panic and stuff their wallets. As James Redden maintains in *Snitch Culture*, "one of the most important developments in the growth of the Snitch Culture is the large and growing role played by media-savvy, politically-oriented advocacy groups."[32] Such groups "publish dubious reports identifying new threats for the government to pursue, testify in support of increased surveillance operations at legislative hearings, and frequently help craft the final versions of the new programs produced by their lobbying."[33] As a result of this type of lobbying, government officials, "feel free to spawn myths of crime and justice and to waste valuable resources on ineffective crime control practices that expand the crime control industry."[34]

Even liberal do-gooder groups have made a buck or two off fueling the myth of teen epidemic-level deviance.

> Well-intentioned youth services justified overstatement on the grounds that modern funders would not turn loose of bucks unless grantees could present evidence of a serious teenage menace. To survive in a hardening climate, sex education, drug and alcohol abuse prevention, gun control, media reform, mental health, and other progressive services wildly hyped youth misbehaviors. Only we, programmers intoned, stand between your wealthy fundee's pleasant suburb-ville and the legions of gnashing superpredators downtown.[35]

Sandia National Laboratories in Albuquerque, New Mexico has certainly cashed in. "With the cold war winding down, this Energy Dept. facility, which was dedicated to providing security for the U.S nuclear arsenal for 50 years, has turned to policing the blackboard jungle."[36] "Rent-a-cops" assigned to schools make a nice wage for assisting in the subjugation of youth, a job pretty darn easy (and safe) in comparison to policing certain areas. Especially those whose primary duty is to man the metal detector. And, as we document in subsequent chapters, snitching can provide an income boost as well. It sure does outside of schools, where the Justice Department employs thousands of people **full-time** to rat on others.[37]

School searches, a.k.a. privacy invasions, also provide some with a career. The war on drugs has been an especially useful method of increasing the number of bureaucrats in Washington, at the state and local level, and even in schools. This is typically at the expense of teens, minorities, and the poor, of course. Schools employ faculty-often known by students as the ass-kickers- whose only job is to deal with discipline. Not a position likely to be necessary if schools did not drum up a lot of kids to punish via locker searches, etc. Some school violence consultants have even capitalized on the post-Columbine paranoia to make the rounds advocating repressive measure and garnering a modest fee to do so.

Another function of our teen hatred and subsequent search policies is that it helps adults to identify the "enemy" and to consequently avoid contact with them whenever possible. In fact, if we can write off a whole generation as drug loser criminals, we don't even have to think about them. We simply up the social control efforts, and turn our minds to more important concerns than our children. Rather than dealing in reality, we gawk at young people on reality TV. Ma and Pa can assure themselves that the school will take care of any problems with their kid.

Hot damn do evil teens make nice pop culture villains as well. Corporate media's support for the manufactured crises of school violence and teen drug use has included news and entertainment programming to public service announcements. Of course, this collusion between media and government to vilify undesirables is not new; there is a long and sordid history of demonizing some people or things to push forward an agenda, such as films that depicted Japanese soldiers as exceedingly barbaric during World War II or the monolithic treatment of Arabic peoples as terrorists in recent years.[38] An example of the ways that government and media are in bed together was exposed by *Salon* magazine in January 2000. Reporter Daniel Forbes revealed that the Office of National Drug Control Policy (ONDCP) secretly paid six major television networks $25 million to include anti-drug themes into popular shows, including *ER, Beverly Hills 90210,* and *The Drew Carey Show.* Even occasional recreational users were to be portrayed as losers or psychopaths. This was part of a bigger program to spend $1 billion over five years on anti-drug ads, starting in 1998. The number of shows with anti-drug themes, according to a White House report, went from 32 in March 1998 to 109 in the winter of 1999. Drug Czar Barry McCaffrey, the brains behind the plan, announced in 2000 that he planned to work closely with Hollywood in order to ensure that films too adhered to the party-line; drugs are bad, teens are bad.[39] It becomes very easy to justify repressive policies when every message adults see is that teen violence and drug use is out of control.

The Easy Way Out

Since adults feel they **have** to react to the scourge of school shooters and druggie burnouts, we use invasive, repressive, and alienating search policies is because they are easy. It's not difficult to find a company who will sell you a metal detector or who will place the stick in the Dixie cup and record if it changes color. These companies are all over. A simple google search for "School Drug Testing" or "School Metal Detectors" reveals a number of companies eager to cash in on the teen fear industry. It's far easier to call the cops and request a visit from Sparky the drug dog than to get to know your student body and to assess how many might be struggling with drug problems. Summing up three of our reasons why schools seem to have little trouble instituting privacy violating "security" measures, Bonnie Hedrick, director of the Ohio Prevention & Education Resource Center at the University of Cincinnati stated, "We're turning to high tech because it's a quick fix and something tangible that administrators can show to their community as their way of securing school premises." And, oh yeah, "Vendors of this technology have seized this opportunity to make money."[40]

Finally, invasive search policies and harsh punishments are a way to support the Republican agenda of privatizing education. According to education specialist Alfie Kohn, even the term "reform" has been co-opted by those with an agenda of ending public schooling. Tongue-in-cheek, Kohn explains that the right has now labeled those who might defend public schools as lacking vision and courage. He says that it is like a memo was circulated stating "Attention. Effective immediately, all our efforts to privatize the schools will be known as 'reform,' and any opposition to those efforts will be known as anti-reform'. That is all."[41] Like the "reform" of environmental laws, which have been eliminated or

extremely diluted, the "reform" of education is following in this
vein. As Kohn explains, some will indeed benefit from this reform,
but it will not be kids.[42] No Child Left Behind, also known as No
Child Left Untested, No Corporation Left Behind, and No Child's
Behind Left, has even been criticized by politicians. Senator James
Jeffords, who chaired the Senate committee on education from
1997 to 2001, called the law "a back-door maneuver that will let
the private sector take over public education, something the
Republicans have wanted for years."[43] Search policies play into
this effort because, as Kohn maintains, "the engine of this legisla-
tion is punishment. NCLB is designed to humiliate and hurt the
schools that, according to its own warped standards, most need
help. Families at those schools are given a green light to abandon
them-and, specifically, to transfer to other schools that don't want
them and probably can't handle them."[44] According to Augustina
Reyes of the University of Houston, "If teachers are told, 'Your
scores go down, you lose your job,' all of a sudden your values shift
very quickly. Teachers think 'With bad kids in my class, I'll have
lower achievement on my tests, so I'll use discretion and remove
that kid'."[45] Mark Soler of the Youth Law Center concurs:
"Principals want to get rid of kids they perceive as trouble."[46]

Although it is not our intention in this book to offer a vast
array of solutions, what schools need to do is quite clear and really
very simple. Stop treating kids as though they're all suspect and
return to not just teaching about civil liberties, but practicing them
as well. If we continue to fail in providing our young people with
their constitutionally guaranteed rights, who can blame them for
telling us all to piss off?

QUESTIONS FOR REVIEW
AND CRITICAL THINKING

In what ways does the media demonize teens, according to
the authors? Do you agree? Is there any variation by type of media,
i.e, film, television, or music? Are there any positive portrayals of
teens?

How have schools responded to Columbine? Do you agree these responses have been extreme in many cases?

What support do the author's offer for the contention that adults are more violent and have greater drug problems than teens? Do you feel this is true?

Have there been any effective anti-drug campaigns?

EXTENSION QUESTIONS AND ACTIVITIES

Are adults truly worse than teens in regard to smoking? Unwed pregnancies? Drinking and drinking-related crimes? Support your argument.

What other groups have been demonized to justify repressive treatment historically? Currently?

Research more about the ways that September 11th has been used to justify civil liberties violations. Who has or stands to profit from these arrangements?

Introduction
Down the Surveillance Highway

> Those who would give up essential liberty to purchase a little temporary safety deserve neither liberty nor safety.
>
> —Benjamin Franklin

> We are discreet sheep. We wait to see how the drove is going, and then go with the drove.
>
> —Mark Twain.

Crotching drugs?" Most Americans are probably unfamiliar with the term, and certainly the idea, that someone might stash their stash in their private region. When we do think about the concept it probably conjures up images of serious drug couriers, not high school special education students. A "crotching" allegation, however, was alleged against a male behaviorally disordered student in the case of Cornfield by Lewis in 1993.[1] It was made by a female teachers' aide, who one day felt that this student's genitals looked larger than usual. After reporting this observation (one wonders what she was doing observing this area in the first place) to the student's teacher and the school's dean, they decided to conduct a strip search. Since the student was under-age they called his mother, who denied permission to search her son. The school proceeded to conduct the search anyways, in the name of school security. He was first taken to the locker room where he was forced to strip to his underwear, was patted down, and even made to hold out his underwear so that they could see nothing was tucked inside. More incredibly, when these measures produced nothing, he was forced to strip completely nude. This was obviously humiliating, especially since school officials found nothing but his natural endowment. His family decided to seek legal recourse, arguing that this was a case of unconstitutional search and seizure, but it was to no avail. The search was deemed justifiable and reasonable by the 7th circuit court.

While this sounds like it can only be part of a cheesy made-for-television movie or a daytime talk show episode, this scenario describes a **real** case. And, while perhaps an especially egregious example of a school's abuse of power and of students' lack of privacy, it is by no means unusual. One would think that Americans would be appalled at such cases. Yet most remain unaware that such things occur, and when they do find out, are generally supportive or at least not critical of school officials. Indicative of adults' attitudes toward teens, a 1997 report from Public Agenda, a non-profit policy group, found that 58% of adults surveyed think today's children and teens will make the world a worse place, or at best, no different, when they grow up.[2] In fact, students in American public schools are subject to a plethora of searches, often on a daily basis, that are considered constitutional in the name of "school safety" or "educational mission." It is ironic that one of the primary directives of our public school system is to educate students in civic virtue, yet we deny them constitutionally guaranteed civil rights. As Louis Brandeis said, "Experience should teach us to be most on our guard to protect liberty when the government's purposes are beneficent." So, why do we do this? Because we've been told how bad our kids are and that we **need** to respond punitively to get them in line and to save ourselves from the onslaught of teen "superpredators." All this is framed by a culture that is supportive of us vs. them approaches that have increasingly eroded privacy in many arenas, not just public schools.

Scare Tactics

We have been snowed into thinking that teen drug and alcohol abuse is a grievous concern. Of course, we all "know" that schools are just full of teens and their drugs, right? Wrong! In the war-on-drugs, scapegoat-youth climate we are currently in, teen drug use has been dramatically distorted. Listening to politicians, you would think that teens are all druggie wastoids. As Mike Males maintains, "The teenage drug crisis is a myth. It was concocted and maintained for political convenience."[3] Here's an example of political drug scare rhetoric: Speaker Denny Hastert's website states, "Drug use is at epidemic levels: Every day parents, teachers and community leaders confirm our worst fears about teenage drug use- not only has the overall number of kids trying drugs increased significantly, but they are using drugs in greater amounts, more frequently, and at younger ages."[4] In reality, the adult rate for drug-related deaths is ten times that of teens, and adults constitute 97% of the emergency room treatment for illegal drugs.[5] According to Males, if surveys are accurate, half of 12-17 year olds never used illegal drugs as juniors or seniors. Of those who have used them, only nine percent use once a month or more, and 80% of this use is marijuana. Contrary to popular opinion, teens use milder drugs, and do so in lower quantities and less frequently than do adults.[6] Further, Monitoring the Future surveys indicate that, on the whole, teen drug use is on the decline and has been since the mid 1990s. Especially significant drops have occurred in the use of heroin and crack cocaine, and even the use of ecstasy, one of the latest media demons, has begun to slow. The 2003 Monitoring the Future survey found an eleven percent decline in drug use by 8th, 10th, and 12th grade students. According to a press release by the National Institute on Drug Abuse, that reduction translates into 400,000 teen drug users in just the last two years.[7] These data are corroborated by other surveys, including those done by PRIDE (Parents' Resource Institute for Drug Education) and the National Household Survey of Drug Abuse.[8] Further, when teens do use drugs and alcohol, they most often do it **with an adult present**.[9] It's curious, then, where Hastert gets his numbers. They certainly serve a political agenda, though.

Of course these data have flaws, as do any statistics. For one, kids may not respond truthfully to pollsters asking about their illegal activities. Yet as Males has noted, other non-self report data tends to show lower, not higher, rates of usage.[10] Second, surveys conducted at school miss a good portion of students, and perhaps those most likely to use drugs; drop-outs, homeless students, and those who are chronically truant. Yet, despite these flaws, many recognize that such surveys measure one thing reliably: drug

trends. Trends show us group usage rates over time. Since there is no reason to believe that kids are more (or less) likely to lie about their usage now, self-reports offer us this macro-level information. Further, since the focus here is on school-related interventions to eliminate the so-called drug problem, what drug use is actually happening in schools is of vital importance.

Teens: A Critical Focus of the War on Drugs?

Yet, despite the evidence that kids are using less drugs and are not the primary drug-using problem in the U.S., our drug war has increasingly been targeted at them. A key point in the war was the first President George Bush's 1989 speech, baggie of crack in hand, about how easy it is for kids to purchase drugs. Despite the fact that Bush's cronies bribed a young African American male to find them drugs in the park across from the White House (he didn't even know where the White House was at first!), the number of citizens who rated drugs as the number one problem in the country rose from an already high 27% prior to the speech to 69% afterwards.[11] The media, of course, seized onto this scenario, as they regularly do with other sensationalistic pieces like it. "Bombarded by the messages of anti-drug bureaucrats, journalists readily embraced the official version of the drug problem."[12] Slick advertising campaigns clearly illustrate that the war on drugs has oft been targeted at youth. For instance, the feds authorized a $10 million ad campaign that premiered during the Superbowl. The premise of this new campaign? If you use drugs, you are abetting the enemy and supporting terrorism. As Huffington proclaims, "Apparently, in The World According to George W. Bush and his drug czar, John Walters, the kids smoking a joint at a party is the moral equivalent of supporting Osama bin Laden or Mohammed Atta."[13] One must wonder whether the $10 million dollars, with $3.5 alone required to air the ads during the Superbowl, was money well spent. And the cost of this particular campaign was merely a fraction of the $130 million spent each year on anti-drug ads. A current anti-drug advertising campaign by the Partnership For A Drug-Free America encourages parents to take invasive measures, such as searching their child's bedroom, in order to keep him or her off drugs, and, amusingly, depicts students as thanking their parents for their efforts! In sum, the drug war,

> Counts on the quietude of the media, whose own car has now been hooked up to the gravy train via a promised billion-dollar anti-drug ad campaign. It counts on maddeningly foolish attitudes such as those the American public expressed toward the war on Vietnam and now the war on drugs-the battle is wrong, destructive, and pointless, but let's escalate until a few hundred thousand more casualties accrue.[14]

We are a drug culture, despite our protestations otherwise. We drug ourselves, literally and figuratively, to "fix" our problems, for simple escape, or even for recreation, yet tell our kids that drug use is bad and expect that they'll understand and be able to distinguish between what we arbitrarily decide are "good" and "bad" drugs. Ritalin is an **amphetamine,** but a good one? The 1980s punk rock band The Dead Kennedys captures this notion nicely in their song, "Drug Me." They state, "I don't want to think. Don't make me care. I wanna melt in with the group. I need the balls to leap out of my shell."[15]

Results of the Drug War Mentality in Schools

This rhetorical attack on teens has been paralleled by aggressive police action and a siege mentality in schools. As Males chronicles, there was a 130.3% rise in drug arrests for teens between 1989 and 1996. Arrest rates for adults also increased, but by a much lesser 29%.[16] Canine searches and drug tests in particular have been used to root out these adolescent users and dealers. So, some argue, if drugs **are** found through these measures, aren't tests and searches worth doing? If we can clean the drugs out of our schools aren't we obligated to do so in any way possible? While seemingly intuitive, this logic breaks down on several different fronts. First, it assumes that these measures are indeed an effective way to root out drugs. The fact is, few canine searches or drug tests turn up the stash; in a California school with 8000 students canine searches revealed **no** drugs. At Vernonia School District, a school with a "major drug crisis," only three positive drug tests were found in over 500 tests of athletes conducted over four years.[17] Of the 505 students who were tested at Tecumseh High School in Oklahoma City (the situation that prompted the *Earls* case in 2002), only three students tested positive.[18] Those students who do have drugs with them at school, in the authors' experience, were quick to outsmart the use of canine searches. Knowing that the dogs cannot legally sniff a student's person, joints and other pills simply ended up deep in jeans pockets. "Congratulations, we're a drug free school," the principal would announce amidst snickers by students and staff who knew or suspected the truth. In addition, there are myriad ways for students to evade drug tests. Since drug testing officials now know of many of them, the response has been to make the tests ever more intrusive. For instance, since testers became aware that students were finding ways to substitute or switch urine samples, many tests now require a tester to actually **watch** the students urinate, rather than listen outside the stall door.

This logic also ignores the fact that such policies might alienate students and undermine the educational mission of schools. Of course, the Supreme Court has paid lip-service to the fact that neither students nor teachers shed their rights at the schoolhouse door; in practice, they have undermined such rights with their decisions, and lower courts generally favor schools in interpreting case decisions. Being an adolescent is now probable cause, despite the evidence that adults, not teens, suffer from more drug addictions. Adults, too, are suffering from intrusive drug testing in the workplace, as will be described later. Thus, "trial by vial" has become an accepted part of America's war on drugs.

Why Repress Teens?
Sounds Good, Cheap, and Easy

Of course, we **have** to do this, because **not** to demonize youth might force some to shift their attention to adults, those who have political, social and economic power. No politician wants to alienate the voter base, but kids are fair game. According to Males, "The art of successful politicking of wedge issues requires blaming vexing national problems on unpopular groups *outside* of the constituencies candidates wish to flatter. By definition, no major political interests would be crazy enough to blame the cohort most known for Big Voting -over-30 adults, whites, 'soccer moms,'-for the worsening state of what this same cohort calls the Big Issuecrime."[19] Further, such anti-teen rhetoric conjures up support for punitive and invasive policies that, in many cases, are financially lucrative, in addition to being a politician's sound-bite dream. Public spending on criminal justice reaches over $100 billion per year, while providing 420,000 jobs in state and federal corrections and 228,000 jobs in local jails.[20] Further, "the popular media seems to see its role as one of uncritically sensationalizing whatever assertions officials utter,"[21] which translates to mean decrying the "moral breakdown" of America, led by today's youth.

Not Just Druggies, They're Thugs Too

"School violence" has provided another rallying cry for punitive policies that invade students' rights to privacy. Yet again, politicians and pundits have excelled at convincing the American citizenry that, while the schools are trying their best to educate students, they are "becoming a resting place for criminals."[22] This concern over school safety more accurately reflects an explosion of media coverage than a real problem. As Sam Smith, commenting on the coverage of the Columbine high shooting, asserted, "One reason America has been moving so effortlessly into a post-constitutional, post-democratic era has been the willingness of the mass media to terrorize the public with stories and images of a country out of control."[23]

School violence can accurately be called a crime myth. According to Criminologists Victor Kappeler, Mark Blumberg, and Gary Potter in *The Mythology of Crime and Criminal Justice*, "crime myths are real in the minds of their believers and have definite social consequences. Crime myths have numerous effects on our perceptions; we may not even be conscious that they are at work."[24]

Most Americans, however, hold on to the nostalgic myth of the "good old days" in school, where the so-called biggest problems were gum-chewing, giggling, talking, and running in the halls. This narrow list of 1930s school problems is a hoax—many if not most of today's problems existed back then. But we have bought into that image, believing that kids today are more criminal than ever before. Thus they require "tough love" interventions. A judge in a privacy-related case harkens back to the good old days, stating that, "crumpled balls of paper, and, at worst, the bully's fists, were the weapons of choice."[25] This is in stark contrast to school shootings like those at Paducah, Columbine, etc. In reality, however, students have a one in a million chance of dying at school, and violence committed against children outside of the school premises occurs forty times more frequently.[26] Only one in ten public schools have reported **any** incidents of violence **ever**.[27] As Vincent Schiraldi, director of the Justice Policy Institute, has stated, "Today's seniors are no more likely than their parents were to be assaulted, injured, threatened or robbed in high school. Ironically, today's seniors are much more likely to be suspended than their parents were. We need to question why a well-behaved generation is being so severely punished by being denied access to education."[28]

But schools all over, with the citizen's support, have responded to this moral panic by implementing punitive, reactionary measures such as metal detectors, officers on campus, drug testing, and dress codes. Filmmaker and author Michael Moore describes the shift in attitude he experienced as a child when he moved from a private to a public school: "Where the nuns had devoted their lives to teaching for no earthly reward, those running the public school had one simple mission: 'Hunt these little pricks down like dogs, then cage them until we can either break their will or ship them off to the glue factory!'"[29] As Kappeler, Blumberg, and Potter point out, the media direct our attention to certain crimes or social issues and limits the discourse about solutions to present policies.[30] Thus the only options for the "teen crime wave," both in and out of schools, seems to be more police, more laws, more prisons and longer, harsher sentences. Even schools with no discernible violence problems have implemented such safety measures. In 1998 an elementary school in Indiana became the first to install a metal detector.[31] Says one principal at a school where administrators decided to install a high-tech video surveillance system costing $93,000, "What we want to do is create the atmosphere that we are thoughtful and prepared."[32] At what cost, though? Clearly the financial cost alone should make us second-guess the need for such actions, but numerous other costs, explored in this book, should make us run away screaming. Merely "pump handle interventions," as Social Psychologist Elliot Aronson calls them, such interventions **sound** good and allow school officials to say they are doing **something,** but do nothing to address root causes of the problem (when there is one).[33]

Who Benefits From the Fear of School Violence? Many Do!

Again, as we saw with the case of the anti-drug industry, certain groups have a vested interest in maintaining the perception that school violence is a social problem. MOSAIC, for instance, dubbed a, "threat assessment software," is designed to "prevent" school violence by profiling students. It is first triggered by a student informant. An administrator then responds to a series of questions, which the software then uses to calculate a threat rating of the student in question on a scale of 1 to 10.[34] Of course, in order to answer the questions school officials must know intimate information about the student and their family. A leading advocate of high-tech school security is Sandia National Labs, based in Albuquerque, New Mexico. Sandia provided security for the U.S nuclear arsenal during the cold war. In search of a new market, Sandia found schools. At their technology conference a few years ago vendors showed off such wears as walk through metal detecting portals, surveillance cameras, x-ray scanners, and drug testing kits.[35]

Lets look at the example of dress codes. Generally implemented as a solution to paranoia about gang infestation, schools all over, even in areas with no known gang presence, have wholeheartedly jumped on the repression bandwagon. Allegedly students do have the right to free expression in schools, as indicated by the Supreme Court's decision in *Tinker v. DesMoines*, which supported the right of students to wear black arm bands in opposition to the Vietnam War. Yet the court was careful to lay the groundwork for generally pro-school interpretations by saying that speech, "which for any reason-whether it stems from time, place, or type of behavior-materially disrupts class work or involves substantial disorder or invasion of the rights of others is…not immunized by the constitutional guarantee of freedom of speech."[36] Referred to as the "material and substantial" test, this verbiage has allowed for few interpretations in favor of students, as it is generally not difficult for teachers and administrators to come up with **some** reason why a slogan on a shirt, for example, will disrupt the educational process. As former teachers, we see several weaknesses in the logic here. First, it assumes that students generally pay attention to what others are wearing. While in some cases this is true, for the most part it was our experience that kids could not care less. Following this, it assumes that, because they are enthralled by Joe's "Big Johnson" tee-shirt (a company known for their use of sexual double entendres) or captivated by Mary's pot symbol necklace, they will be unable to learn. But we are not as concerned that many come to class either starving from not eating breakfast or on a sugar high from their Mountain Dew and Little Debbie combo, we merely want to apply more stringent bodily social controls. As Aronson notes, everything adults do in schools sends a message to students.[37] Is repression and totalitarianism **really** the message we want to send?

The Rise of the Superpredator?

As any educated person knows, schools do not exist in a vacuum; what happens on campuses reflects what is happening in the broader society. Thus these anti-teen school policies, like drug testing, canine searching and use of metal detectors, merely mirror a larger societal movement to demonize teens. According to some academics and most politicians, the 1990s was to be the era of the "superpredator," where a large population of teens was plotting carnage and destruction. "Kids killing kids" was a media-prompt for tougher punishments, yet 90% of all murder victims under 18 are killed by adults.[38] Like we saw with drug testing, crime is **really** an adult problem. While index crimes (eight serious felonies tracked in the FBI's Uniform Crime Reports collected from police agencies) declined five to ten percent for youth ages 13-17 in the last two decades, the index crime rate for adults ages 30 to 49 has risen by thirty percent over the same time period.[39] Ignoring the fact that this wave of teen-crime never came, in fact, teen crime has been on the decline since the mid 1990s, law-makers pushed for ever- punitive policies for adolescents and adults who read and hear about such policies believe that juvenile crime is rampant. Polls clearly show that adults are likely to exaggerate the incidence of violent crime committed by juveniles, while ignoring the more egregious case of adult violence **against** youth.[40]

Such demonization serves an ideological purpose. As Peter Elikann, author of *Superpredators*, maintains, "it is easier and more acceptable for us to beat up on monstrous animals than on kids."[41] And beat up we have. A mid 1980s trend that continues unabated is to try juveniles as adults. Twenty states do not even have a lower limit on the age at which a juvenile can be tried as an adult.[42] The juvenile justice system, established with the importance of judicial discretion in mind, has become more and more like the repressive adult criminal justice system. Between 1992 and 1995, for example, fifteen states plus Washington D.C. added mandatory minimum sentences for juveniles, a policy once reserved only for the adult courts.[43] While juvenile sentences once ended at age 21, the trend is to hold teens longer. Some states now hold juveniles until age 25, while others have declared no definite age.[44] Kids are being increasingly detained in adult prisons, despite mounds of evidence that their risk of suicide and of being beaten and/or sexually abused by guards and fellow inmates is much greater.[45] According to Kappeler, Blumberg, and Potter, teens in adult prisons are eight times more likely to commit suicide, five times more likely to suffer from sexual assault, and two times more likely to be beaten by prison staff than teens housed in juvenile facilities.[46] Juvenile records, once expunged or sealed upon a youth's reaching adulthood, are now often made available to the military, politicians and others.[47] By 1997, 42 states allowed press access to juveniles' name, address, and/or picture during and after trial, while 30 states allow certain juvenile cases to be open to the public.[48] Several studies indicate that sentences are more lenient when a similar sex offense is committed by an adult, rather than a teen, against a child. We continue to be one of six countries that still allow the execution of juveniles, and are in company with such human rights standouts as Iran, Nigeria, Pakistan, Saudi Arabia, and Yemen.[49]

Other countries see the U.S as excessively punitive as well. In 1989 the United Nations General Assembly adopted the Convention of the Rights of the Child. By 1998, 91 countries had ratified the document, recognizing that children do indeed have certain inalienable rights. In an act of lip-service President Clinton signed it as well, but then never took the crucial step of sending it to the senate for ratification.[50] Essentially required by the 1994 Safe and Drug Free Schools and Communities Act, all schools now have some form of zero tolerance law mandating the expulsion of students who have weapons or drugs on campus. While on its face this sounds like a move with student safety in mind, we can all think of ludicrous examples (the boy who pointed a chicken wing at a peer, said "bang," and was suspended for threatening behavior) of how such laws are being misused. Even more problematic is the way that they have been targeted at minority youth; African American males have been suspended and expelled at very disproportionate rates, and often for things such as "persistent disobedience." The American Journal of Trial Advocacy found that African American males were being suspended and/or expelled at rates 250 times higher than their white counterparts.[51]

This vilifying of our youth, both figuratively and literally, has been coupled with a continued failure to address **real** problems faced by children in America. Rising poverty rates, disintegrating families and communities, lack of access to adequate healthcare, and too easy access to firearms are legitimate concerns that some kids deal with every day in America, yet our focus is on preempting the next pot party and punishing kids who bring butter knives to school. Many adults have virtually stopped supporting their schools financially, as evidenced by the failure of whole communities to pass needed school improvement bonds. As Elikann maintains, much of the draconian response is due to their perception that what was once a minority problem has now become one for middle-class, white and "apparently mainstream" kids.[52] For instance, a school shooting occurred in a predominantly black part of town in New Orleans in early April, 2003. In opposition to previous coverage of school shootings in largely white schools, however, our local paper, the *Rocky Mountain News*, only contained one picture and a caption of the incident in the days afterward. It's as if blacks are **supposed** to do those things; when white kids do them it's suddenly newsworthy.

Surveillance Everywhere You Go

While teens have been the target of many of the repressive "safety" and "anti-drug" measures and are the focus of this book, this has all taken place within a general erosion of privacy rights. Many of us have found our bodily privacy and our privacy in other settings, such as the workplace and even on public streets, subject to attack. For instance, the Supreme Court, in 1986's *Bowers v. Hardwick*, upheld as constitutional Georgia's anti-sodomy law, even stating that the case was not about privacy but about "protect[ing] our society's values."[53] It is hard to imagine anything more private than a personal sexual decision, but what should we expect from the

Supreme Court? As attorney Jeffrey Rosen states, "It is not surprising that Supreme Court justices, who are secluded in a marble palace and have spent most of their careers in cosseted solitude in lower courts and universities, aren't terribly good at predicting how much privacy ordinary Americans expect..."[54] According to Gloria Feldt, president of the Planned Parenthood Federation of America (PPFA), the current Bush "regime" has pushed forward "the worst threat [to abortion rights] in thirty years of this work."[55] Bodily surveillance now begins prior to birth, as doctors keep detailed files on pregnant women and may, in the event that drug abuse is detected, turn this information over to law enforcement and social services without the mother's knowledge or consent.[56]

Workplace privacy has perhaps eroded even farther, as it impacts all of us rather than a few homosexuals selected for application of the state's sodomy laws. One way that privacy has been reduced at work is through the increasing use of drug tests. In 1986, President Reagan signed an executive order requiring federal agencies to drug test employees. This policy spread rapidly through the public and private sector, with 81% of the companies who reported to the American Management Association in 1996 conducting employee drug tests. The impetus behind Reagan's move was to further his war on drugs. It is much easier to extend the reach of the war on drugs if employers are on board. Federal employees, unlike minorities and welfare recipients, are often beyond the normally extended tentacles of the drug warriors. But with a cooperative employer mandating their drug testing (whether willingly so or not), they, too, were an accessible population. The executive order was accompanied by a plethora of scare tactics designed to get employers on board. Warnings of diminished productivity and profits, lack of worker reliability and heavy absenteeism, as well as more accidents and workers compensation claims provided the needed ideology for cut-throat, bottom-line employers to be sold on the idea. Employers were also told that drug testing is the most cost effective means by which they could address employee drug use. Of course, what most failed to note is that the primary source of such data was the drug testing promoters themselves.[57]

The National Academy of Sciences, the oldest and most prestigious scientific body in the country, released a study of employee drug testing in 1994 and found that, contrary to the drug testing industry and politician's claims, "the data…do not provide clear evidence of the deleterious effects of drugs other than alcohol on safety and other job performance indicators."[58] What **has** been found is that drug testing, while failing to deliver on any of its promises, has consequences that may inhibit, rather than promote, organizational goals. It has been found that work force drug testing deters qualified applicants from applying, and negatively impacts workplace morale, especially of those from certain cultures and amongst women. Further, work place drug testing creates fear among employees that their legally prescribed medications will become public information. Urinalysis in many cases reveals not only the presence of illegal drugs but also of other physical and medical conditions, including pregnancy. The ACLU reports that, in 1988, the police department in Washington, D.C. admitted that they had used urine samples they collected for drug tests to screen for pregnancy without informing or receiving consent from the women involved.[59] In an era of corporate downsizing, employees are concerned that false positives may lead to their unwarranted termination. Such policies also can reduce worker productivity, as they do not feel as though they are being treated with dignity and respect, not to mention the broader impact of perpetual bodily surveillance. Imagine you are a fifty year old, modest mother of four. You have not undressed in front of anyone but your husband for over thirty years, yet in order to keep your job you are forced to urinate in front of a drug testing official, despite no evidence of any wrongdoing. One woman, much like the one described here, has this to say about her drug testing experience: "Nothing I have ever done in my life equals or deserves the humiliation, degradation and mortification I felt."[60] Degrading? Yes. Humiliating? Yes. Effective at curtailing drug abuse? No.

Sadly, the U.S. has exported our notion that drug testing is good policy. President Bush's good pal Tony Blair announced in 2004 that workplace testing will now occur in the U.K. Demonstrating that what happens in schools mirrors larger social moves, this announcement was followed closely by Blair's decision to allow drug testing in U.K. schools, despite fierce opposition by teachers.[61]

It's About Our Rights!

"If you have nothing to hide, then who cares?" is the common response by conservatives and others to such policies. This response has been used for years on end by law enforcement in order to trick people into consenting to searches that should require a warrant or to taking part in interrogations without their attorney present.[62] President Clinton even called up such logic post-Columbine when trying to convince a group of students at a Virginia High School to report fellow students exhibiting "antisocial behavior."[63] Such a response drastically oversimplifies a complex question of inherent privacy rights and places the ownership for probable cause, a once necessary element of all searches and seizure, in the hands of the wrong side. As John Raines states in *Attack on Privacy*, "one wonders where our pride as free citizens has gone that 'they' should not first of all have to explain themselves to us; that the censorial power should come to reside in the government over the people."[64] And, as University of Oregon law professor Garret Epps notes,

> "The truth is, everyone has something to hide. For most people, it's not a crime; it may be a health condition that could expose them to discrimination, an unfashionable political allegiance, a deeply held personal religious commitment, a painful family secret or just a juvenile sense of humor. For each of us there is something we choose not to share with people we do not know well. And when these personal foibles are stripped bare, the people exposed often feel a deep sense of violation and may lose friends, jobs or spouses."[65]

Surveillance Via Technology

Another example of workplace privacy invasions is through technological monitoring. Lets picture a thirty-something database technician for a company with a variety of contracts. He is unexpectedly called into his manager's office. Curious, he figures perhaps he is getting a raise, as he knows he has done his job well and certainly has not done anything wrong. His manager says, "Bill, we have a problem. I have data here documenting your use of company time to visit pornographic websites." Bill is shocked and knows he has done no such thing. Yet his manager insists, and produces a layout of spreadsheets provided by a software program that monitors computer use, tracking exact URLs and classifying them as pornographic. Bill looks at the list, only to find that both were legitimate places he had visited but neither were pornographic; one was the publishing company Feralhouse, and the other was an online horror story magazine. Yet, since the software, Telemate, identified them as pornographic, Bill's manager tried to force him to sign a document admitting his guilt and declaring that future incidents would result in disciplinary action, possibly termination. Bill refused, and saw no other option but to resign.

The scenario described above is based on an actual event that occurred in a Seattle-based company and is told by Redden in his book, *Snitch Culture*.[66] It is by no means an exception. And, while the goal of software programs like Telemate is to collect information for consumer purposes, it is easy to see how they can be misused. A survey of 1000 large corporations by the American Management Association in 1999 revealed that 45% monitored their employees' e-mail, computer files, and phone calls.[67] E-mail, even after it is "deleted," is a permanent record, and we regularly leave our "electronic footprints" in the form of our web history.[68] Examples of even more problematic surveillance abound. Postal workers in New York City learned several years ago, to their horror, that management had installed video cameras in the restroom stalls, while female workers at a department store in the northeast found a hidden video camera in an area regularly used as a changing room.[69] Personal genetic information is being used more frequently by both insurance agencies and employers; according to an American Management Association survey in 1997, 6-10% of employers already use this information as a condition of employment, a situation that could possibly get worse with the completion of the human genome project.[70] Like the film *Gattaca*, we could find ourselves in a world where our only job interview is a blood test. Few things, it seems, are private in the modern workplace.

Privacy of our most intimate, personal information is needed in order to protect ourselves from misinterpretation. It is also the foundation of intimate relationships, something increasingly absent in a "me" based country. As Sociologist Erving Goffman has pointed out, we all (even kids!) need a backstage, a place where we can let down the masks we all wear in public.[71] Yet, as Jeffrey Rosen asserts, "it is surprising how recent changes in law and technology have been permitted to undermine sanctuaries of privacy that Americans took for granted throughout most of our history. But even more surprising has been our tepid response to the increasing surveillance of our personal and private life."[72] We are living, it seems, in Bentham's modern-day panopticon, where we no longer question the surveillance we are subject to and merely submit to the power of the all-seeing eye. Privacy intrusions, rather than raising our ire, have become common sense.

Law-Enforcement Surveillance

Police are regularly using intrusive surveillance techniques to track alleged "subversives." Columnist Katha Pollitt reports a branch of the ACLU in Colorado discovered that the Denver Police Department had been conducting surveillance and maintaining intelligence files since the 1950s. Their targets? Pacifists, advocates for reproductive rights, and Native American activists.[73] The Denver Police has since admitted that this was the case, but defends their policy on the grounds of homeland security.

"Surveillance practices long associated with prison have spilled into communities, as law enforcers and security guards increasingly monitor public places."[74] Indeed they have. Designed to monitor traffic patterns, video cameras are being placed on major streets and intersections. Of course, they can and are also being used to track individual cars. Some cities have followed the

lead of the UK in using mobile radar cameras to take pictures of
speeding cars or other traffic violations by capturing on film the
offenders' license plates.[75] If you plan to attend the Superbowl in
future years, be aware that you will be treated as a suspected crim-
inal. "Facetrac," an electronic imaging technology, debuted at the
2001 game. It recorded all of the faces of the spectators and com-
pared them on 128 different facial characteristics with a database
of known criminals.

Perhaps most disturbing is the suggestion that DNA should
be collected from all newborn babies. While the stated reason is to
help locate children who become victims of kidnappings, it is easy
to see the potential for abuse once we are all "in the system."
Current federal law requires that all 50 states collect DNA samples
from convicted felons and send them to a database housed at the
FBI. Twenty-four states already take such samples from juveniles in
trouble with the law or any teens.[76] Reminiscent of Orwell's Big
Brother, the NSA already runs a satellite-based surveillance system
called Echelon that is capable of tracking virtually **all** electronic
communications.[77]

Can It Get Worse? Yep-Post 9-11!

The terrorist attacks of September 11th served to further the
government's intrusions that, amazingly, have generally been sup-
ported by Americans. From President Bush's first post-September
11th speech he has claimed that terrorists attacked us because they
hate our freedoms. Yet over a year later, according to attorney and
professor David Cole, "it appears that the greatest threat to our
freedoms is posed not by the terrorists themselves but by our own
government's response."[78] We have, in the name of "homeland
security," authorized the government to keep track of our purchas-
es and movements, often using a corps of citizen snoops to do so.
The "Patriot Act" allows the government to run wiretaps and
searches without probable cause, providing they claim they are
seeking to gather foreign intelligence.[79] As James Redden points
out in *Snitch Culture*, "In addition to the new laws and policies,

government officials began planning a dizzying array of high tech systems to track our every move."[80] The proposals include: routing all Internet traffic through centralized computer servers monitored by the FBI; national ID cards with embedded microchips containing all our financial, medical and educational data; facial recognition cameras in all public places tied into computer databases; and retinal-scanning devices built into all computers to verify the identity of anyone who logs onto the Internet.

We have turned our public schools into military recruiting zones and, in the process, violated the privacy of our children. Buried deep in the 670 page No Child Left Behind legislation is a statement requiring schools receiving federal aid (i.e., all public schools) to provide recruiters with access as well as personal information.[81] We sure are "leaving no child behind"; at least no minority or poor kids that might be required to fight in our next quest for global imperialism and oil access.

As Nikolaus Mills has documented in *The Triumph of Meanness*, we are living in a culture of meanness. This culture allows us to maintain the self-righteous position that American society is generally fair and that those who succeed have done so on their own merit. By contrast, those who are at the bottom must **deserve** to be there.[82] And no one is further toward the bottom than our teens. "Meanness in any one area-institutional, social, or personal-makes meanness in every other areas easier to achieve."[83] In need of an enemy (one would think Saddam, Osama, and Kim Jong Il would be adequate), we have turned on our own offspring. While we should follow the words of Nietsche, who suggested that we fear all in whom the urge to punish is great, we have instead embraced the punishers as our saviors and protectors from demon superpredator teens. And our failure to critically assess our privacy intrusions and our so-called safety measures may be having grievous consequences. As Ayers, Dohrn, and Ayers assert in their book *Zero Tolerance*, "Ironically, elaborate security hardware fails to create school safety. Recent research indicates that as schools become more militarized they become less safe, in large part because the first casualty is the central, critical relationship between teacher and student, a relationship that is now being damaged or broken in favor of tough-sounding, impersonal, uniform procedures."[84] Negative, punitive policies are likely to do the exact **opposite** of the intention; for example, they may push already alienated youth toward drug abusing peers, and encourage dishonesty.[85] Likewise, installing search devices like metal detectors in schools may convince students that school **is** a dangerous place, whether that impression is accurate or not.[86]

QUESTIONS FOR REVIEW AND CRITICAL THINKING

Why has the public generally approved or failed to question search policies in schools?

What are examples of technology being created or used for surveillance? Can these or other examples of technology help **ensure** privacy?

Are the "good old days" of school truly a nostalgic myth? Ask around-do adults think so?

How has the government abandoned schools financially? What is their responsibility for funding schools?

EXTENSION QUESTIONS AND ACTIVITIES

Research more on how anti-teenism has manifested in juvenile courts.

According to the authors, how does the U.S. rate in its treatment of juveniles compared to other nations? Find out more about searches and discipline policy in schools in other countries.

Read George Orwell's 1984. Do you believe any of what he predicted has or is likely to happen?

Research historical and current examples of law enforcement surveillance. One topic might be the FBI's infamous COINTEL-PRO program.

CHAPTER ONE

The Big Three
The Supreme Court
and Student Privacy Rights

> We cannot expect people to have respect for law
> and order until we teach respect to those we have entrust-
> ed to enforce those laws."
> —Hunter S. Thompson

The Supreme Court has heard three cases regarding search and seizure in public schools. Each has established important yet problematic precedents regarding students' rights to privacy, and each has failed to conclusively answer the critical questions about school searches. This chapter looks at each case in chronological order, first describing the main arguments considered by the court and the logic used in their majority, concurring, and dissenting opinions, then offering critique and implications of each decision. The critique of many of the issues that arise from these cases is also taken up in later chapters.

New Jersey v. T.L.O 469 U.S. 325 (1985)

T.L.O, a fourteen year old, and another female student at Piscataway High School in New Jersey were discovered standing in a haze of smoke by a high school teacher. While neither student was actually observed with a cigarette in her mouth, the teacher assumed that they had been smoking, in violation of school rules as well as state law, and asked them if this was true. T.L.O's companion admitted that she had been smoking and was punished accordingly. Conversely, T.L.O denied that she had smoked anything, arguing she was merely caught in the cloud of the other girl's smoke. The teacher did not believe T.L.O, and demanded that she go to the assistant principal's office, where the assistant principal, Theodore Choplick, asked her to empty her purse. There he found cigarettes, as well as an item he deemed suspicious; rolling papers, often used for marijuana. Choplick then decided that these finds gave him adequate cause to further search T.L.O's purse, opening a zippered enclosure. There he found a pipe, generally used for smoking marijuana, plastic baggies, a small amount of marijuana, and an index card listing "people who owe me money." Assuming this to be adequate evidence that T.L.O was selling drugs, he also looked through some of her personal letters for corroboration. T.L.O argued that the search of her purse was a violation of her Fourth Amendment right to be free of unwanted governmental intrusions of her privacy and that, according to the exclusionary rule, none of the evidence obtained should be used against her. The exclusionary rule prevents police from presenting any evidence that is unlawfully obtained to prosecutors to be used in court. The rationale is that if police know the evidence they obtain will not be usable, they will refrain from conducting illegal searches. While not disputing the assistant principal's belief that the evidence was related to possible sale of marijuana, T.L.O argued that reading the letters was excessive in scope.[1]

New Jersey v. T.L.O was the first time that the Supreme Court heard a case regarding searches at school, although there had been several lower court decisions in this regard. One of the first questions the court had to address was whether students have any legitimate expectation of privacy in a school setting, as the Fourth Amendment only applies to those privacy concerns deemed "legitimate." The state of New Jersey argued that, based on the school's supervisory role over students, they have no expectation of privacy regarding articles "unnecessarily carried into school."[2] Thus T.L.O had no expectation of privacy in her purse. Since the search of T.L.O was not a bodily search, the court did not address whether students have a legitimate expectation of privacy on their persons while in school.

The Supreme Court rejected the state's logic, arguing that the twin premises that privacy is inconsistent with education and that kids shouldn't bring personal items to school are both severely flawed. The court rejected a comparison of students to prisoners confined to their cells, arguing that the school's need for discipline is not so dire that this parallel applies. Further, the court said that students **do** need personal items at school. At minimum they need study supplies, personal hygiene items, and other non-disruptive items like photos, letters, and diaries. Many students may also need certain personal items in order to participate in extra curricular activities.[3] The court determined, then, that students do indeed have a legitimate expectation of privacy in their personal effects at school. They did not address whether students have a legitimate expectation of privacy in lockers, desks, or other school property.

A second question before the court was how to characterize the role of teachers and administrators in regard to their ability to conduct searches. If school faculty are akin to police or law enforcement agents, they are subject to the same probable cause standard. If school faculty serve more as parents than as police, any searches and seizures they conduct are not protected under the Fourth Amendment, which only covers governmental intrusions, not those of private citizens. While recognizing that school faculty act in loco parentis, or as an ideal parent would, the court also recognized that education is compulsory. School faculty have been considered as state actors in regard to other civil rights issues, including challenges to students' First Amendment, due process, and Fourteenth Amendment rights. In addition, the court said that schools must balance the need for order and discipline with students' privacy rights, as well as protect the health and welfare of students. The court stated, "in recent years, school disorder has often taken particularly ugly forms: drug use and violent crime in the schools have become major problems,"[4] demonstrating a misconception with disastrous impact.

Balancing the two apparently competing definitions of the role of school faculty, the court decided that the Fourth Amendment does indeed apply in a school setting, but set the standard for searching at "reasonable suspicion," rather than the more rigorous requirement of probable cause. Probable cause refers to virtual certainty that a search will produce contraband, and must generally be articulated to a third party (a judge or magistrate). Reasonable suspicion has been defined as a "belief or opinion based upon facts or circumstances that do not amount to proof."[5] Justice Byron White, writing for the majority, argued that probable cause "is not an irreducible requirement of a valid search. The fundamental command of the Fourth Amendment is that searches and seizures be reasonable, and although both the concept of probable cause and the requirement of a warrant bear on the reasonableness of a search...in certain limited circumstances neither is required."[6] The warrant requirement, said the court, is unsuitable for a school setting, as to require such would "unduly interfere with the maintenance of the swift and informal disciplinary procedures needed in the schools."[7] The reasonableness standard, then, also applies in cases where students are suspected of violent activity, and to seizures as well as to searches. In essence, searches based on the T.L.O standard "place discretion in the hands of school personnel,"[8] as the critical element in considering a possible Fourth Amendment violation is the school official's articulation of reasonable suspicion.

The "reasonableness" standard must apply across two important dimensions; whether the search was justified at its inception, and whether the intrusiveness of the search is reasonably related to the objectives of the search. To be justified at its inception, school officials must have "reasonable grounds for suspecting that the search will turn up evidence that the student has violated or is violating either the law or the rules of the school."[9] The court admitted, and subsequent cases have supported, that adequate reasonable suspicion can be based on tips from students, staff, or others, on observations, or on a variety of other means. The degree of intrusiveness of a search is assessed by considering whether the "measures adopted are reasonably related to the objectives of the search and not excessively intrusive in light of the age and sex of the student and the nature of the infraction."[10] Thus, "excessively intrusive searches must be supported by a relatively strong degree of suspicion by the school officials."[11] In addition to the above two standards, the court also decided that the context of the search matters. "What is reasonable depends on the context within which the search takes place."[12]For example, the court felt that cases with loosely articulated factual background related to a **specific** violation were "too nebulous" to support reasonable suspicion.[13] Unfortunately schools must have missed this part of the decision (or disregarded it), as have later courts.

Another important question before the court was whether school officials need individualized suspicion that a particular student has some type of contraband prior to commencing a search. While not addressing this question specifically, as they felt it was not pertinent to the case of T.L.O (where it was clear that the assistant principal's suspicious was indeed individualized), the court did state that, "some individualized suspicion is essential as a prerequisite to a constitutional search."[14] This is taken from the language of the Fourth Amendment, which requires a warrant, based on probable cause, to search a person or their possessions. The warrant must specify the place to be searched and the persons or things to be seized. Subsequent cases have varied in their interpretation of the need for individualized suspicion. For instance, in a case where the luggage of an entire school band on a trip was searched the court ruled that individualized suspicion was required, yet another court found differently in a similar case.[15] Some argue that this opposing interpretation may be in light of "increased seriousness of drug and weapon use in school."[16] As we will make clear throughout this book, the perception of increased drug and weapon use is a farce. In general, the trend has been to defer to group searches if the situation is dangerous. Group locker searches, absent individualized suspicion, have generally been considered acceptable, as lower courts have ruled that students have a lower expectation of privacy in school-owned property. Typically locker searches are confined to items in plain view, however.[17]

In regard to the specific case before them, the court decided that the search of T.L.O was not in violation of the Fourth Amendment. Two searches were actually conducted; the initial search for cigarettes, and the second search for marijuana. The first search, according to the court, provided suspicion for the second. The initial search was justified based on T.L.O's denial that she had been smoking, which "corroborates the suspicion that she had been smoking" and "casts doubt on her credibility."[18] Choplick's suspicion for the initial search was also based on the teacher's report of what was observed in the bathroom, and the court felt that her purse seemed an obvious place to begin the search. Upon observing the rolling papers in the first search, the assistant principal was justified in further searching for marijuana. T.L.O contended that Choplick should not have reached into her purse to remove the cigarettes, as this action is what allowed him to see the rolling papers and thus prompted the subsequent searches. She claimed that no school rule forbid her from having cigarettes in her possession, since students, faculty and others were allowed to smoke in certain designated areas. The court rejected this argument as "hairsplitting" and said such logic had no place in the inquiry into reasonableness.[19]

Since they determined that the searches were reasonable, the court did not address the issue of whether the exclusionary rule applies to items seized through searches of public school students by school officials. The New Jersey Supreme Court, however, had decided that the exclusionary rule did indeed apply in this case. Stevens, Marshall and Brennan also supported the New Jersey court's finding that the exclusionary rule should apply, writing in their partial affirmation, partial dissent, "if the Nation's students can be convicted through the use of arbitrary methods destructive of personal liberty, they cannot help but feel that they have been dealt with unfairly."[20] The court also refused to address whether the same reasonable suspicion standard applies in regard to school searches in conjunction with or at the behest of law enforcement.

In the concurring opinion written by Justice Powell, which Justice O'Connor joined, he stressed the importance of the close relationship between teachers and students in a public school setting, arguing that such a relationship precludes some of the expectation of privacy students might have. The important distinction, as Powell and O' Connor saw it, was that the relationship was not adversarial, like that between citizens and law enforcement.[21]

Justices Brennan and Marshall, in their partial affirmation, partial dissent, described the reasonable suspicion standard as an "unclear, unprecedented, and unnecessary departure from generally applicable Fourth Amendment standards."[22] Further, they emphasized that a purse contains highly personal items. Searching such an item, especially of shy or sensitive students, can prove to be embarrassing, at least. Justices Stevens, Marshall, and Brennan, in their partial affirmation, partial dissent, expressed certain fears they had regarding the outcome of the case. They expressed "fear that the concerns that motivated the court's activism have produced a holding that will permit school administrators to search students suspected of violating only the most trivial school regulations and guidelines for behavior."[23] A primary concern is that the search was prompted by an alleged school rule infraction, not evidence of criminal activity. "The court's standard for deciding whether a search is justified 'at its inception' treats all violations of the rules of the school as though they were fungible. For the court, a search for curlers and sunglasses in order to enforce the school dress code is apparently as important as a search for evidence of heroin addiction or violent gang activity."[24] The school's handbook allows for a search in order to find evidence of violation of school rules in the following areas: establishment of secret societies, driving to school, prohibited use of the school parking lot, direction of traffic in the hallways, presence in the hallways without a pass, profanity, attendance at athletic events, cafeteria use and cleanup, eating lunch off campus, and unauthorized absence.[25]

Following *T.L.O*, a few courts have interpreted whether a search is justified at its inception very narrowly, requiring that there be evidence to support a specific rule violation by a specific student. For instance, in *Cales v. Howell Public Schools*, 635 F Supp. 454 (ED Mich. 1985), a student was found by a security guard ducking behind cars in the school's parking lot. The guard assumed she was using or had drugs and commenced searching her purse. The court ruled that her presence in the parking lot could be explained by any number of reasons, both legitimate and illegitimate, therefore it was unreasonable to search her purse.[26]

Yet, in general, the trend has been to broaden the search rights of school officials, while obviously reducing the privacy rights of students. One way this has occurred is through expansion of the use of group testing. In most cases, the denial of student privacy rights is couched in war rhetoric; either the war on drugs or war on violence, regardless of whether such assertions hold true. "In the 1990s, however, as the level of violence in schools reached dramatic new heights, the question arose as to whether searches of students were constitutionally permissible based on reasonable suspicion in relation to a group, rather than an individual."[27]

There are a variety of concerns brought forward by the court's decision in T.L.O, including those questions they refused to address. First, the court expressed concern that to require the more stringent probable cause standard would unduly burden school officials. Implied here is the notion that school officials are untrained to ascertain what probable cause would be, which is likely true. Most teacher preparation programs offer nothing in the way of understanding how law applies in school settings. Yet, according to the logic of the T.L.O decision, these same untrained school officials are capable of determining what is reasonable suspicion and can now search students more easily than can qualified and trained law enforcement officers. As was noted, this allows them incredible discretion. Moreover, precisely what reasonable suspicion is seems to be somewhat vague, and it is clear from this decision as well as many others that this vagueness serves the interests of the school, not the students. So, are the justices concerned about teachers and administrators being unprepared to conduct searches or not?

The court apparently gave little to no consideration to the messages being sent by their decision. Many students already feel as though school is a prison, it's not likely that expanding the control techniques of the school to include increased surveillance will reduce this feeling. "Entwined in the brutality and suffering caused by violence are assumptions that shape reactions to the problem-reactions that can, at times, exacerbate the problem."[28] It seems that school staff have been given permission to "battle the imaginary at the expense of the real,"[29] allowing searches based on scanty evidence in the name of "violence prevention" or "drug use deterrence." As will be discussed in greater detail later, such punitive actions in schools may only serve to increase student apathy and resistance and decrease student ability to learn, allegedly the primary objective of schooling.

The logic of the court was also based on some faulty premises. For instance, the notion of rampant school violence and teen violence in general permeated the court's logic in a number of places in order to reinforce the school's disciplinary/safety goals, yet there is little evidence that this was indeed the case at that time. Nor is it true now. The teen population fell from 1977 to 1992, during the time period in question, yet the amount of serious crime rose, suggesting that teens were **not** the main perpetrators.[30] While there was an increase in the rate of homicides committed by juveniles between 1984 and 1993[31], it is not clear that, a) the court heard any actual evidence of this; and, b) it would have been relevant to the case at hand, as T.L.O's offense was significantly less serious than homicide. Even in the peak year of 1994, less than 1 percent of all young people were arrested for a violent crime, and those were highly localized in a few major cities.[32] Thus the court seems to have bought into the misperception of evil teens committing crimes at will. Interestingly, the court heard this case shortly after the publication of the 1983 A Nation At Risk report, which demonized American schools, and their students, on a number of different fronts, so perhaps that is where some of their perception came from.[33]

A problem noted by the dissenters was that the decision in this specific case, as well as the precedent set by the court's majority opinion, is that it is equally acceptable to search students for evidence of violation of school rules as for violation of criminal laws. The majority stated, "We are unwilling to adopt a standard under which the legality of a search is dependent upon a judge's evaluation of the relative importance of various school rules."[34] Clearly school searches are about social control efforts, not (in general) about safety. The court, and the general public, have come to believe that, "students can be controlled if they are convinced of the nearly omniscient power of the school to watch, apprehend, and to quickly serve punishment."[35] Once again, the court couched their decision behind popular "tough on crime" rhetoric taken at face value.

The court also seemed to imply that, if a school creates a policy about a particular search-related issue, then they're all set; mere existence of a policy exempts the school from scrutiny regarding whether that policy is really necessary and constitutional. Hence the fact that the Supreme Court, in essence, okayed searching students based on their failure to have a hall pass or their cursing at a classmate.

In the specific case of T.L.O, the notion that her denial of smoking provided suspicion for school officials to search is quite problematic. So now any time a student denies an allegation, whether that allegation has any independent merit or not, they are suspect?

Finally, there are several important issues the court left unaddressed. As noted earlier, they did not consider whether students have a legitimate expectation of privacy in regard to searches of school property, nor did they decide whether police involvement in school-based searches changes anything. They failed to address the distinctions between group and individual searches, as well as whether the exclusionary rule applies to school searches. These are all critical questions, and by failing to address them, the court allowed schools to conduct such searches unencumbered until years later when a challenge was finally brought (an unsuccessful one, at that).

Vernonia School District 47J v. Acton, 575 U.S. 646 (1995)

Let us be upfront: It is our belief that testing for pot—a purely recreational drug—should be discouraged or eliminated. But in athletics, where athletes compete for awards and in some case to be put on professional teams later, they should not be permitted to take steroids, which give them an unfair advantage over other competitors. Being stoned is an individual issue. Beating others because you have the unfair advantage of steroids should be prevented because it is decidedly **not** just an individual issue. Sadly, the focus of most drug-testing of athletes, at least in schools, is not on performance enhancing substance. The issue of steroid use is addressed again in Chapter Six.

It was ten years before the highest court addressed another school search case. By then "the situation in schools had worsened," or at least the perception of it had. In the late 1980s, increased use of drugs and alcohol had prompted an increase in disciplinary actions at the Vernonia School District in Oregon, a district with one high school and three grade schools. In the 1988-89 school year disciplinary referrals were two times higher than they had been in the early 1980s. It was determined by school officials that athletes were leaders of this "drug culture."[36] The school provided stories of student-athletes dancing and singing loudly at inappropriate times in class as evidence that they were involved with drugs. Further, student-athletes had been bragging about the drug culture and boasted that there was nothing the school could do about it.[37] A teacher reported observing small groups of students passing joints back and forth at a restaurant across the street from the school, both before and during school hours. Another caught students skipping school and using drugs at a student's house.[38]

The school initially responded by introducing more drug education programs, then by calling in canines for searches, but neither method seemed effective. The school then instituted a drug test policy for all students involved in interscholastic sports.[39] Prior to officially instituting the policy the school held a parent input night to discuss the proposal. Those in attendance gave unanimous approval, and the policy was approved for the fall of 1989.[40]

Each student who chose to partake in sports was tested at the beginning of the season. Ten percent of all of the athletes were randomly selected each week for additional testing. Students were required to disclose any prescription drugs they were taking as well as provide a copy of the prescription for school officials. The actual test took place in a bathroom with an adult, same-sex monitor. Boys provided a urine sample at a urinal, with their back to the monitor. Girls were allowed to provide their sample from inside a stall, while the monitor stood outside to hear but not see the procurement of the sample. The urine samples were then sent to an independent laboratory and the identity of the student providing the sample remained anonymous. Results of the tests were mailed to the superintendent. Others who had access to test results included the principal, vice principal, and athletic director. Students who tested positively were notified by school administration, and a positive test immediately prompted a second test. If the second test was positive parents were notified and the student had the option of attending six weeks of drug counseling, including weekly drug testing, or a suspension for the remainder of the playing season and another athletic season. Students were also retested at the beginning of the next eligible season. If a student tested positive a second time, they were automatically suspended for the remaining season and one more. A third offense resulted in suspension of two full seasons in addition to whatever remained of the current season.[41]

James Acton, a 12 year old, wanted to play football at his grade school in the fall of 1991. He refused to consent to the mandatory drug test. According to his attorney, "James should not be subject to an intrusive bodily search when there was no reason to believe he was taking drugs."[42] Thus Acton argued that the blanket drug test policy was in violation of the Fourth Amendment. A district court dismissed the claim, but the Ninth Circuit Court reversed, agreeing with Acton that the drug test was indeed a violation of his privacy rights. In 1995 the case came before the Supreme Court, who ruled 6-3 that the search was reasonable.

The first order of business was to affirm that a drug test is indeed a search. Prior cases, although not in reference to drug tests of students, had determined that drug or alcohol tests, whether by blood, urine, or breath, are searches. Two key cases in 1989 affirmed this, and set the precedent that individualized suspicion of drug use is not required in cases where there is a prevailing safety concern. In *Skinner v. Railway Labor Executives Association* 489 U.S. 602 (1989), it was determined that the health and safety concerns associated with railroad work outweighed the need for individualized suspicion. In *National Treasury Employees v. Von Raab*, 489 U.S. 656 (1989), a case dealing with drug testing of customs agents, the courts determined that the government also had a compelling interest in public safety, as the agents were armed, and thus it was acceptable to drug test them without individualized suspicion.[43] The court did not address the constitutionality of drug testing in order to **detect and deter** drug use in either case, however, as was the issue in question with Acton.

In writing for the majority, Justice Scalia admitted that kids in school do have Fourth Amendment rights, but that these rights are weaker than those of adults. Thus the court referred back to *T.L.O* to determine that no warrant was needed for a search. Essentially, the court considered four main factors. In determining whether there is a legitimate expectation of privacy, the court stated, "What expectations are legitimate varies, of course, with context…depending, for example, upon whether the individual asserting the privacy interest is at home, at work, in a car, or in a public park. In addition, the legitimacy of certain privacy expectations vis-à-vis the state may depend upon the individual's legal relationship with the state."[44] The court deemed it central in this case that the policy deals with children who are in "the custody" of the state as schoolmaster. Thus, the "'reasonableness' inquiry cannot disregard the schools' custodial and tutelary responsibility for the children."[45] Athletes have an even further reduced expectation of privacy, as they regularly change clothes and shower in communal locker rooms. According to the court's logic, sports are not for the bashful. In addition, those who chose to go out for the team voluntarily subject themselves to greater regulation by school officials than students in general. For instance, they are typically required to have a pre-season physical examination, prove that they have insurance, maintain a minimum grade point average, and comply with the rules of their sport.[46]

In considering the intrusiveness of the search, the court recognized that collecting urine samples indeed intrudes on an area normally afforded great privacy, yet argued that the degree of intrusiveness here depended on the manner of monitoring. The conditions of Vernonia's monitoring were said to be "nearly identical to those typically encountered in public restrooms."[47] Citing *Skinner*, the court determined that "The Fourth Amendment does not require that the 'least intrusive' search be conducted."[48] The court also considered the issue of privacy in regard to the information disclosed through a urine test. Since the officials at Vernonia were only looking for evidence of drugs, not, for example, pregnancy or disease, and because the drugs they were looking for were standard (did not vary across students), the court felt that the information disclosed was not overly intrusive. In regard to the specific concern about disclosure of prescription medications, the court stated that, "we have never indicated that requiring advance disclosure of medications is *per se* unreasonable."[49] Also considered was the fact that there was limited disclosure of the test results and none of the results were given to law enforcement.

The court also addressed the nature of the governmental concern. It was decided that the government, in this case the school, has a compelling interest in deterring drug use. They determined that the crisis of drug use at Vernonia was "obvious and immediate."[50] "It is self-evident that the drug problem was largely fueled by the 'role model' effect of athletes' drug use,"[51] so the drug test policy was considered an effective means to address that problem. The court clearly did not question the involvement of athletes in the drug culture, nor the contention that student-athletes serve as role models for other students. The majority also noted the special health dangers that drug use poses for athletes, stating, "school years are the time when the physical, psychological, and addictive effects of drugs are most severe."[52] Psychological effects described to the court included impairment of judgment, slowed reaction time, and a lessened perception of pain. Addressing specific drugs, they were provided with evidence that amphetamines can result in artificially induced heart rate increases, increased blood pressure, and can mask normal fatigue. Marijuana causes irregular blood pressure, a reduction in the oxygen carrying capacity of blood, and an inhibition of normal sweating, leading to increased body temperature. Cocaine use results in increased blood pressure, and possible coronary artery spasms and myocardial infarction. The court also determined that "the effects of a drug infested school are not visited just upon the users, but upon the entire student body and faculty, as the educational process is disrupted."[53]

Further, an additional issue considered by the court was the efficacy of the means. It was noted that the record showed no parental objections to the policy, other than the Actons. "The most significant element in this case is…that the policy was undertaken in furtherance of the government's responsibilities, under a public school system, as guardian and tutor of children entrusted in its care."[54] In this case, the court felt that a blanket policy was as effective, or perhaps even more effective, than individual suspicion would be at rooting out drug users. The court did, however, caution against using such blanket searches in other contexts. In particular, Justice Ginsburg, in her concurring opinion, stressed the special problem of drug use at Vernonia and maintained that the ruling did not necessarily extend to random testing of all students.[55]

Justice O' Connor wrote for the three dissenters. She accused the majority of casting aside the main premise of the Fourth Amendment- the belief that **an individual** has done something wrong. She argued that the Fourth Amendment was drafted to prevent searches of this very nature; blanket, suspicionless searches. She also disagreed with the court's majority that the privacy invasion of the Vernonia drug tests was "negligible." She argued that the "state-compelled and monitored collection of urine is particularly destructive of privacy and offensive to personal dignity."[56]

Further, O' Connor critiqued the blanket drug testing policy, arguing it was not necessary to combat Vernonia's drug problem. Blanket policies can be considered worse than those conducted on individualized suspicion, she expressed, because they impact multiple people, not just one person. Since students, including athletes, are supervised by school officials on a daily basis, O' Connor maintained that it would be easy to test based on individualized suspicion. Moreover, most of the evidence that seemed to indicate that athletes had a drug problem (dancing and singing loudly in class, for example) also clearly provided individualized suspicion.[57] Of specific concern was the fact that these instances occurred at the high school; there was no evidence of a drug problem at Washington Grade School, which the petitioner attended.[58] In response to the argument that the blanket policy treated all students fairly, O'Connor explained that the court had previously stated that, "evenhanded treatment was no substitute for the individualized suspicion requirement." She explained, "Thus it remains that the police cannot, say, subject to drug testing every person entering or leaving a certain drug ridden neighborhood in order to find evidence of crime."[59]

A key element of the court's decision was that athletes have a reduced expectation of privacy. Much attention was given to the nature of communal locker rooms and showers, and to the fact that sports are not for bashful students. Yet this fails to take into account the number of athletes who **never** do either of these things; they change clothes in an enclosed stall or prior to arriving at a practice or game, and they wait to shower until they are in the safety of their family's bathroom. This is likely to hold true to a greater degree among younger students, as we know that middle school is a time when students are especially conscious of their growing and changing bodies. There also is a big difference between changing in a locker room where your peers are doing likewise and being searched by authorities. Yet the court felt that such an assumption was valid for a student who attended a **grade school**. Further, the court held that athletes have less privacy because they are required to take pre-season physicals, get insurance, and are, in a number of ways, subject to greater scrutiny than is the average student. However, such items are qualitatively different than urinating in front of a stranger. For instance, a pre-season physical may be conducted by a family doctor with whom the student has a lifelong relationship, whereas the drug test monitor is unlikely to have known and treated the student since birth. Likewise, it is difficult to see that urine testing and expecting athletes to carry a minimum grade point average are comparable requirements, as the court asserted. In sum, having someone observe you urinating is **inherently** intrusive, regardless of the monitoring technique. The court could have held that the least intrusive search is what is most reasonable in any case, but refused to do so.[60]

Another questionable assumption made by the court is that the state, in this case, the school, has a compelling interest in deterring drug use among students. While in and of itself this is not problematic, it becomes shakier when we look at actual drug use data. For the state to have a compelling interest in something, one would think there would need to be a compelling problem. While this issue will be explored in greater detail in the chapter on drug testing, in brief, the data do not suggest a rampant drug problem for teens. The number of teens in drug abuse treatment declined by 70 percent between 1980 and the mid 1990s. According to Mike Males, "America's drug problem has indeed grown to crisis proportions. But teenagers have not made up any significant part of it in two decades."[61]

The court took as givens the notions that athletes are role models and that drug use poses special concerns for athletes. Yet the role model argument is not necessarily so, and the court failed to require that the school prove that the athletes were leading others to use drugs, a key point in showing that they were "leaders of the drug culture." Additionally, there is little evidence that, in aggregate, athletes use drugs more frequently than do non-athletes nor that they are more greatly affected by drug use. A study of 1515 high school athletes, for instance, found that the athletes reported less use of marijuana in the last year than non-athletes. Athletes also used less cocaine and psychedelic drugs.[62] Again, it seems as though the assumptions of the court's majority were based on their perceptions of a problem, not necessarily on reality.

It would seem as though the court would want to see evidence that drug testing in general, and specifically Vernonia's policy, is effective, yet no such evidence was requested nor provided. Simply because it is easy to implement a drug test policy is not evidence that such a policy works. As noted in the Introduction, only three positive tests were found in over four years of testing at Vernonia.[63] A recent study by Monitoring the Future has shown that drug testing does not deter drug use. The researchers found nearly identical drug use rates at schools that don't have drug testing. Seven schools in their sample even use random testing of the entire student body, yet this does not significantly alter student drug use.[64] Other research addressing the effectiveness of drug testing is provided in Chapter Six.

Justice O'Connor brought up the important point that the Fourth Amendment was intended to prohibit just this sort of blanket, suspicionless search. Her point that, in this case specifically and likely in most cases, there is enough individualized suspicion to conduct a search is also valid. As the court admitted that athletes are more supervised than other students, it is unclear why it would be so difficult to obtain individualized suspicion. Nor does arguing that all were treated the same under the policy (regarding the process and consequences of a positive test) change the problems inherent in using such a policy with schoolchildren.

Above all, the drug test policy approved by the court sends the message that all athletes are suspect and that school officials are not obligated to grant students basic privacy rights. It may also serve to deter kids, not from drug use but from athletic participation, either as a way to continue their drug use, or, more likely, because being tested makes students feel like criminals. Another effect may be to increase alcohol use among athletes, as this is not usually included in the testing procedures and is harder to detect if it is.[65] Further, some research has shown that students in schools with drug tests may perceive drug use to be a bigger problem than it actually is.[66] It's easy to see how students may think, "The school wouldn't test if there wasn't a problem, so there **must** be a problem." Research has shown that students do indeed do this with other issues, such as the hiring of school resources officers or the installing of metal detectors. Thus students not only get a faulty impression of their classmates, but may be even more likely to engage in drinking or drug use. They can justify it by saying that everyone is doing it, the very message being sent by their school and the courts.

Board of Education of Independent School District No. 92 of Pottawatomie County v. Earls (2002)

In 2002 the court again heard a case regarding a challenge to student privacy rights. It was the first federal challenge to drug and alcohol testing of students in extra curricular activities, and, in some cases, in academic courses. In practice, the policy in question was applied only to those students involved in competitive extra curricular activities. Lindsay Earls and Daniel James, both 16 year old juniors at Tecumseh High School, and Lindsay's sister Lacey, brought the suit against the school, asserting that being forced to submit to a drug test is a violation of the Fourth Amendment. Lindsay was a part of the school's choir and marching band and wanted to remain so. She was also a member of the school's Academic Team and the National Honor Society. Daniel was seeking membership in the Academic Team.[67] Yet involvement in such activities made these two students suspect (since they are extra-curricular), and subject to the school's drug test policy.

Tecumseh High instituted their policy in 1998. All 7th through 12th grade students who wanted to be in any extra curricular activity were expected to consent to be drug tested as a condition of their participation. As in *Vernonia*, the urine sample was procured in a stall with a same sex monitor listening to but not seeing the student urinate. Results were released to school employees on a need-to-know basis and were not given to law enforcement agents. The thinking was that such activities were voluntary, and thus students who elect to be involved subject themselves to greater scrutiny. Yet Academic Team, Band, and Choir were part of the school's curriculum and helped to fill a fine arts requirement.

Refusal to submit to the testing resulted in the student earning no credit for those courses. Earls actually was tested two or three times, all negative. In fact, of the 505 students tested in total, only three students tested positive. All three were athletes, although two of the three also participated in other extra curricular activities.[68]

A positive test at Tecumseh resulted in drug-related counseling. If the student agreed to get the counseling they could remain on their team or as a participant in the activity of their choice as long as they could show they had signed up for a counseling program within five days of receiving the test results and agreed to submit to a second drug test in two weeks; if they refused they were barred from competition. A second positive test resulted in a suspension from participation in the extra curricular activity for 14 days, the mandatory completion of 14 hours of substance abuse counseling, and monthly drug tests. Students testing positive for a third time were suspended from participation in extra curricular activities for the remainder of the school year or 88 days, whichever was longer. The policy was allegedly based on a drug problem in the district since the 1970s, yet some who testified said there was little evidence of such a problem.[69]

Arguments about the constitutionality of testing students involved in extra curricular activities were quite heated before the court, with at least one justice, Kennedy, berating Earls, her attorney, and her family, despite her negative test results. Graham Boyd, an ACLU attorney representing the Earls' and James, argued, "When courts have upheld blanket drug-testing, it has been on some dangerous activity," such as sports, yet "there's nothing about singing in the choir that poses any danger."[70] Further, he maintained that, "the district's drug test policy is more about symbolism than substance. Tecumseh officials initiated urine testing without any evidence of a drug problem at the school and at a time when government reports show that teen drug use is on the decline nationally."[71] Justice Ginsburg expressed concern that it was illogical to drug test those students involved in extra curricular activities, based on lower court testimony that those students posed less of a drug problem than those not involved in an after-school activity. "Even if students might be deterred from drug use in order to preserve their extra curricular eligibility, it is at least as likely that other students might forgo their extra curricular involvement in order to avoid detection of their drug use."[72] Yet Justice Scalia argued that the district was simply "trying to train and raise these young people to be responsible adults."[73]

Ginsburg noted the lack of evidence of a drug problem at the school, which would be required based on *Vernonia*. She referred especially to the fact that, throughout the case, the Superintendent repeatedly said drug use was not a major problem. In response, Justice Scalia angrily asked, "So long as you have a bunch of druggies who are orderly in class, the school can take no action. That's what you want us to rule?"[74] Justice Kennedy was also quite abrupt: "It seems to be that if a school district is better than other districts, with less drug use, they're entitled to keep it that way. You seem to be saying that there has to be a great crisis, where we lose a few years to drugs,"[75] and, in a voice laced with sarcasm, "it is hardly a revelation that the government is concerned about drugs among our youth. This is not exactly rocket science."[76] While some members of the court felt as though there was some evidence of a drug problem at Tecumseh, they also stated that, "a demonstrated drug problem is not always necessary to the validity of a testing regime," citing *Chandler v. Miller*, 520 U.S. 304, 309 (1997), yet backtracking on their logic in *Vernonia*.[77]

Kennedy likened the intrusiveness of the search to that of asking students to wear school uniforms. The invasion of privacy associated with the urinalysis was not significant, considering the "minimally intrusive nature of the sample collection and the limited use to which the test results are put."[78] Justice Breyer, in his concurring opinion, expressed concern that the privacy intrusion was not negligible, but liked the fact that the school had held public forums to discuss this and other issues.[79] Later in the arguments Kennedy became more rude, stating nastily to Earl's lawyer during a discussion of whether a district might have two schools, a good one (with drug testing, of course) and a "druggie" one, "No parent would send a child to that school, except maybe your client."[80] Justice Breyer felt that a positive element of the school's policy was that no one who tested positive was arrested but was offered the opportunity to attend counseling.[81]

The court decided 5-4 that the drug test policy at Tecumseh High School was not in violation of the Fourth Amendment. Citing *Treasury Employees v. Von Raab,* 489 U.S. 656, 667-668 (1989) as well as *T.L.O* and *Vernonia,* the court affirmed that probable cause was not necessary in order to conduct a search. In fact, probable cause "may be unsuited to determining the reasonableness of administrative searches where the government seeks to *prevent* the development of hazardous conditions,"[82] thus drug testing was seen as a form of administrative search. Probable cause was not really an issue of contention in this case anyway, as the policy was not related to any criminal investigation. In addressing the nature of the privacy interest, the court considered the context of the school setting. Like *T.L.O* and *Vernonia,* the court held that the special needs of a school setting due to disciplinary, health and safety concerns preclude the individualized suspicion requirement. To require individualized suspicion would impose an additional burden on already burdened teachers.[83] Further, "a program of individualized suspicion might unfairly target members of unpopular groups. The fear of lawsuits resulting from such targeted searches may chill enforcement of the program, rendering it ineffective in combating drug use."[84]

The court also determined that students choosing to participate in closely monitored activities such as extra curricular activities have a reduced expectation of privacy. In response to the concern that there is a privacy distinction between athletes and non-athletes, the majority proclaimed that this distinction was not essential, citing that the primary logic of the *Vernonia* decision to support a drug testing policy was the custodial responsibility and authority of the school.[85]

In regard to the character of the intrusion, the court mainly addressed the manner of the urine monitoring, as per *Vernonia.* They determined that the policy at Tecumseh was virtually identical to that which they had upheld in *Vernonia*; in fact, it was more protective of student's privacy by allowing male as well as female students to use a stall to produce their sample. The respondents argued that the school was careless in protecting the disclosure of test results, citing as an example the fact that the choir teacher looked at the list of prescription drugs being used by students and left the list exposed where students could see it. The court, however, maintained that the choir teacher had access to such information prior to the drug testing policy, and had a need to know this information because she takes students off campus on occasion. Further, since there was no evidence that another student actually saw the list, the court found this to be non-problematic.[86]

Regarding the nature and immediacy of the governments concerns and the efficacy of the policy in meeting them, the court stated, "The drug abuse problem among our Nation's youth has hardly abated since *Vernonia* was decided in 1995. In fact, evidence suggests that it has only grown worse."[87] Citing Monitoring the Future survey results, the court determined, "As we cannot articulate a threshold level of drug use that would suffice to justify a drug testing program for schoolchildren, we refuse to fashion what would in effect be a constitutional quantum of drug use necessary to show a 'drug problem.'"[88] In his concurring opinion, Justice Breyer cited statistics that indicate drug use is responsible for 20,000 deaths and $160 billion in economic costs each year in the U.S. In response to the respondents contention that the testing of non-athletes does not rest on a safety issue, which was allegedly a key part of the special needs framework, the majority stated that the, "safety interest furthered by drug testing is undoubtedly substantial for all children, athletes and nonathletes alike. We know all too well that drug use carries a variety of health risks for children, including death from overdose."[89]

The majority felt that testing those in extra curricular activities is a reasonably effective means of detecting and preventing drug use. Since supply-side interventions have not reduced drug use, and schools are obligated to address it or else they run the risk of losing students to private or parochial schools, Justice Breyer indicated that the drug testing policy at Tecumseh addresses the most important factor leading children to drugs; peer pressure. The policy thus "offers a nonthreatening reason to decline his friends' drug use invitation." Admitting that *Vernonia* had the issue of athletes as role models that was not present here, the majority explained that this was not essential to their decision.[90]

In describing the prevailing logic of the majority of the court, Justice Scalia stated that the tests were needed in order to avoid the danger of getting "young people used to a drug culture."[91] The Bush administration expressed their support for the school's drug test policy by sending a representative of the Justice Department to the oral arguments. In fact, the administration has spoken out in favor of testing of **all** students.[92]

Justices Souter, Stevens and O'Connor, as in *Vernonia*, were three of the dissenters. Souter's primary concern was that the extra curricular activities students partake in are not necessarily voluntary. He argued that it is impossible for students to get into a competitive college if they do not partake in any extra curricular activities. "Participation in such activities is a key component of school life, essential in reality for students applying to college and, for all participants, a significant contributor to the breadth and quality of the education experience."[93] Breyer responded in his concurring opinion, arguing that a "conscientious objector" has an option, refusal, and although this brings a consequence (ineligibility to participate), that consequence is much less severe than expulsion. In Earls' case, a refusal to be tested made her ineligible to be part of the band or choir. While technically there were other courses offered that satisfied the same fine arts requirement, neither ceramics nor music appreciation offered the competitive outlet she was seeking.[94] The dissenters also expressed concern that non-athletic extra curricular activities serve all kinds of students, including the shy and reserved, rendering moot the contention in *Vernonia* that sports are "not for the bashful." Citing research by the American Academy of Pediatrics, Ginsburg stated such activities "afford opportunities to gain self-assurance, to 'come to know faculty members in a less formal setting than the typical classroom,' and to acquire 'positive social supports and networks [that] play a critical role in periods of heightened stress."[95]

An interesting exchange occurred during oral arguments and is reflected in Justice Ginsburg's dissent. The petitioners cited dangers associated with certain extra curricular activities that, in many people's (including Ginsburg's) eyes were absolutely ludicrous. The petitioners maintained there were safety risks associated with being in the band, as members were "required to perform extremely precise routines with heavy equipment and instruments in close proximity to other students" and with students in the Future Farmers of America (FFA), who are "required to individually control and restrain animals as large as 1500 pounds." Ginsburg responded: "notwithstanding nightmarish images of out-of-control flatware, livestock run amok, and colliding tubas disturbing the peace and quiet at Tecumseh, the great majority of students the school district seeks to test in truth are engaged in activities that are not safety sensitive to an unusual degree." Further, she was concerned that students involved in this type of activity show no special predeliction toward drug use. "Many children, like many adults, engage in dangerous activities on their own time; that the children are enrolled in school scarcely allows government to monitor all such activities."[96]

That the court completely backtracked on their *Vernonia* decision that schools must provide evidence of a drug problem and/or a safety need at their specific school prior to implementing a drug testing policy is problematic. Further, the logic of the court in *Earls* seems to open the door for potential testing of all students, something increasingly likely, as the current presidential administration has expressed support. As attorney Boyd pointed out, not only was there little evidence of a drug problem at Tecumseh, but surveys indicate that, nationwide, drug use is on the decline. Our drug war rhetoric, however, overshadows the actual evidence and allows most citizens, including the justices of our highest court, to assume the worst about teens and drugs.

The impact of a drug test policy on students who chose to participate in positive activities at their school could be substantial. As Ginsburg pointed out, it may deter kids from getting involved. These students should be rewarded for their choice to support their school, not accused. A study of drug testing policies found attitudes toward school were much less positive among students in schools with a drug testing policy than comparable students who were not.[97] Allegedly, having to face a drug test offers students an easy way to say no to drugs when pressured by their peers to use them, but this research found students did not believe this to be the case.[98] Further, as was noted here and presented in *Vernonia*, there is simply no evidence that testing students in extra curricular activities will prove effective, as many studies show they are the **least** likely to be involved in drug use. Having worked in public schools for several years, drug use among choir members or FFA members was never a salient issue. Finally, Justice Kennedy's assertion that to require urine samples from students is no less intrusive than to require them to wear school uniforms is simply ludicrous. Evidently the public is to believe that urinating with a monitor nearby is akin to being told you must wear navy blue pants and a white top.

QUESTIONS FOR REVIEW AND CRITICAL THINKING

1. According to T.L.O v. New Jersey, why do school officials and teachers need reasonable suspicion instead of probable cause to commence a search?

2. Do you agree the searches of T.L.O were justified at their inception and reasonable in scope?

3. What are the arguments in favor of requiring schools to always have individualized suspicion of a student prior to searching him or her? What are the arguments in favor of conducting group searches absent individualized suspicion?

4. Should school officials be allowed to search students for violations of school policy?

5. Do you agree with the court in the *Vernonia* decision that athletes have reduced expectations of privacy?

6. Do you agree that schools have a "compelling interest" in reducing or eliminating drug use?

EXTENSION QUESTIONS AND ACTIVITIES

In what other settings is denial cause for further accusation? Research court cases that have addressed this issue, i.e, whether running from the police provides probable cause.

Find out what the research says regarding whether kids involved in sports and other extra curricular activities do better in school and have fewer disciplinary, legal, and social problems.

CHAPTER TWO

Property Disputes and the Coercive Effect of Johnny Law

School Searches Involving Police

> It behooves every man who values liberty of conscience for himself, to resist invasions of it in the case of others: or their case may, by change of circumstances, become his own.
>
> —Thomas Jefferson

> We know that freedom cannot be served by the devices of the tyrant. As it is an ancient truth that freedom cannot be legislated into existence, so it is no less obvious that freedom cannot be censored into existence. And any who act as if freedom's defenses are to be found in suppression and suspicion and fear confess a doctrine that is alien to America.
>
> —Dwight D. Eisenhower

While the Supreme Court has never heard a case regarding searches of or on school property, lower courts have heard a number of challenges in this regard. Almost all have, to date, upheld these searches as constitutional, regardless of the questionable circumstances or the significant diminishment of students' privacy rights. The rulings have sent mixed messages regarding whether students even have a legitimate expectation of privacy in their lockers or vehicles. Nonetheless, the courts tend to side with the schools as they affirm search after search. These searches are all a part of the "righteous onslaught" against our demon youth, who are presumed to be hyper-violent and drug-dealing ganja freaks. The school administrators aren't the only ones policing students. Police officers have long been involved in school searches in a variety of roles. This is likely to increase as the pressure to monitor our kids prompts communities to demand more School Resource Officers (SROs). The New York City Board of Education employed over 3200 uniformed school safety officers, more than the entire Boston Police Department, in the mid 1990s.[1] According to a U.S Department of Education study, approximately 19% of public schools had a full-time officer present on campus during the 1996-7 school year.[2] The use of SROs was supported, if not required, by Bush the Elder's "Goals 2000" malarkey.[3] Additional federal funding to the tune of more than $350 million has facilitated the growth of officers on school campuses.[4]

The best advice for students who wish to keep their personal effects private, as the case law will demonstrate, is to carry everything they own in their backpacks or their pockets, don't ever look nervous, and, by all means, never associate with classmates who might be considered sketchy; you could be guilty by association, or, perhaps worse, they could turn snitch on you. In spite of the fact that the courts pay lip service to the notion that students have some, albeit diminished, privacy rights, their decisions indicate that in the eyes of the law, schools can do no wrong when they conduct questionable searches of both lockers and vehicles.

The Ends Justifies the Means

Even in cases in which the courts agree that students have privacy rights regarding personal belongings in their lockers, the court is willing to cast these rights aside when presented with a case in which the administrators actually **find** something. Thus the ends justify the means, even though the purpose of the Fourth Amendment is to ensure that the means are always appropriate and fair in achieving the ends. Not for students, though. For instance, in the case of *In re Patrick* 124 Md. App. 604; 723 A 2d 523; 1999 Md. App. in 1999, the Court of Special Appeals of Maryland admitted that students have a legitimate expectation of privacy in their lockers, even though such a right can be limited when there are significant safety and discipline issues the school must address. In this case the "significant safety issue" was an anonymous tip that there might be drugs or weapons on campus. Unbelievably, Mark Twain Middle School security guard Patrick Rooney could not even remember the source that gave him the tip. Regardless, this allegedly justified a random search of **all** middle school students' lockers.[5] In clarifying the expectation of privacy in lockers, the Supreme Court of California, in *People v. William G.*, 221 Cal. Rptr. 118, 127 (1985) had stated, "a student always has the highest privacy interests in his or her own person, belongings, and physical enclaves, such as lockers."[6] Someone forgot to relay that message to Maryland. Or most of the other fifty states.

Little Privacy In Your Vehicle Outside of School

A similar issue is whether students have a legitimate expectation of privacy in their vehicles parked on school property. More generally, the Supreme Court has repeatedly held that vehicle searches are an exception to the warrant rule. They have continued to chip away at the privacy rights of all U.S citizens by expanding what and who can be investigated in the course of a vehicle search. A prohibition-era case, *Carroll v. United States*, 267 U.S. 132 (1925), first established that vehicles are an exception to the warrant rule.[7] The decision was reaffirmed in 1982 in *United States v. Ross*, 456 U.S. 798 (1982), where the high court stated that "police officers who have legitimately stopped an automobile and who have probable cause to believe that contraband is concealed somewhere within may conduct a warrantless search of the vehicle that is as thorough as a magistrate could authorize by warrant."[8] These decisions stemmed from the potential mobility of the vehicle, with the court asserting that, if contraband was within a vehicle and officers had to wait to get a warrant in order to search, that vehicle is likely to be moved. More recently, the court has upheld the right of police to remove passengers suspected of no wrongdoing from vehicles they have stopped (*Maryland v. U.S.*, 519 U.S. 408), and has determined that it is acceptable for police to search the belongings of passengers who are not suspect (*Wyoming v. Houghton*, 526 U.S 295).[9] In a 9-0 ruling in 2004, the Supreme Court gave officers even greater flexibility with the probable cause standard when searching for drugs. Joseph Jermaine Pringle was a passenger in a car stopped for speeding. Officers found crack in a rear seat armrest and arrested all three individuals in the car because none confessed to crack ownership.[10] Happen to be riding with a lead-footed driver? Better keep any personal effects in your pockets, as that is the only remaining place the police still need probable cause to search. Additionally, the court has upheld the use of anonymous tips as the sole evidence to search a vehicle.[11] It is not surprising that such violations of a person's privacy within their own vehicle have trickled into our schools, only to a much worse degree.

Nor In School!

The courts have admitted on numerous occasions that students have more privacy rights in their vehicles than in lockers, which are school-owned property. For example, one court held that "student's expectation of privacy in a school locker is considerably less than he would have in the privacy of his home or even his automobile."[12] Yet again, this seems to be more rhetoric than reality. As with other types of school searches, the courts have generally required a reasonable suspicion standard in order to search a vehicle. Of course, simply parking on school property now provides this suspicion in some schools. Schools in many locations have posted signs that are visible upon entering the parking lot which state that, by parking there, students and/or staff have consented to searches of their vehicles with or without cause by school officials or police officers. School officials have likened such signs to entering courthouse grounds and being subject to a metal detector test.[13] Incredible that students parking their cars in an attempt to enter a place they are **required by law to attend** is viewed the same as the legitimate safety concerns that accompany a public building like the courthouse. The courts have repeatedly held that teachers and students have a non-adversarial relationship and this is certainly distinct from the nature of relationships between people at the local courthouse. Thus it is difficult to see the parallel between parking at school and entering court.

Never Fear, Kids, They're After the Staff As Well!

If it makes students feel any better, teachers are not immune to such surveillance tactics and subsequent harassment; in *Hearn v. Board of Public Education* 191 F. 3d; 1999 U.S. App. Sherry Hearn's car was searched and a partially smoked joint was found. Given that she had been in class all day, the car window was unrolled and the joint was still warm, she felt it reasonable to decline a drug test with the explanation that it obviously wasn't hers. After talking to a lawyer she agreed to be tested the next day. Despite her negative test for marijuana, she was fired because she failed to take the test within the two-hour period required by school policy. Hardly a fitting send off for an award-winning teaching of twenty-seven years.[14]

Private Effects in Lockers and Vehicles Are Fair Game For Searching

In addition to the fact that students do-but-don't really have a legitimate expectation of privacy in their lockers or vehicles, a different but related issue that requires consideration is whether personal effects contained within those lockers or vehicles are private. The courts generally ignore this concern altogether, evidently assuming that once the school is "in," everything else is fair game. By failing to specifically address whether students' personal effects within their lockers are private, the courts seem to be answering in the negative. To those who might wonder why students would need personal effects at school or whether they have any expectation to even a modicum of privacy, the court has already addressed this issue. As discussed in the previous chapter, in *T.L.O.* the Supreme Court affirmed that students do have some privacy rights in schools and need access to some personal items, such as keys, diaries, money, and items required for personal hygiene. Again, students receive mixed messages about their privacy rights. The case of students enrolled in physical education classes highlights this concern. Clearly it is not reasonable to expect a female student to play volleyball with her purse hanging from her arm, yet if she leaves it in her gym locker can she be assured that it will not be searched?[15] The answer, sadly, is a resounding "No." In another case, *State v. Brooks*, 43 Wn. App. 560, 718 P. 2d 837 (1986), the court upheld a search of a locked metal box housed within a locker, which was found to contain drugs.[16] One must wonder to what degree school officials are going on fishing expeditions when they require the opening of locked items within school lockers, especially when it is done absent individualized suspicion, as is the trend in locker searching.

While the courts have generally tended to uphold locker searches, even under some quite convoluted logic, some states are attempting to make the process even **easier**. For instance, Michigan passed a law in 2000 allowing random locker searches in all schools. The bill was prompted by the discovery of a pipe bomb near Holland Woods Middle School in Port Huron.[17] If this is ever contested, chances are good the courts will side with the school, as they have previously held that uniformity of procedures is a nice protection for schools when they conduct what should otherwise be unlawful group searches.[18] While of course no one wants a pipe bomb in schools, the reaction that we must now search **all** kids is overbroad and overzealous.

What About Personal Effects in Vehicles? Nope!

In regard to items within vehicles, an important case was heard by the Appeals Court of Washington; *State v. Slattery 56 Wn. App. 820; 787 P. 2d 932* in 1990. A student's tip to Thomas Jefferson High School Vice-Principal Sterling Thurston prompted the search. The student told Thurston that another student, Mike Slattery, was selling marijuana in the school parking lot. Thurston

says that he believed this student was a reliable source of informa-
tion because of his past experience with the student, as well as the
fact that he had heard other reports about Slattery using drugs.
Every future administrator and teacher should be so well trained in
rumor-mill evidence gathering. Thurston called Slattery into his
office and asked him to empty his pockets. Slattery complied,
revealing $230 in cash in small bills and a paper with a pager num-
ber listed on it. Thurston knew that drug dealers often have cash
on them and use pagers to make their deals, and assumed this to be
the case with Slattery. He called a school security officer, who
searched Slattery's locker but found no evidence of contraband.
The search should have ended there, as clearly Slattery had no
contraband in the school. But Thurston pressed on, asking Slattery
if he would consent to a search of his vehicle. Slattery **denied** con-
sent, to which the security officer responded that they would get
into his car "one way or another." Clearly this comment raises ter-
rific concerns about coercive consent issues that will be addressed
later in the chapter. Slattery next spoke to his mother, who advised
him to allow the vehicle search, which he did. In his car school
officials found a pager and a notebook with a list of names and dol-
lar amounts written next to them. They proceeded to open his
locked trunk where they found a locked briefcase. Slattery said that
he did not know the combination to the lock, so the security offi-
cers pried it open. Inside they found 80.2 grams of marijuana. The
police were then summoned to the scene, where they arrested
Slattery.[19]

The court held that the search was part of the school search
exception to the warrant rule, thus no warrant was needed to
search Slattery, his locker, nor his vehicle. Slattery did not dispute
the searches of his person or his locker as reasonable, but argued
that searching the vehicle and locked briefcase were not justified.
His argument, in essence, is that the Fourth Amendment protects
against fishing expeditions of this ilk. Citing *Brooks*, where the
court upheld a similar search of a locked metal box found in a lock-
er that turned up evidence of drugs, the court determined that the
vehicle and briefcase searches in question were not unconstitu-

tional. In their ruling, they stated that drug use was a serious, ongoing problem at Thomas Jefferson High. The magic words were spoken. Even in pre-*Vernonia* days school administrators needed only to scream that they were warriors in the war on the drugs and even the most egregious searches were condoned. Further, the situation apparently required immediate action because Slattery, or someone else, could have moved the vehicle. Yet no evidence was presented to suggest that Slattery had access to the vehicle during the school day or was in any way planning a hasty getaway from the scene.[20] Once they found that Slattery had no drugs on him or in his locker, the court held that his vehicle was the next logical place for administrators to search. Aside from being quite presumptive, this logic allows for administrators to wage further pogroms against youth. And so the prevailing logic in schools seems to be, if the item of concern is not where we thought it was, well we'll just keep searching until we find it somewhere, Fourth Amendment be damned.

The TIPS Standard: In Law and In Reality

Using the precedent set in *T.L.O*, the lower courts typically assess the constitutionality of a locker or vehicle search based on its overall reasonableness. This includes whether it was justified at its inception and whether it was reasonable in scope. While seemingly simple, determining whether a search of lockers or vehicles was justified involves the balancing of many different factors. School privacy experts Rossow and Stefkovich recommend use of the TIPS formula in determining the legality of a search. The "T" represents the "thing" or contraband to be seized, i.e, what you are looking for, while the "I" represents the "information" that prompted the search. The "P" and the "S" address the reasonableness of the scope of the search, where the "P" refers to the place or person to be searched and the "S" refers to the search method.[21] The "T" and "I" represent the first prong of the reasonableness test, whether the search is justified at its inception. As a general proposition, the higher the degree of danger presented by the "thing" that is being sought out, the less suspicion required,[22] and the courts seem to have deemed drug-related queries as "high danger." A search is supposedly unlawful if it is "predicated on mere curiosity, rumor, or hunch."[23] But, according to a Missouri Superintendent, student tips are an excellent source of reasonable suspicion. He said, "We can identify kids who may be a threat because kids many times know best. They have hunches."[24] Thus the game of semantics begins. Will this district initiate searches based on these hunches? Likely. And could a student challenge them on constitutional grounds? Certainly. And will the story then become that the search was based on a tip rather than a hunch? Absolutely. And will the courts affirm the search as constitutional, calling it reasonable suspicion? Without question.

Any Old Informant Is Credible

In *People v. Joseph G.*, 38 Cal. Rptr. 2d 902, 904-05 (1995) the courts upheld a locker search based only on an anonymous phone call, allegedly because the item of concern was a handgun.[25] While it is obvious that a gun on campus poses a significant danger, typically it should not be difficult for the schools to corroborate a tip with additional information. Sadly, court rulings make this increasingly unlikely, as schools know that their searches will be upheld without doing so. What is their advantage in conducting further investigations? Upholding the Constitution? Not usually an important part of the cost-benefit analysis.

Outside of a school setting, the standard for assessing the reliability of information comes from *Illinois v. Gates* 462 U.S. 213 (1983). Here the Supreme Court held that an analysis of the totality of circumstances must ensue, "where the basis of knowledge of the informant is weighed to decide whether there is probable cause to believe that contraband or evidence is located in a particular place."[26] While tips from school personnel are arguably fairly credible, tips from students "need to be weighed carefully."[27] But are they? The Supreme Court of Mississippi, in *In re South Carolina*, 583 So. 2d 188, 192 (1991), stated that, "absent information that a particular student informant may be untrustworthy, school offi-cials may ordinarily accept at face value the information they sup-ply."[28] Evidently high school students, who have been deemed irre-sponsible by the law in virtually all other venues (they can't drink a beer, vote, or in some cases even drive a moped), suddenly become reliable as informants by virtue of **not** being proven the opposite. So we have identified at least one situation in which we trust our youth; when we think they're ratting on each other! Some schools have even gone so far as to pay students for their tips. As James Redden states in *Snitch Culture*, "Snitching is almost a required subject these days."[29]

In an especially dubious example of a student-informant's tip prompting a search, the appellate court of Mississippi heard the appeal of S.C., a new student at Long Beach High School in *S.C. v. State* 583 So. 2d 188; 1991 Miss. Allegedly S.C. tried to sell handguns to student Derek Laster. At noon Laster reported this to an assistant principal, who absurdly requested that Laster interro-gate S.C. and see whether he had any guns on campus. Laster did as asked and S.C allegedly replied that he did. No school official ever questioned S.C., or any other students for that matter. The assistant principal, upon hearing the update, contacted a colleague and the two obtained S.C.'s locker number. It was locked, so they went to S.C.'s classroom and asked whether he would accompany them to his locker while they opened it. He agreed, and they found a black bag hanging in the locker. One of the assistant principals picked up the bag, unzipped it, and removed two guns. S.C. was subsequently taken to the office, where school officials called his grandparents, with whom he was staying, as well as the police. In the end, S.C. was adjudicated a delinquent child in Harrison County Family Court and was to spend time in a Juvenile Training School.[30]

In court, one of S.C.'s main arguments was that, per *T.L.O*, there was no reasonable suspicion to conduct the search. His con-cern was that Laster was the only source of information regarding the weapons, and that Laster had never actually **seen** any guns. Laster could be a complete wack-job, or simply someone who took an immediate disliking to S.C. The court admitted that normally relying solely on an informant's tip would be problematic, stating, "In the larger world we expend considerable judicial energy searching out the reliability of informants and the basis of their knowledge. We do this because experience has taught that informants often act out of self interest and, more generally, they are not among our more reliable citizens." Yet, they felt that "High school students would seem to fall into a different and generally less suspect class."[31] In fact, rather than independently question S.C. to verify Laster's allegations, the school officials initial response was, frighteningly, to send the untrained and potentially unreliable Laster back to pump information from a potential gun runner. Brilliant. Instead of finding this problematic, the appellate court determined that "a responsible school official under the circumstances would and should have regarded this information sufficient that he take action."[32] While the seriousness of potentially having guns on campus makes it readily apparent that action was necessary, it is equally apparent that sending a student on a covert fact-finding mission is dangerous and moronic. And by condoning the methods employed by the authorities, the court, in effect, sends the message that it is appropriate to use students as undercover agents in their quest to maintain control. More on the use of tips to justify searches will be provided in a subsequent chapter.

As noted above, vehicle searches have generally been considered an exception to the warrant rule based on the mobility argument. Yet one must wonder whether this is a valid assumption in a school setting. According to school legal experts Rossow and Stefkovich,

> Whether or not students have access to their cars during the day has a bearing on the degree of interest the school has in a search and therefore the degree of reasonable suspicion needed for a search. If students do not have access to their cars, the extent to which the cars become part of the routine in the school environment is minimal to nonexistent. In that case the expectation of privacy in the car is treated more like that of the home than that of the locker.[33]

Sounds good, but it doesn't seem to be what actually happens. For instance, in the previously mentioned *State v. Slattery*, the search of his vehicle, and items within it, was upheld despite any evidence that Slattery could or would access his car during the school day. Apparently the car will be searched just like a locker when the locker search fails to prove fruitful. [34]

Even a Shady School Policy Seemingly Forestalls Complaint

Generally, courts have been less sympathetic (if that is possible) to student privacy claims when the school has a pre-existing policy regarding ownership and searching of lockers. For example, in the case of *Isaiah B. v. State*, 500 N.W. 2d 637, 638 (Wis. 1993) in Milwaukee, the courts upheld a random locker search for weapons because the search was covered by a very detailed school policy. It stated that the lockers belonged to the school and that school officials would conduct periodic inspections, at any time, for any reason, and without notice, student consent, or a warrant.[35] Sometimes, however, schools craft ambiguous or confusing policies yet the courts seem to feel as though **any** policy is good enough.

In an ironic twist, the courts will even uphold cases in which the school's actions directly **violate** their own policy. Mark Twain Middle School had a policy which stated that the school "subscribed to the Montgomery County Public School's Search and Seizure policy, which provides that the principal or the administration's designee may conduct a search of a student or of the student's locker if there is probable cause to believe that the student has in his/her possession an item, the possession of which constitutes a criminal offense under the laws of the State of Maryland."[36] In the aforementioned case of *In re Patrick Y 124 Md. App. 604* the Court of Special Appeals of Maryland determined that a search prompted by some kind of tip to security guard Patrick Rooney (who, as noted, could not recall the source of that tip) justified a random search of all middle school students' lockers. The appellant contested the search, arguing that the wording regarding "probable cause" requires the school to actually **meet** that standard. It is questionable that they did in light of the fact that the search was prompted by an anonymous source's non-individualized tip. In addressing the specific wording of the school's policy, the court stated that they did not read it to prohibit searches absent probable cause.[37] Of course not. Even though the policy flat-out says "probable cause," it certainly can't really mean that if we then have to toss out some juicy evidence. They argued that, "the statement, read as a whole, explains the consequences of students' actions. It does not purport to be a complete statement of disciplinary policy, nor does it purport to be a limitation on the school administrators' need to maintain safety and order in the school."[38] The court even admitted that, if the policy explicitly acknowledged students' privacy in their lockers, under the circumstances of this case they would have felt a search was justified. Translation: The student gets the shaft either way.

In court, defendants are allowed to confront or cross-examine their accusers. No one seems too worried, however, that Patrick was unable to do so because the school's highly trained law enforcement agent cannot seem to recall what prompted him to paw through a pre-teen's personal items. And because Rooney is an officer of the law we should assume he is automatically credible? Tell that to the victims in Tulia, Texas, where clearly an officer was anything **but** credible. In this heinous example of law-enforcement, a private investigator was called in to "fix" a non-existent drug problem in this small town. Allegedly a town that could barely keep open a Dairy Queen was home to more than forty big-time drug dealers, who all just happened to be black or intimately involved with blacks. Tom Coleman, the private investigator, collected no actual evidence of drugs, drug paraphernalia, or the fruits of drug sales (large houses, expensive cars, weapons, etc.) but did manage to record his observations about the drug exchanges on his hand, enough to convince an all-white jury to convict.

Your Consent Is Irrelevant

Whether consent to search is required in schools is another issue the courts have struggled with. Outside of schools, consent is an exception to the warrant rule. In other words, if an officer asks if they can search your bedroom, for example, and you say "yes," then the search can proceed without a warrant. Yet in order to give permission, it would seem, one must be aware of the repercussions of that consent and one must not be coerced or intimidated by their social position or lack of legal knowledge. Not so, however, which will be discussed more thoroughly later in the chapter. Definitely not so in schools. A Massachusetts court, in the case of *Commonwealth v. Snyder*, 413 Mass. 52; 597 N. E. 2d. 1363; 1992 Mass, determined that locker searches absent student consent or presence are fair. A teacher reported to an assistant principal that a student told her that Snyder had a video-cassette case containing three bags of marijuana in it, which he had put in his book bag after he tried to sell the drugs.[39]

The assistant principal and another school official opened Snyder's locker while he was in class, after determining that it would be too disruptive to discuss the issue with him while he was in the student center at lunch time. Isn't it touching that the school cared about embarrassing a student? But did they really? More likely they were waiting to search the locker at a time when they could avoid the possibility that Snyder would object. Sneaky tactics, but who cares? It's only an adolescent. They found Snyder's book bag, and the three bags of marijuana in the video-cassette case in his locker, as alleged. Snyder contended that the search was in violation of his privacy rights and that the school needed a warrant.[40]

The court did conclude that Snyder had a legitimate expectation of privacy in his locker, in fact, that all students do, unless there is some "express understanding to the contrary."[41] In this case the student code said that students had the right "not to have his/her locker subjected to unreasonable search,"[42] which clearly implies a right to privacy. The court still held, however, that the search was reasonable, citing *T.L.O.* They determined that the school did not need a warrant, as there was an imminent threat that the marijuana would be either removed or sold. Yet clearly Snyder was not doing this in any haste, as he did not attempt to move the items during lunch or between classes, which would seem to be the prime time for drug sales. Must be he was planning a covert operation to sneak out of his class undetected to peddle his wares. The court felt that it was acceptable that the school officials searched Snyder's locker without talking to him due to their judgment that it would be disruptive to do so in the student center and due to the need for immediacy.

So the kid had drugs and got busted and we should all be happy. Right? Wrong. One kid whispers in a teacher's ear and the search is on? And another kid's right to know that someone is rifling through his personals is ignored because telling him might cause a disruption? Well, apparently there's a new formula for effective administration for all the aspiring principals out there: Search away but keep it real quiet. Sounds like a part of the Patriot Act. Hate to have some Constitution-loving kid cause a disruption while you're ransacking his SpongeBob lunch pail.

In another case dealing with student consent, *Shamberg v. State*, 762 P. 2d 488, 490 (Alaska Ct. App. 1988), despite admitting that student Matthew Nolan's consent to search his vehicle was not free nor voluntary, the court still upheld the search. Thankfully, not all courts agree that searches with student consent should be upheld.[43] In *Jones v. Latexo Independent School District* 499 F. Supp. 223 (E.D. Tex. 1980) drug-sniffing dogs indicated at cars and the school officials asked the students for permission to conduct searches. Although the students gave consent, the court, in suppressing the evidence, held that "students in school are afraid not to cooperate with school authorities."[44] Yes! Finally someone seems to understand that teens may not be on equal footing with officers, an idea to which we will return.

Searching in a Timely Fashion, Or Whenever Works Best To Get the Goods

Finally, the issue of the timeliness of a search is of great concern, both to school officials as well as to the students being searched. Clearly if there is a threat of imminent danger a school must act in a timely fashion to squelch that threat. Yet, again, we see that schools have abused this duty and that courts generally ignore their abuses. As the above case demonstrates, timeliness was cited as a reason why the search was justified, yet administrators waited over an hour before conducting the search in order to make the process smoother. And is smoother really just sneakier? We're afraid so. "Make my job easy" seems to be the request of administrators, rather than "help me treat my students like American citizens."

Searches By or With Police

According to Rossow and Stefkovitch, when police search in schools they must meet a higher standard than school officials; probable cause and the warrant rule apply to officer-driven searches, rather than the reasonable suspicion standard. If school officials search a student at the urging of the police, they supposedly are assumed to be acting as agents of the police, and are therefore required to have probable cause. Yet if police merely give the school "tips" but are not substantially involved in the searching, the courts have generally supported a reasonable suspicion standard.[45] Likewise, the lower standard applies when police are present but do not initiate the search, as in *Cason v. Cook* 810 F. 2d 188 (8th Cir. 1987).[46] It is to officers' advantage, then, if they feel as though a search should be conducted, to convince school officials of the need and to have the school officials themselves actually do the searching. This has been referred to as the "silver platter doctrine," as school officials are figuratively handing police evidence on a silver platter and it was brought up as a concern in *T.L.O*, even though the court did not address police involvement at that time. The ACLU submitted an amicus curiae brief expressing apprehension that police would merely receive evidence from school officials without having to do any investigatory work.[47] And, more importantly, such evidence would be allowable in court, especially as some states and local school boards did (and still do) require school officials to notify police when a crime has occurred. While supposedly the silver platter doctrine is not acceptable practice, an early case determined that it **is** constitutional. In *People v. Overton*, 20 N.Y. 2d 360, 283 N.Y.S 2d 22, 229 N.E. 2d 596 (1969) three detectives from the Mount Vernon Police Department obtained a warrant to search two high school students and their lockers. The detectives presented the warrant to the school's vice-principal, Dr. Adolph Panitz, who summoned the boys from class. The detectives searched the boys in Panitz's office but found nothing. After briefly interrogating the boys, two of the detectives took one to his locker, leaving the other boy, the defendant, in the office with the vice-principal and the remaining detective. Overton was asked whether he had marijuana in his locker, to which he did not respond but nodded in an uncertain manner. The detective asked him again, and Overton responded, "I guess so," or "Maybe." The detective, Panitz, and the school custodian then went to Overton's locker, opened it with Panitz's master key, and found marijuana cigarettes in Overton's jacket.[48]

It was later held that the warrant that prompted the action was ineffective, so Overton moved to suppress the marijuana as evidence in the proceedings against him as a youthful offender. The Court of Appeals determined that Dr. Panitz had consented to the search, which was binding on the defendant. It was determined that the locker belonged to the school, not Overton, so Panitz's consent was adequate.[49] Huh? Another person can give consent to search **my** stuff? Once again, only if you're a minor. As a spouse, for instance, I can only give consent for an officer to search shared areas. Thus I **cannot** give an officer permission to search my husband's golf bag, for instance, as that is not a shared item.

The Court of Appeals drew on another case that was heard by the U.S. Supreme Court, *Bumper v. North Carolina* 391 U.S. 543

(1968) in further addressing the issue of consent. In *Bumper*, four white law enforcement officials, who claimed they had a warrant, were determined to enter the home of an elderly black woman living in rural North Carolina. Later, it was found that the warrant was ineffective. She meekly told them to go ahead. As in *Overton*, the prosecution argued that the search was still valid because they had obtained consent. Further, since both searches (in *Bumper* as well as *Overton*) turned up contraband, the prosecution argued that they were indeed valid. The ends justify the means, again. The Supreme Court thankfully rejected both arguments in *Bumper*. In regard to consent, the court stated, "When a law enforcement officer claims authority to search a home under a warrant, he announces that the occupant has no right to resist the search. The situation is instinct with coercion-albeit quasi-lawful coercion. Where there is coercion there cannot be consent."[50] Meaning that because a warrant had been presented, the defendant could no longer give meaningful consent because they might believe they had no right to resist the search.

Yet the appellate court determined that the case at Mount Vernon High lacked the "lawful coercion" found in *Bumper*. Elaborating on who owned the lockers, the court stated that the administrators of all the buildings in the district operate those buildings as representatives of the Board of Education. The court felt that the student's consent was not relevant, as in *Bumper*, based on Panitz's delegated duty to oversee the school's property.[51] Thus the coercion factor was completely ignored.

The dissenters argued that Panitz opened the locker not out of any supervisory role, but because he felt obligated to because the police could not (since the warrant was ineffective). They stated, "no matter how the record is read, the coercive effect of this bad search warrant on the principal as well as on the defendant is inescapable. Dr. Panitz himself testified that in permitting the search of the defendant's locker he was 'honoring the search warrant'."[52] Although not brought up by the dissenters, another important component of searches conducted by police is the **inherently** coercive nature of their role. According to David Friedman in his chapter on Privacy and Technology in *The Right To Privacy*, "governments almost always have an overwhelming superiority of physical force over the individual citizen."[53] To this important area we turn next.

Police and Kids: An Adversarial Relationship?

In several other cases, cited below, the courts have also ignored the frequently adversarial relationship between teens and police that everyone (except perhaps school faculty and court justices) knows exists. The Supreme Court has adopted what they call a "reasonable person" standard in regard to consent, not just in schools but everywhere. This standard is "patently fictional, and allows the police to engage in substantial coercion under the rubric of 'consent' without any limits on the persons to whom the coercion can be applied."[54] Thus the courts may only find coercion when it is above and beyond that of an officer's inherent authority. This "one-size-fits-all reasonable person standard fails to take into account that citizens may be differently situated with respect to encounters with the police."[55] Evidently the justices feel that a fourteen-year old has the same capacity to deny consent to a police officer as does a fifty-year old Congressman. Alida Brill's insights regarding privacy hold especially true here: "The more vulnerable you are, the less likely it is that you will feel empowered or enabled to protect your privacy."[56]

In a more recent case, *Stockton v. City of Freeport*, 147 F. Supp. 2d 642 (S. D. Tex. 2001), officers clearly used their authority for nefarious means. Officers from the local police department entered Brazosport High School in Freeport, Texas at the behest of school officials, who had found a "threatening" letter on the Friday after the Columbine shootings. They suspected one student in particular, and knew that this student hung around with 14 other students during lunch. The officers rounded up the students, frisked them, handcuffed them, and led them out of the building. They were placed in police cars and driven to the municipal courthouse. No one explained to the students why this was happening, but allegedly the officers used profane language toward them during the drive. They also threatened to place the students in the municipal jail, where they would "suffer mightily at the hands of the inmates."[57] The students were ordered to stay in an empty courtroom and threatened with five-year prison terms if they tried to leave. At no time did the officers produce a warrant for the searches or for the students' arrest. After an hour wait the students were told to call their parents, who were lectured by the police and the principal upon their arrival. The mother of one of the students, Jeremy D., insisted that she could not wait through the lecture and left with her son. Before he left a detective told him that they knew he had done nothing wrong and that the whole incident was a "show of force, intended to impress upon the students that the authorities were monitoring them."[58]

The next morning the principal explained to the student body during an assembly that none of the arrested students were guilty of anything and that the school was safe. He admonished them not to bother the fourteen students in any way, but his words were clearly ignored. Too little, too late. Several of the detained students complained of harassment by peers. Jeremy received in-school suspension two times because he tried to exonerate himself from accusations levied by classmates during geometry class. He suffered from stress, resulting in a loss of sleep. After falling asleep in class once, Jeremy's teacher, appallingly, threw a glass of water at him while the students laughed. His mother's complaint to the principal about this treatment was met with the suggestion that she remove him from the school. She refused, but one of the other detainees did elect to be home schooled rather than face the accusations and poor treatment by fellow students. Jeremy and two of the other detainees filed suit in February of 2000, claiming that their detention was an unreasonable seizure.[59]

The federal district court dismissed the case. The court followed precedent in considering the nature of the governmental concern and the efficacy of the means. Their logic demonstrates the post-Columbine hysteria that swept the nation but it leaves much to be desired. While we definitely acknowledge Columbine was a horrific event, it should not have been co-opted by schools and police to engage in widespread anti-teenism in violation of constitutional guarantees. The court essentially upheld the students' guilt by association in determining that the detained students were socially connected to the student suspected of leaving the threatening letter. This logic is especially asinine if we apply it to situations outside of school. Take, for instance, some evidence that a member of a bridge club from a senior citizens home has written a potentially threatening letter and left it at the table during the group's weekly meeting. The police should have to investigate all the other seniors, since they are "socially connected," right? The court stated, "It is difficult to conceive of a scenario in which a greater government interest is invoked than the threat of indiscriminate violence at school."[60] Perhaps, but it is also difficult to conceive of a scenario more reprehensible than the scare tactics used here with no justification.

As the event happened within a week of Columbine, the court also considered that, "the officials in the Columbine massacre were harshly criticized for *failing* to take action regarding prior signs of problems."[61] Although the court admitted there was some concern about the supposed immediacy of the threat, as several days separated the finding of the letter from the police action, they felt that the concern was still weighty enough to justify the police response. So they were worried about **not** acting, but then waited days before they acted? In regard to the efficacy of the means, the court gave the school and the police wide latitude. They did acknowledge that less intrusive means were available, but still determined that what occurred was in the bounds of what is constitutional.

In response to the claim that the actions by the school and police were simply post-Columbine hysteria, the court countered, "in the aftermath of the Columbine High violence, some period of hypersensitivity among school officials...indeed should be lauded," and "it simply is not improper to overreact."[62] To overreact means to act excessively; isn't that, by nature, improper? And, in an era of Zero Tolerance and knee-jerk reactions, the consequences of overreacting are more profound than ever. Again, if administrators scream "safety concern" they are given carte blanche to run amok and then pat themselves on the back for a job well done. And, of course, how long this "period of hypersensitivity" should last is an important question; it certainly does not seem to have abated in 2004.

The plaintiff's attorney, Robert Rosenberg, articulated one of the major problems with the court's decision. He said, "School, as well as police, officials need to take a course in civics and study the Constitution before taking such knee-jerk reactions. Otherwise, they will be providing the breeding ground for future attorneys like me, who will dedicate their careers to making schools places where the Constitution is taught in not only word but deed."[63] The get-tough tactics used by the police, at the behest of the school, could have easily been replaced by an investigation. Yet the court, rather than nipping such coercive actions in the bud, has allowed for police to continue pushing the edges of acceptable conduct in the name of school safety.

More Intimidation Tactics, Er...Consent

In 2000 the Fifth Circuit Court of Appeals again denied that police have a coercive effect on youth in the case of *Milligan v. City of Slidell*, 226 F. 3d 652; 2000 U.S. App. On January 26, 1997, a fight took place between several students from Salmen High School and two brothers from Slidell High School in Slidell, Louisiana. Two days later a Salmen High School student, David Gilis, contacted the father of the two from Slidell, Louis Thompson, and told him there was to be a retaliatory fight, possibly including weapons, at Slidell High. Thompson first called the football coach at Salmen, as Gilis had told him that some football players might have been involved in the altercation. He then called Sgt. Emery of the local police, and the three possied up and went to Salmen High to "diffuse" the situation. Thompson also had his sons compile a list of students involved in the altercation and anyone they would consider to be their "known" enemies.[64]

Are we dealing with the mob here?

Upon arrival at the school, Thompson and Emery asked Vice-Principal Smith to call some of the students on the list out of class and question them, which he did. Prior to this Emery and some other officers had met with the football coach and the players in question, who confirmed that there was to be a fight at Slidell with baseball bats. The plaintiffs were questioned about the fight and warned against engaging in future altercations. Plaintiff Eric Milligan said that he felt physically intimidated by the officers and was not free to leave the meeting. The officers claimed that no physical contact occurred and that the students seemed comfortable talking.[65]

The appeals court overturned the district court, which had ruled that this was an "investigative detention" as per *Terry v. Ohio*, 392 U.S (1968). According to *Terry*, the officers were required to have reasonable suspicion of past or incipient criminal activity, which they did not have. The appeals court stated that the application of *Terry* was questionable, and that even if *Terry* did apply the district had ignored the importance of the school context. Further, the appeals court ruled that it was not clear that students have a right **not** to be summoned and detained for questioning.[66]

Regarding the nature and immediacy of the concerns, the appeals court held that the school had a compelling interest in acting with immediacy. Good thing the posse arrived, then, to facilitate the process. Additionally, the court addressed the efficacy of the means, holding that the means were indeed appropriate. The officers involved had used appropriate channels in first talking to the football coach, then the vice-principal. The court also reaffirmed that there is no constitutional guarantee that the least intrusive method will be used during a search, as in the previous case in Brazosport.

When the School Calls in the Law

The opposite of the searches described above is also true; a school can request assistance with a search or give police permission to search lockers or vehicles. It is likely that the police officer will be held to a reasonable suspicion standard in this case. The purpose of the search **supposedly** matters. If the police are involved then the implication is (in theory, at least) that some criminal evidence is to be turned up. According to Rossow and Stefkovitch, "the police have no interest in internal school disciplinary matters."[67] This no longer seems to hold true, however, as courts have affirmed many searches in which police are involved but no criminal evidence is in question. For instance, in *Cason v. Cook*, cited earlier, the court ruled that a search in which an officer assigned to the school assisted was acceptable. The search was for a missing change purse. The officer's contribution was to patdown a student, which was, according to the court, minimal.[68] As *Cason v. Cook* brings up, with more surveillance at schools in the form of School Resource Officers, the picture becomes much grayer in regard to characterizing precisely the role of police in school searches. School Resource Officers are trained police officers, not certified teachers or administrators. They typically wear their uniform, including their handgun, and are paid by the police force, not the school. Yet the courts seem to see their role as akin to educators, holding them to the lower standard of reasonable suspicion as opposed to the probable cause standard. Given their training and that the police pay their wages, this is a dubious precedent for the courts to establish.

Teachers, Police: Who Knows the Difference?

The Appeals Court of California determined that school-based police officers are more like teachers than they are like police in the case of *In re Frederick B.*, 192 Cal. App. 3d. 79; 237 Cal. Rptr. 338; 1987 Cal All. (1987). In determining the specific status of Bartlett, an officer assigned to Richmond Unified School District the court drew on Education Code 39670, which states that school guards are peace officers. They fall into a "special category," however, which the court failed to articulate. Bartlett had observed two students apparently exchanging money in a "high crime" area of the school and questioned and detained them. As Frederick B. tried to leave a scuffle ensued and it was discovered that he had a pistol. The court deemed this particular situation as one of a detention rather than a search, so they determined that Bartlett did not need probable cause. While the court admitted that the student's behavior was "consistent with innocent activity" and they had previously been skeptical of the "high crime area" argument, they avoided the issue of whether school officers need probable cause to search or reasonable suspicion. By failing to address the issue they really gave their answer; whatever you do, as long as you do it to students, is all right by us.[69]

In another case heard by the Supreme Court of California, *People v. Randy G.* 26 Cal. 4th 556: 28 P. 3d 239; 110 Cal. Rptr. 2d 516; 2001, in which it was affirmed that School Resource Officers are not really paid officers but more like teaching faculty, Cathy Worthy, a campus security officer at a Los Angeles county high school, observed two students standing in an area off limits to students. When Randy G. saw Worthy he "fixed his pocket very nervously,"[70] but some of the lining in his left pocket was still hanging out. Rather than assuming he was a) playing with change in his pocket; b) adjusting himself; or c) some combination of both, Worthy assumed the worst. After demanding that the boys go to class, she followed them because she felt that Randy G. was acting "very paranoid and nervous."[71] She notified her supervisor and, at his direction, summoned another officer. When the two officers arrived at Randy G.'s classroom, Worthy asked if she could see him outside. Once there she inquired whether he had anything on him, to which he replied he did not. The second officer asked Randy for consent to search his bag, which he gave. Worthy again asked if he had anything on him and Randy again reaffirmed that he did not. Still, the second officer asked Randy if they could pat him down, to which he gave his consent. The pat down revealed a knife, later found to have a locking blade, in his left pocket.[72]

Randy G. contended that the officer lacked reasonable suspicion to detain or search him. He also contended that his consent was a product of the unlawful detention and should not be taken as voluntary.[73] Essentially, he argued that the officers coerced his consent.

The first question the appeals court addressed was whether or not this was a detention. Citing *Terry v. Ohio*, the court defined a detention as "only when the officer, by means of physical force or show of authority, has in some way restrained the liberty of a citizen..."[74] In this case they determined that a minor at school "can hardly be said to be free to continue on his or her way," as students are required to be in school. However, they also stated that a part of daily life in schools involves various types of detention, such as when students are told to remain in or leave a classroom, are given errands, or are called to the office. Unlike citizens on the street, students are "subject to the ordering and direction of teachers and administrators...[A student is] not free to roam the halls or remain in [the] classroom as long as she please[s], even if she behave[s] herself."[75] Thus when a school official stops a student, that student's liberty has not been violated above the limitations already in place by being in attendance at a public school. It sure seems that a teacher asking students to stay after class to discuss their conduct is distinct from a security officer demanding that her questions be answered, but unfortunately the court did not think so. Based on this frightening logic, it was determined that Randy G. had not been "detained." The court did allow that students could challenge the conduct of school officials as arbitrary, capricious, or harassing, but did not feel that was the case here.[76] So apparently rooting around in your pockets is a no-no. And looking nervous when being interrogated about it will only make matters worse.

Since the court determined the major issue of the case was a seizure, not a search, they held that a standard different than that provided by *T.L.O* must apply. Seizures are considered generally less intrusive than searches, so require even **less** suspicion. This hardly seems possible. According to the court, "To require teachers and school officials to have reasonable suspicion before merely questioning a student would destroy the informality of the student teacher relationship...Instead teachers and school officials would be forced to conduct surveillance, traditionally a law enforcement function, before questioning a student about conduct which poses a serious threat to the safety of the students for whom they are responsible."[77] Additionally, the court held that school officials "must be permitted to exercise their broad supervisory and disciplinary powers, without worrying that every encounter with a student will be converted into an opportunity for constitutional review."[78] We wouldn't want teachers and school officials to have to actually work while at work, would we? The reason courts have developed such protections as the exclusionary rule is precisely **because** authority figures weren't spending enough time considering the fact that their encounters with citizens should **always** be constitutional. But in the hallowed halls of today's schools, where our President has just decried the state of students' knowledge of civics, we are teaching a new generation an anti-civics lesson; how to distort and selectively apply our constitutionally guaranteed rights. It's ironic that the court mentions surveillance. Perhaps they should all just send student snoops out to shake down their fellow students, as in S.C.

Randy further argued that, even if the reasonable suspicion standard did not apply to the conduct of the teachers and administrators here, it should apply to the security officers. The court declined to,

> distinguish the power of school security officers over students from that of other school personnel, whose authority over student conduct may have been delegated to those officers. The same observation and investigation here could well have been undertaken by a teacher, coach, or even the school principal or vice-principal. If we were to draw the distinction urged by the minor, the extent of a student's rights would depend not on the nature of the asserted infringement but on the happenstance of the status of the employee who observed and investigated the conduct.[79]

The problem is that the same observation and investigation **was not** made by a teacher or administrator. And the status of the employee who observed and investigated the conduct **should** matter, as this person has an entirely different relationship to students than a teacher or administrator does, not to mention completely disparate training. It should be possible to consider both the student's conduct **and** the student's relationship to the person conducting the search. Unless, of course, it doesn't behoove the system to consider both things. Hasn't the court repeatedly held that, in assessing the legality of school searches, they must perform balancing acts? But here they would be unable to do so? Further, the court stated that if they determined that school security officers had less authority to enforce school rules and investigate misconduct than other school personnel, there would be no point in hiring them. Now finally there's a good idea!

So it seems to boil down to this: Faculty must only have reasonable suspicion to conduct a search because they aren't police and apparently can't understand that really complicated probable cause concept. But when we add cops to the equation, who had better understand probable cause, we allow them to operate under the lower standard. Why? Because otherwise their snooping would be limited and they might not catch those teeming hordes of drug-dealers they would have us believe are terrorizing our schools in epidemic proportions.

QUESTIONS FOR REVIEW AND CRITICAL THINKING

1. Do the ends ever justify the means? If they do, under what circumstances?

2. Why have the courts repeatedly determined vehicle searches are an exception to the warrant rule? Do you agree? How has this been applied in schools?

3. Should teachers be subject to the same search policies as students?

4. Who should have input into school policies? What should be included in school search policies? Should a student's consent to search their locker or vehicle be included?

5. Under which standard should police officers work when in a school setting, reasonable suspicion or probable cause? Should security guards and School Resource Officers follow the same standard?

6. Do you agree police and students have an adversarial relationship? What is the impact of this relationship on a student's ability to consent to a search, according to the authors?

EXTENSION QUESTIONS AND ACTIVITIES

What does the research say about the effectiveness of School Resource Officers in regard to actual and perceived school safety? Explore student, faculty, and parental perspectives.

Research the most current vehicle search cases. Does the trend to expand this exception seem to be continuing?

How have school search policies been applied against teachers to date?

Find out more about court decisions regarding consent. Are police required to **tell** citizens they can refuse consent for a search? Should they be?

CHAPTER THREE

Rover and the Magical Wand

Drug-Sniffing Canines and Metal Detectors in Schools

> The greatest glory of a free-born people is to transmit that freedom to their children
>
> —William Howard

> Since adults, not kids, commit the vast majority of drug abuse, sex crimes, weapons carrying, and violence, we are now holding school boys to higher standards of behavior, greater scrutiny, and lower standards of legal protection, than adults.
>
> —Aaron Kipnis, author of
> *Angry Young Men.*

Can't Afford to Pay the Staff, But Let's Up the Surveillance

Budget cuts are taking a heavy toll on public schools across the nation in the early twenty-first century. Oregon, for instance, actually cut days from the 2002-03 school year in order to save money and, presumably, teaching jobs. While part of this is due to economic recession, much of it can be attributed to the government's lack of support for public schools. The U.S. government is more concerned with financing the next war on terrorism than ensuring all a quality education, despite lip-service to the contrary. Yet, somehow, districts all over have still scrounged up the funds to finance the installation of metal detectors and to pay for visits from drug and weapon detecting canines, generally with public approval. As school districts work to stretch their funds, the industry supplying these surveillance services are often receiving an ample share, as advertised on Interquest's web site (www.interquestk9.com). Interquest is the nation's leader in providing canine-based searches to schools. Their site advertises that their franchisees can expect to bring in a tidy $60,000 to $90,000 income per year. And that's with only one dog.[1]

Such a phenomena is not exclusive to schools; we are not only in an era of greater than ever surveillance, but we are also increasingly dependent on technology as the means to fix our social problems. According to school violence expert Ronnie Casella, "The security build up is not just the result of zero tolerance, it is also an outcome of private security companies that have seen schools, like businesses and homes before them, as a new niche in which to sell their wares."[2] Many school boards are more than willing to take advantage of this new technology because they believe it "sends an important message" to students. While we agree that it sends messages, they may be very different from those that are intended.

And, in addition to the many costs of implementing technological "solutions" to the perceived problems with teens, there are some heinous emotional costs for students. Here is what one female student had to say about the "minimally intrusive" handheld metal detector searches she was forced to endure from a male security guard in her New York City public high school: "I feel like they are trying to know my body...I hear the comments or I see the looks from the guards to the other girls. And through that and through the scanning, they get closer than they ever can get in a normal way...I'm sure they're getting off on it."[3]More on this later.

Canine Costs

In 1999 the federal government spent over $20 million on drug prevention efforts specifically aimed at youth, with a great deal more targeted in general. While some of that goes toward the largely unsuccessful D.A.R.E. program, a portion of that total is also used to fund drug dogs in many districts.[4] The Los Angeles Unified School District even went so far as to purchase their own dogs, rather than contract with a private firm, as most schools do. One dog cost the district $5,000, the other was donated and they are hoping to be able to purchase ten more shortly. The funds, the district is hoping, will come from donations, due to the district's budget crisis.[5] Those schools that arrange to bring in drug dogs from a private company, like Interquest, will generally pay about $600 per dog, per day. The company recommends that schools have a minimum of two visits per month, generally with more than one dog.[6] One wonders how the quality of schools could improve with tax-payers' money being dedicated to new textbooks, after-school art programs, or myriad other uplifting educational programs, rather than periodic visits from Rover and the gang.

Costs of Metal Detectors

Metal detectors, another drain on educational budgets, range in cost, depending on whether a school board approves the more costly but higher technology walk through models more common to airports and courtrooms or the more economical hand-held wands. One company, "Super Metal Detectors," advertised a blowout sale in June of 2003 whereby a "Ranger Security Hand Held" detector could be purchased for $99.99 and a walk through model for just under $5,000.[7] A metal detector purchased from Garrett Electronics would cost a district anywhere from $119 to approximately $5,500.[8] While this may not sound excessively pricey, there are numerous other non-financial costs associated with such purchases, as we will show. If metal detectors were great weapons deterrents schools might be justified in incurring their costs, financial and otherwise. As the reader will see, however, this is not the case either.

Frequency of Metal Detectors and Canine Searches

How prevalent are these types of searches? A 1998 report from the U.S. Department of Education and Justice stated that four percent of schools were using metal detectors, and one-percent were using them daily.[9] A National School Board Association survey of more than 700 districts found that 39% of urban schools use metal detectors.[10] While this may sound minimal, usage has definitely expanded. A 1999 *Newsweek* article indicates that one Texas manufacturer of metal detectors saw their school orders quadruple in 1999.[11] A Dallas, Texas school recently revealed their new "security conscious" facility, containing 37 surveillance cameras, six metal detectors, and a security command center, costing a total of $41 million.[12] Public support for the use of metal detectors, at fifty percent in a 1999 Associated Press poll, virtually ensures that districts will continue to purchase metal detectors.[13] And this is encouraged, of course, by the companies in the surveillance industry. In the words of an Interquest representative: "I'd like to think that dogs will be common, in most schools, in the very near future. Our experience is that once one school district in a region takes advantage of our services, it becomes a 'me too' phenomenon, and it dominoes through all the other schools in the area."[14] Assess your own needs as a school district? Why bother? Just call Interquest or another company like them and get on board the super snoop bandwagon.

Canine searches are also being used more frequently. Hundreds of schools in California alone use drug dogs. Interquest, for example, has contracts with 300 schools in that state and 41 franchises in 23 states. A representative of the company stated in February 2003 that they had 1300 contracts nationwide.[15]

Are They Necessary? No!

If districts are spending money for metal detectors and canines, there must be a need for them, right? Not necessarily. Many districts have installed metal detectors, for example, absent any indication of a weapons problem. Proponents often rely on unfounded fears and perceptions of school violence to justify their use. Yet, as Michael Ferrarracio asserts in his critical analysis of metal detector use, "perceptions of school violence as a nationwide problem do not justify the use of metal detectors in local districts which have never had, and may never have, a problem with violence."[16] The companies that provide these services are fully aware of the paranoia many Americans have about school violence and they milk it for all it's worth. Take, for instance, this guarantee from a supplier of school safety equipment: "By simply screening small packages, book bags, backpacks, briefcases, handbags, boxes, and mailed items for explosives, weapons, and other contraband, a school can almost guarantee the safety of all their students, faculty and staff."[17] The bottom line is that searching the whole laundry list of items that kids will legitimately have with them as they arrive for a school day is neither "simple" nor is it constitutional. The assertion that a school could, or should, search every purse and package that enters in an effort to "guarantee safety" underscores that attempting to guarantee safety via these means can only guarantee a loss of rights for students. Apparently the suppliers of school safety equipment are comfortable with these measures. As discussed below, we are not.

Likewise, misconceptions about the prevalence of drugs in schools have fueled use of drug-sniffing canines. And, even if there is no evidence of a drug problem in a particular school, a school board can just fire up the "deterrent" argument and generally win support for the institution of canine searches. Citing studies that suggest that D.A.R.E. is ineffective, those on the canine-bandwagon over-generalize that **all** preventative measures are ineffective. With preventative measures out of the way, "deterrents are key in the interim."[18] School police in the Los Angeles Unified School District admit that actual confiscations are rare, but concur that the goal of using the two dogs is also to discourage kids from bringing drugs to school.[19] A police captain in Salt Lake City, who just negotiated with school administrators to begin using canines to sniff lockers and cars in the school's parking lot actually stated,

"Nothing prompted us to do this on a regular basis other than it's a good tool to avoid problems. It's not that we have a drug problem…we are putting ourselves into a preventative mode."[20] Well, bully for you; You've ignored Supreme Court decisions, like *Vernonia*, that suggest there must be at least **some** need in order to put in place an intrusive intervention. According to one of the dog handlers, the canines are "getting the message across that no knapsack, locker or car is safe."[21] Great. Big Brother and the knapsack patrol have arrived.

The Murky World of Canine and Metal Detector Search Standards

A concern common to both metal detectors and canines is under what standard their use should be governed. As often police officers, or School Resource Officers, are involved in both types of investigations, the probable cause standard should be required. Yet, in fact, these two types of searches are generally governed by even less stringent guidelines than the typical school standard of reasonable suspicion. In one of the primary cases dealing with metal detectors, *People v. Dukes*, 580 N.Y.S. 2d 850 (N. Y. Crim. Ct. 1992), the court deemed the use of hand-held metal detectors, manned by school police officers, as administrative searches, which are an exception to the warrant rule.[22]

Similarly, the Supreme Court has ruled that canine searches aren't actually searches. In *United States v. Place* (462 U.S. 696 (1983)), the court determined that a canine sniff is not a search within the meaning of the Fourth Amendment.[23] In *Horton v. California* (496 U.S. 128 (1990)) they expanded this logic, stating that, since a canine sniff is not a search, no reasonable suspicion, probable cause, or even consent is needed to conduct that sniff. Further, none of the normal standards for searching are required of sniffs of property, including cars, parcels, trains, and luggage. The dog alert, generally a series of nudges with the dog's snout, the dog scratching vigorously, or the dog sitting down, is taken to **provide** the probable cause for the search, per *United States v. Place*.[24] The courts are unwilling to rule the obvious, that a police-conducted search is exactly that, regardless of what implement is involved and what pseudo-reason is provided. Of course, schools can easily get around any potential concern in this regard by involving a private company in their canine searching instead of the police. In fact, this is a primary marketing strategy used by Interquest: "As a private agency, we are able to provide service to your campus or school location without the challenges and difficulties faced when law enforcement agencies are present."[25] It's so nice schools can virtually circumvent the law while they preach to students that they must not engage in unlawful behavior. The hypocrisy is astounding.

No Need for Individualized Suspicion of Students

A final issue common to both metal detector and canine searches is their whole-scale lack of individualized suspicion. A New York court, in *People v. Dukes*, held that metal detector searches of students entering the school were not in violation of the Fourth Amendment, despite the lack of individualized suspicion. Special police forces from the local school safety task force set up metal detecting scanning posts in the school's lobby, as per a new school board policy. Hand-held wands were used to scan all students, unless lines became too long. At that point officers used a "random" system of scanning every three or four students. In addition to the scan of the student, any items within his or her possession were also searched. If the detector was activated while scanning a bag, the officers requested that the bag be opened as they looked inside. If the detector indicated something on the student, he or she was told to remove any metal objects and was re-scanned. If the detector was activated during the second scan the student was escorted to a nearby private area. A same-sex officer then patted him or her down.[26]

In ruling that the search was constitutional, the court affirmed that metal detectors are administrative searches and therefore individualized suspicion is not needed. They also made the false analogy to metal detector searches in airports and other public buildings (more on this later). Further, since the court held that metal detectors are "minimally intrusive," they felt blanket searches were acceptable.[27] The decision that metal detectors do not require individualized suspicion was reaffirmed in the case of *In re F.B.* 658 A. 2d 1378 (Pa. Super. 1995) several years later. In that case the court used similar justification, and also added that the uniformity of the procedures were a safeguard against intrusiveness. The court said, "The officers who conducted the student searches followed a uniform procedure as they searched each student; after each student's personal belongings were searched, the student was scanned by a metal detector. This uniformity served to safeguard the students from the discretion of those conducting the search."[28] Right. The court's position, that uniform procedures safeguard people, is patently offensive. Uniform procedures, as in this case, often just manage to offend people in a uniform fashion, as dependable as clockwork.

Metal Detectors and the Law

The first federal court to address metal detector searches was the United States Court of Appeals for the Eighth Circuit in *Thompson v. Carthage School District,* 87 F.3d 979 (8th Cir. 1996).[29] In this case a bus driver's report of fresh slashes in the bus seats prompted a search of all students in the sixth through twelfth grades. Students were moved by class into an empty room and told to remove their outer clothing and empty their pockets. Each student was then checked with a hand-held scanner. If the scanner activated, which it did frequently because of the metal buttons and studs on the blue jeans most were wearing, the student was patted down. In addition to affirming that individualized suspicion was not required (why should the administration have to actually investigate who was on the bus that morning?), the court held that the exclusionary rule (which ensures that evidence obtained through unlawful means cannot be utilized in court) does not apply. During the course of the search one student was found with crack cocaine in his pocket and had sought to exclude the evidence. The court determined that students in school have no right to the exclusionary rule, as "application of the rule would seriously deter educators from undertaking disciplinary proceedings that are needed to keep schools safe," and, because they are not law enforcement agents with an adversarial relationship, the rule is not needed to deter misconduct on the part of school officials.[30]

They Are Too Intrusive

Metal detector searches, especially those conducted with hand-held devices, are most certainly intrusive. Recall, for instance, the quote at the beginning of the chapter from a female student who feels sexually assaulted by her school's search procedure. In another example, an African-American female felt forced to transfer to another school because a guard made suggestive comments to her as he moved the scanner around her legs.[31] While these cases may seem extreme, the way the hand held scanners are used, and abused, almost ensures that many students will be made to feel uncomfortable at the beginning of every school day.

In addition, the clothing that students wear, as was seen in *Thompson*, will frequently result in an activation of the detector during the initial scan. Items such as belt buckles, bras, eyelets on boots and brads on blue jeans can activate a scanner. Once activated, as evidenced in the above cases, the policy is typically to perform a pat down. Despite the claims of metal detector proponents, then, it is likely that many students will actually be physically searched by security guards, rather than simply be scanned unobtrusively. Further, as Ferrarracio maintains, metal detectors are intrusive based on the results they yield. Since the machines are indiscriminate about what metal objects will set them off, an activation of the metal detector may lead to a search of a student's purse or backpack, which might in turn reveal some very personal items that are not contraband.[32]

By deciding that students may not use the exclusionary rule, the courts have effectively shut down any legal recourse students might have if they are unlawfully searched. Further, the court's logic is flawed; many students do indeed have an adversarial relationship with school administration. Yet the court held, "there is a commonality of interests between teachers and their pupils."[33] While given there are teachers who have this type of relationship with their students, many other students would wonder what planet the justices were on. And any one who has spent time in schools knows that administrators do target particular kids by watching them more closely than others. Much like the refrain in the film *Field of Dreams*, "if you build it they will come," one can argue, "if you watch them you will find." In other words, the more closely you police particular demographics, the more likely you are to catch that group in some wrongdoing. Lacking the necessary checks and balances provide by the exclusionary rule, school officials have received permission to go ahead and target certain students indiscriminately.

Canine searches are also blanket searches and have, on several occasions, been upheld in courts without individualized suspicion. In an interesting twist of logic, though, as noted earlier, the dog's indication is not considered a search, but is used to provide the needed suspicion to do so. Yet what prompts the dog to be in the location in the first place? Again, while it should be based, at minimum, on reasonable suspicion that there is contraband in the place of the sniff/search, schools have not typically been required by the courts to provide evidence of either an individualized or even a school-wide suspicion of drug use.

Canine Use Outside of Schools: There Really ARE Some Standards

In the world outside of schools, courts often find that some additional, specific information is required in order to bring dogs onto the scene. For instance, in two recent cases the Minnesota Court of Appeals found that police were using the dogs to engage in illegal searches. In *State v. Miller*, 659 N.W. 2d 275 (Minn. Ct. App. 2003) the police believed there were drugs in the appellant's car based solely on evidence that the driver and passenger had been at a home which they knew as a "drug house" (despite the fact that the last time the house was searched no drugs were found). The police, lacking probable cause, brought out a dog and found drugs in the car. The judge ruled for the driver and called the search a "fishing expedition."[34]   In *State v, Buchta*, 2003 WL 1815874 (Min. Ct. App. 2003), the appellate court held that a stop for a broken taillight was not sufficient to call in the dogs.[35]

As these cases demonstrate, in the adult world the police must have justification to drag Rover out of the squad car. However, if school officials want to let Rover roam the halls no evidence of a past problem, current problem, or even potential problem is needed. Thankfully one court, in *B.C. v. Plumas Unified School District*, 192 F. 3d 1260 (9th Cir. 1999), did hold that absent evidence of a drug problem or crisis, use of canines requires individualized suspicion, but this case seems to be the exception.[36]

As with metal detectors, sniffs of lockers, other belongings, and vehicles are considered to be minimally intrusive. And, according to some schools that use canines regularly, it's the least obtrusive way to keep drugs off school grounds. Sure it is, only if the dog doesn't indicate at or near your locker or car. At that point a full-on rifling through your personal items will commence, sanctioned by the law. In addition, as will be discussed later, part of the intrusiveness of the search is that in most cases school officials notify parents of a dog's indication, regardless of whether the actual search was fruitful.

Metal Detectors: Schools are NOT Airports

Proponents of metal detector use often cite the fact that people are asked to walk through or be scanned by hand held detectors in airports, courthouses, and other public places, and we generally do so with little complaint. As the argument goes, requiring students to be scanned prior to entering the school is the same as if they were entering these other buildings, so the kids should just submit to it like travelers at airports. According to one of the

judges in the *Dukes* case, "Weapons in schools, like terrorist bomb-
ings at airports and courthouses, are dangers which demand an
appropriate response...In my opinion the government interest
underlying this type of search is equal to if not greater than the
interest justifying the airport and courthouse searches."[37]

The argument falls apart, however, when we consider that
schools are qualitatively different than these other locations. First,
students are compelled by law to attend school, whereas a person
can choose not to fly or can elect to leave a courthouse without
any consequence. If a student makes this choice, we slap a truancy
label on them and punish them and sometimes even their parents.
Second, the time spent in each location is considerably different.
A person flying may spend one to two hours in the check-in
process, and may do so a few times in a year. Similarly, those called
to be potential jurors, for instance, may spend a few eight-hour
days in the courthouse in a given year (although in rare instances
they must do duty on longer trials). Students, on the other hand,
spend approximately 180 seven-hour days in the school each year
for twelve years, thus are potentially submitting to 180 plus search-
es a year. Third, schools have quite a different purpose than do
these other locations and school employees, in theory, at least,
should have quite a different relationship with students than do
court employees with those entering the court or airport personnel
with those seeking to fly. Schools are allegedly a place where stu-
dents can form bonds with others as they learn and grow. They are
not, or should not be, impersonal monoliths in which visitors are
treated like numbers. Airports, on the other hand, are essentially
impersonal places that offer no promise of nurturing.

Another argument made by proponents of metal detectors is
that, because they are "random," they are not in violation of any-
one's rights. The randomness argument is simply bunk; searching
every third student is hardly an intricate pattern that students can't
figure out. A more likely scenario is that guards or other school
personnel manning the detectors, especially if they are hand-held,
will create a "random pattern" that, in reality, targets only those
students they **want** to search. Kids dressed in all black, smokers,

and rebellious teens had better watch out.

So if Johnny wants to get his gun into the building, he can do one of several things to decrease the likelihood of being caught. First, he could arrive late, when lines are backing up and the school officials are no longer able to check every kid. Then he could count off and position himself accordingly to ensure that he is not the next to be searched. And if he is often targeted by the "random" searches, he could employ some other student to mule in his weapon. Heck, he could even have an accomplice hand him a weapon later in the day through an open window. If we can't keep weapons and drugs out of prisons do we really believe that these means will keep them out of schools? And don't fear that we just gave Johnny any tips on beating the system. Any average students bent on shooting up a school can easily work out the sizable loopholes in the system for themselves. For instance, the perpetrator in the school shooting near New Orleans in April 2003 managed to get his AK-47 and handgun past security guards and a metal detector to kill one student and wound three others.[38]

In finding that individualized suspicion is not required, the court held in *In re F. B.* that, "if schools cannot operate in a violence-free atmosphere, then education will suffer, a result which ultimately threatens the well being of everyone."[39] One would think that education would also suffer if a student misses half a class period because he or she is waiting in line to be scanned and probed, as John Devine describes in the New York City public schools.[40] At least one court, the Superior Court of Pennsylvania in *Commonwealth of Pennsylvania v. Vincent Francis Cass*, 446 Pa. Super. 66: 666 A. 2d 313; 1995, however, has concluded that canine sniff searches of student lockers absent reasonable suspicion are unlawful.[41] At least someone's got it right.

While metal detectors may be effective at keeping some weapons off of school grounds, so too would any blanket search of a sizable population. Knocking on the doors of every house in the vicinity of a college and then poking around the insides, for example, would likely yield a plethora of illegal substances. However, there is nothing in the wording of the Fourth Amendment that indicates effective search methods are necessarily or should be considered lawful. In fact, this is precisely what the drafters of the constitution planned to avoid. Of course the British could find contraband in the colonists' homes when they were allowed free reign to rummage through them, but such a state of affairs was decidedly unpalatable and thus became an integral part of the Bill of Rights. Further, evidence of metal detector's effectiveness is questionable. Despite sporadic use of metal detectors, there was a steady decline, from seventeen to twelve percent, of students in grades nine through twelve who reported bringing a weapon to school one or more days in the previous month.[42] This is likely due in great part to the fact that teens in general report carrying weapons **anywhere** less frequently than in prior years.[43]

Canine Effectiveness

A primary issue of concern with canine searches is whether they are effective at preventing and/or deterring drug use, as proponents allege. Some dogs are simply not effective. Nowhere was this more obvious than in the case of the dogs from Detector Dogs Against Drugs and Explosives (DDADE). Founder Russ Ebersole had marketed the services of his canines to several government agencies shortly after September 11th, as well as to schools. He is now being charged with 26 counts of wire fraud and 2 counts of making false claims to the U.S government. The reason? His dogs failed to detect 50 pounds of TNT, 50 pounds of dynamite, and 15 pounds of C-4. Ebersole, if found guilty, could face five years in prison for each of the counts and a fine of up to $1.4 million. The government was alerted to the possibility that Ebersole's claims about the ability of his dogs were exaggerated and decided to set up a sting. Three trucks carrying explosives were driven to three different entrances of the Federal Reserve. The dogs failed to stop any of the trucks. Additionally, ATF agents gave six of the dogs working at the State Department an explosives test later that month; all failed.[44]

While the DDADE case may be an extreme example of

canine failure, even dogs held to the most stringent standard still have a relatively high acceptable error rate. The ATF standards for effectiveness are that a dog can have two false positives out of thirty indications.[45] Dogs can, and do, indicate at lockers and cars that prove to hold no contraband items. And, because the dogs are not always positive which locker contains the item that triggered their reaction, typically lockers adjacent to the trigger are also searched. For example, in *Commonwealth of Pennsylvania v. Vincent Francis Cass*, "Rudy" sniffed all 2000 student lockers, indicating at eighteen. Each of the eighteen lockers, plus those adjacent to them, was searched. Of the 54 total lockers searched, one yielded a small bag of marijuana. Contrary to typical proceedings, the search was deemed unconstitutional because, as the court put it, "Vague, unsubstantiated reports do not amount to reasonable suspicion that was necessary to conduct the canine sniff search."[46] Thankfully the court did not believe the school principal's assertion that increased note-passing between students and more trash in the counseling center (which was allegedly because more students were using the center to discuss their drug problems) was valid.[47] But more importantly, the ratio of one "find" for eighteen "hits" and 54 searches demonstrates that this is no exact science. Perhaps "Rudy" had a bad day.

Since the searches are always conducted unannounced, supposedly at least some of the "druggies" will have their stash with them at school. Yet time after time accounts of canine searches yield little or no drugs. For instance, a search conducted with eight dogs yielded only one suspicious substance in an Allegheny County school in Pennsylvania.[48] Using the price of $600 per dog per day, as frequently is the going rate, the school spent $4800 and rooted out one joint.

Perhaps, as proponents claim, the failure to find drugs is because the knowledge that the dogs **might** conduct a search on any given day has deterred students from bringing in their stash. Steve Essler, President of Kontraband Interdiction, Inc., suggests that this is the primary purpose of his canine services. He says, "We give kids another out. If somebody says, 'Hey, try this,' the kid can say, 'But what if the dogs show up today?'"[49] Yet kids don't believe this to be the case, nor do the teachers or administrators who actually **think** about it. A board member at a Pennsylvania school that recently voted to begin using drug dogs said students have told board members and administrators that drugs are carried on person, which the dogs cannot detect because they are not allowed to sniff actual people, only property.[50] In our experience, students were well aware that the dogs could not approach them and so carrying their drugs was, in a sense, safe. They would generally remark during drug-dog sweeps that, "Any student dumb enough to leave his stuff in his locker deserves to get caught. That's what pockets are for."

Further, the logic of deterrence assumes that people a) know the consequences of their actions; b) weigh out the costs and benefits of their actions; and c) make a rational decision in favor of maximizing benefits and minimizing costs. There is little evidence to suggest that adults, let alone juveniles, actually go through such a weighing out process. Juveniles can be somewhat impulsive and are prone to "I won't get caught" thinking, so they are especially unlikely to make a decision after weighing the costs. In addition, if dogs come through, at the most, two days per month, if a student was to weigh out their chances of being caught with drugs on campus, this might seem like pretty good odds. The shortcomings of deterrence theory logic will also be addressed in Chapter Seven.

In addition to the flawed logic of deterrence theory, the assumption that drug dogs are needed in order to give students an "out" is insulting. Per usual, we give our students absolutely no credit. We assume that they would need an occasional visit by canines in order not to succumb to the drug pusher, rather than simply teaching them to decline on their own grounds. Further, by responding that they don't want drugs, "because the dogs might come," they unwittingly send the message that they may be interested under other circumstances, almost inviting a dealer to approach them again. This response also fails to show any disapproval of a classmate pedaling drugs on campus. Perhaps kids would be less likely to push drugs if their offers were simply met with a stern, "NO" rather than a "maybe next time, don't want to get caught today."

Narc the Kids Out, Even if Nothing Was Found

Surely if the dog indicates at a locker or vehicle but the subsequent search yields nothing, everyone just goes about their business, right? Wrong again. Many schools have as part of their search policy a statement that parents will be notified of **any** canine indications. Huh? One can only imagine how this actually plays out. Here's a likely scenario: "Hi Mrs. Jones. This is Principal Smith. Well, we've had some trouble down here at the school. The canines came through the school today and one of them indicated at Bobby's locker. Well, no, nothing was actually found, but we think you should start watching Bobby more closely. Maybe check out the kids he hangs around with. Our canine service will also search his bedroom, for a modest fee, if you want to be absolutely sure he's not a stoner or a meth-head." All of this because "Rudy" or another dog like him had another bad day. Many adolescents have strained relationships with their parents. One can imagine that reporting a student in such a manner to the parent—when there is no evidence of wrong doing—could have a serious negative impact on the student's well being.

Widening the Net

In the event that something is found, many schools immediately turn the evidence over to the police. Of course this seems logical, but brings up an issue that criminologists refer to as "widening the net," or involving students in criminal justice for issues that would have at one time been dealt with informally. As Randy Beger explains in his *Social Justice* article, some states even require that police be involved in searches and that schools report any evidence obtained from a search.[51] Concurrent with the addition of such policies is the dramatic increase in penalties for crimes committed on school property.[52] The concern about widening the net is addressed in detail in Chapter Eight.

The Message To Students?

A final concern with both metal detector and canine search-es is the overall message students receive when they are used. There is quite a bit of evidence that installing metal detectors in communities with little or no need actually creates **more** fear. Students often ask themselves what they were missing before; if the school spent money to install detectors, the logic goes, then there must be a problem of which we were unaware. Even in schools that have had a history of weapons concerns, students know that if a classmate really wanted to smuggle in a gun or drugs they'd have no trouble, and thus see the new technology as nothing more than a waste of time and money. Often these same schools fail to pro-vide students with the most basic items, like textbooks and even tolerable classrooms. Jonathon Kozol, in *Savage Inequalities*, chron-icles how some schools in inner-city environments actually hold classes in bathrooms due to lack of usable classroom space.[53] In addition to fear, students may resent the intrusion and rebel against the system. Aaron Kipnis, in his book *Angry Young Men*, connects his research with his own life experience as a "bad boy." He states, "the more adults treated me like a bad boy, the more I began to think of myself that way. Eventually, rather than be crushed by shame, I began to take pride in the role."[54] Much like the labeling theory used in criminology, Kipnis is arguing that if students are repeatedly accused of being deviant, they have nothing to lose in actually **becoming** deviant.

Military Lingo and Practices "Invade" the Schools

What metal detectors and canines have done, however, is change the culture, even the language, used in schools. "Scan days" and "holding pens" are just two examples of the new lingo to invade schools.[55] Like something out of *Minority Report*, whose basic plot revolved around someone who worked in a "pre-crime department" nabbing criminals before they did anything, they conjure up images more familiar to a correctional setting than an educational institution. In fact, Gordon Crews and Jeffrey Tipton of the Koch Crime Institute have compiled a list of ways that schools are like prisons that is, frankly, terrifying. Here is a partial list of the characteristics that some schools and prisons have in common:

> Both use metal detectors.
> Both have surveillance cameras.
> Searches of personal property are conducted by administration.
> Both lock perimeter doors.
> Officers are assigned to the premises.
> Controlled movements of "clients."[56]

Mari McLean, as cited in DiGuilio's *Educate, Meditate, or Litigate?*, concurs: "When students view schools as prisons and teachers and administrators as guards and wardens, they will begin to behave more like prisoners than students, and violence in the schools will become its own self fulfilling prophecy."[57] Funny, we didn't see that quote on the Interquest web site.

As Webber explains in *Failure To Hold: The Politics Of School Violence*, "these forms of monitoring and control do chip away at the confidence students may have and the trust they feel for one another. Specifically, these disciplinary procedures act as subtle forms of fear-based indoctrination."[58] An ACLU representative from southern California addresses the atmosphere created by the use of canines: "It makes schools more like a World War II prison camp. That's not a conducive atmosphere to learning."[59] Crews and Tipton maintain that an overly controlled environment can stifle creativity and individualism, not to mention overall academic development.[60] Of course, who **really** thinks that schools exist to foster creative geniuses? Rather, schools seem to be in the business of creating future automatons that will not question authority but simply accept their lot. Makes for darn good employees, maybe they can get jobs in the drug detection industry.

Why Don't They Complain? Who Would Hear?

Some school officials claim that few students complain about the surveillance in their schools, so they must not be bothered by it. Yet one wonders if students even have a voice to complain with? Isn't it likely that they know by now that to complain would be futile? Or, worse, it could be seen as some type of evidence of wrongdoing, prompting further repression? Additionally, the fear of school violence and myth of rampant drug use has a hegemonic effect, whereby some students have come to be convinced that their school is full of would-be gunmen and crackheads seeking to push their goods on the innocents. Thus students who should be complaining are pressured to believe that only those who have something to hide care about their privacy rights, and those with something to hide are all stoners, so who cares.

Law enforcement tactics are replacing tradition educational interventions, such as good-old discussions with students who might be troubled. As school violence expert Ronnie Casella asserts, "Security equipment, for example, while having a utilitarian purpose, also legitimizes the moral right of schools to watch over students but not to interact with them."[61] In the event that someone is called in to intervene, too often now it is the police, not educators or counselors. In a troublesome onslaught of student-rights assaults, some school districts are not only teaming with local police but with federal agents, including Customs, to bring in the dogs.[62] And regardless of the legality (questionable as it may be) of such searches, there's no getting around that students will **perceive** this as a law enforcement issue. So now our teens are worthy of attention from the feds? What next? The CIA infiltrates the public high school?

The daily surveillance in schools provided by metal detectors and canines essentially tells students that they cannot be trusted. Schools can be as sneaky as they want to, however, all the while perversely accusing their students of wrongdoing. As one canine supervisor stated, "If we're searching lockers, the kids won't even know. A dog can search an entire floor of lockers in about five minutes."[63] Let the self-lauding commence, folks, we've tricked and violated our youth and they never even knew it. According to Kris Bosworth, a drug-prevention expert at the University of Arizona in Tucson, the best way to address potential school problems is to allow students a voice, which gives them power to change their school culture.[64] Yet to increase security, and consequently, mistrust students, is to stifle the open communication needed to address real concerns about drugs and violence.

Things Are Looking Up?

The good news, however, is that dog handler's are attempting to minimize the negative feelings associated with the intrusions they lead. Says one of the officers who handles a dog used in the Los Angeles schools: "we try as hard as we can to make this as good an experience for the kids as possible."[65] Thanks officer, maybe next time we can jazz "Buddy" up in a ballet tutu and teach him to dance a jig for the students. Then Sally won't be so upset when her parents get the call that she might be a drug dealer even though her locker was clean. Beger sums up the problem with police in schools nicely:

> The nation's courts no longer seem interested in scrutinizing the specific facts surrounding the search of a student to determine if police had probable cause or even reasonable suspicion. Instead, courts search for a policy justification-e.g., minimizing disruptions to school order or protecting the safety of students and teachers-to uphold the search, even when police use evidence seized under lower and increasingly porous search standards to convict minors in adult criminal court.[66]

QUESTIONS FOR REVIEW AND CRITICAL THINKING

What are the costs and benefits of using metal detectors?

Canine searches?

What does it mean to widen the net? What are other examples of how this happens in schools? In other institutions?

Do you agree that schools often bear striking similarity to prisons? In what ways?

EXTENSION QUESTIONS AND ACTIVITIES

Examine the use of canines and metal detectors in other settings. Are search standards more or less rigorous than in schools?

What is the impact of people coming to expect continued surveillance? Are they more palatable in certain settings? Are people more comfortable with metal detector use in airports after September 11th? Compare the use of metal detectors in the U.S. with their use in other countries.

CHAPTER FOUR

Observations, Tips, and Shoes Gone Missing

If you want a Big Brother, you get all that comes with it.

—Erich Fromm

Teacher, Leave Them Kids Alone

Teachers are granted a great deal of authority over youth in the United States. They are responsible not only for teaching important content, but to help teach civic virtue and values, to mold students into "good citizens." Recently we have given teachers carte blanche to lord over their minions. We have allowed them, as well as other school officials, to become Big Brother incarnate, the all-seeing and knowing eye. It must be that those who pursue a career in education also have superior senses, as lower courts have, on several occasions, deemed teachers' vision and sense of smell as reasonable suspicion to search students. And, in true Big Brother fashion, teacher allegations are not to be questioned, only accepted. Thus if a teacher alleges that a student is out of class without a pass or notices a student in a location he or she is not authorized to be in, the next logical step, according to many courts, is to commence with a search. Similarly, it seems as though missing items in schools also provide reasonable suspicion to search students, especially when such items are reported missing by teachers.

While the unwavering acceptance of teachers' and other school faculty members' observations is questionable enough, even more problematic is the use of tips from other sources to prompt searches. As described in Chapter Two, students can and do provide tips. In many cases courts have upheld searches based on tips from anonymous sources and when no effort was made to verify the information or the credibility of the informant. In fact, some courts have found no problem with school officials not only condoning students' snitching on one another but actually **asking, and paying,** them to do so. On other occasions the courts have upheld the use of prior information about a student to justify searches, so kids with a "reputation" generally have no recourse if they are searched. But most disturbing of all is the use of undercover agents in schools. These infiltrations often lead not only to privacy violations, but a host of other equally egregious effects.

Teachers As Scent Police

The olfactory detection skills of teachers were in question in the 1992 case of *Widener v. Frye*, 809 F. Supp. 35; 1992 U.S. Dist. An Ohio high school teacher noticed an odor of marijuana, allegedly coming from a particular student, during a class test. The teacher alerted the school security guard, who took the student to the principal's office. Both the guard and the principal claimed to smell marijuana as well, and felt that the student was "sluggish." They summoned yet another security officer, lest the supposed pothead go on a rampage, demanding potato chips and Twinkies. They received permission to search the boy's jacket and bag and also patted him down and asked him to empty his pockets. None of these searches revealed marijuana. The female principal then left the office so that the two male security guards could probe further. They had him remove his socks and shoes, lift his shirt, lower his pants, and, finally, pull his underwear tight around his genitals so that they could observe his crotch.[1] Envision a mortified teenager giving himself a wedgie with his whitey-tighties in front of two grown men. Is this a legitimate search or a summer camp hazing ritual? They never did find any drugs on the poor kid.

The Ohio court found this search to be reasonable. In affirming the search, the court implied that teachers and administrators must have superior odor detection abilities which, combined with the students' sluggish appearance, signaled the need to search.

Evidently it never dawned on them that the test he was taking might have been making him sluggish. Further, while the boy was "quite understandably embarrassed to some degree," strip-searching him for weed was apparently reasonable in scope.[2]

You Look Sketchy and You Dress Weird

Teachers and administrators have also been granted the opposite of the adage, "Never judge a book by its cover." A student's appearance, as described by a school official who is not trained in identifying signs of drug or alcohol use, can provide justification for a search. For instance, in *Martinez v. School District No. 60*, 852 P. 2d 1275; 1992 Colo. App., a school dance monitor's assertion that some students at the dance were inebriated prompted a unique type of search; the students were taken to a private office and made to blow in her face.[3] Hopefully everyone spritzed with Binaca before the dance.

In another case that exemplifies the all-too-common post-Columbine paranoia, a teacher's impressions of students' dress prompted a search. Three South Carolina high school students who wore black coats to school were searched and suspended. One was interrogated about the Chemistry book in his bag, as this suggested he was planning to make a bomb.[4] We most certainly would not want our students to dress, or worse yet, think, uniquely for themselves. This "ownlife," as Orwell described it,[5] is dangerous to the status quo, and it seems schools are all about maintaining the status quo. In his book *Geeks*, Jon Katz describes several similar cases in which students are terrorized for looking or acting "different." The book chronicles Katz's relationship with two students as they leave high school and move to Chicago. Both are self-defined computer geeks and found school, for the most part, to be miserable because they were teased and targeted by fellow students and faculty. In a conversation shortly after Columbine, one of the guys, Jesse, expressed the following concern: "You watch, they'll blame the geeks," with "they" referring to the media and so-called experts.[6] He was right. In further explaining, Jesse said,

You never want to hurt anybody. But there are a lot of days when I was at Middleton that I'm glad I didn't have a gun around. It's a piecemeal, gradual, daily grinding down of you as a human. First, there's the school, where you have to leave the Constitution and all your rights at the door. They tell you what to think, where to sit, what to wear. They tell you what you can and can't read.[7]

Katz then posted a series of columns on slashdot.com critiquing the public and school responses to Columbine, which garnered a plethora of horrendous stories from geeks nation-wide. One example came from "Anika" in Chicago. She described how she was stopped at the door of her high school for wearing a trench coat. She was given the option of going home or taking the coat off. She refused both options, and was made to report to the principal's office by two school security guards. The guards then called the school nurse, a female, who demanded that she remove the coat and undress. She took the coat off but refused to undress further, and, thankfully, the nurse did not force the issue. The guards did thoroughly examine her coat for evidence of god-knows-what, guns, presumably, but of course found nothing.[8]

Not all searches based on a teacher's observations are as whimsical in nature as the aforementioned cases, but some are handled just as poorly. In *Shade v. City of Farmington, Minn.*, 309 F.3d 1054 (8th Cir. 2002), a teacher observed a student using a pocketknife to open a juice can on a bus trip. Rather than approach the student and confiscate the knife immediately, the teacher waited until they arrived at their destination to call for backup. The principal and another school official were joined by two liaison officers who informed the students that they would be searched. The student produced the knife at that time. End of story, right? Wrong. The school officials searched the class anyway. Why, you ask? Well, as the court asserted, searching the others was reasonable because nobody knew whether other students had weapons as well.[9] Thus a simple situation becomes a fiasco because one teacher won't say to a kid, "Hey, give me that pocketknife," and a problem that used to result in a phone call home now results in searches, expulsions and lawsuits.

In the Right Place?

In addition to being searched for smelling funky, having odd clothes or having a good time at a dance, the following events, sadly, can lead to searches at school; being seen in the wrong place during school hours, trying to cut class and, worst of all, being around when any item goes missing. While there are, fortunately, some notable exceptions, for the most part, courts have held that students who are not where they "should" be are subject to searches. For instance, a California court held in *In re Bobby B.*, 172 Cal. App. 3d 377; 218 Cal. Rptr. 253; 1985 Cal. App., that it was acceptable to search two boys who were found in a bathroom without a pass. Of course, they did appear nervous, and that couldn't be due to the fact they knew they were in trouble for the pass violation. And the school's dean did know that kids sometimes smoke in the bathrooms, so of course these two must have been as well.[10]

In *Coronado v. State*, 8355 W. 2d 636; 1992 Tex. Crim. App., a student attempted to leave the school under false pretenses. Because that student had previously been found to be "carrying evidence of drug dealing," the principal felt that his faked excuse to leave school was justification to search him. Coronado was using the age-old school skipping excuse that his grandfather died, which school officials found to be untrue upon verification from his family. In testimony before the court, the school's assistant principal admitted that the only evidence of any violation Coronado might conceivably be guilty of at that time was truancy. The court found that the initial pat-down search of Coronado was justified based on his attempt to leave school, but that the subsequent searches of his clothing and person, locker, and vehicle were too intrusive in light of the skipping infraction and therefore in violation of Coronado's rights.[11] While at least that portion of their decision makes sense, it is illogical to search all students who attempt to skip school. Of course, if Coronado had been in-line for class Valedictorian honors, it is unlikely that even the pat down would have occurred. More likely everyone would have had a good laugh about the good kid trying to be sneaky and using the lame grandpa-death story, and he would have been sent back to class unpunished.

In *Brousseau v. Town of Westerly,* 11F. Supp. 2d 177; 1998 U.S. Dist., a Rhode Island court upheld pat down searches of all students who had been present in the school's lunchroom when a cafeteria employee reported a nine-inch serrated knife (used to penetrate greasy school-lunch pizzas) had gone missing. After an announcement asking the perpetrators to come forward was met with no success, the assistant principal received permission from the principal to pat all the students down. Males and females were separated into two lines and patted down by same-sex school employees. No knife was found on the students; it later turned up in an empty pizza box in a dumpster outside of the school.[12] Evidently it never dawned on the administration at this school that the knife could have been merely misplaced. Prior to searching the students the administrators made a cursory look around the cafeteria, which was enough to convince the court that they had exhausted all other options prior to commencing with the search.

In *DesRoches v. Caprio,* 156 F. 3d 571; 1998 U.S. App., a report of some missing shoes prompted pat down searches of all students in a high school art class. Shamra Hursey placed her tennis shoes on a desk and left them there while the class dismissed for lunch. The teacher stayed in the room for the lunch period but was in the closet some of the time and could not see the shoes. When Shamra returned she found the shoes missing. James DesRoches and several others assisted in a search for the shoes, to no avail. The dean of students was alerted and was told by the teacher that only three students had been in the classroom during lunchtime (DesRoches was not one of them). The principal spoke to these students, but none of them knew anything about the shoes. For some reason the dean was not told at this time that DesRoches had been seen in the cafeteria through the entire lunch period and that he had his backpack with him, making him an unlikely suspect.[13]

The dean announced that he was going to search the belongings of the nineteen students in the class, and asked if anyone objected. DesRoches and one other student did, to which the dean responded that the school's policy allowed for a ten-day suspension if they refused. Nice-violate their rights and punish them if they call you on it. The other student then complied, but DesRoches still refused. The bags of all the other students were searched, revealing nothing. DesRoches was then taken to the principal's office, where he still refused to consent to have his things searched. His parents were called and he was suspended for ten days.[14]

At issue for the court was exactly how to define "inception" when determining if the search was justified. DesRoches argued that the search should be judged based on when it was first announced and the school official's knowledge and suspicion at that point. Thus they had no reason to suspect nor search him; in fact, had they done their legwork, they would have found he was accounted for during the lunch period. The district court agreed with this logic, arguing that to search first the consenters and then the non-consenters allows "one's constitutional rights...[to] wax and wane according to whether others stand upon their...right."[15]

The school argued that the search of DesRoches began when he was actually suspended, and that by this time they had suspicion of him, evidently based on his refusals. The court felt that the school gave DesRoches plenty of opportunity to consent. How noble of them. Further, the search of DesRoches was reasonable because the searches of the other students had not revealed anything. So, by process of elimination it was acceptable to search DesRoches.[16] Nice logic. If at first you don't succeed, try, try again. In addition, the court held that the school had a compelling interest in conducting the search. Citing *Camara v. Municipal*, 387 U.S. 523 (1967) and *Skinner v. Railway*, 489 U.S, the court felt that a search could be upheld where the government's interest are "substantial—important enough to override the individual's acknowledged privacy interest, [and] sufficiently vital to suppress the Fourth Amendment's normal requirement of individualized suspicion."[17] So, are we to believe that a missing pair of Keds presents a substantial government interest? Substantial enough to override the rights of an entire classroom of students? We are hardly convinced that this is analogous to maintaining the public safety, as was the government's interest in *Skinner*. Nor is there a legitimate health concern, as in the administrative search of an apartment in *Camara*. The court also determined that this group was sufficiently small that they could be searched without violating the individual suspicion requirement. So, apparently, students better hope they are in larger classes in the future if they wants to ensure their privacy rights.

Students Have Credibility
As Informants, If Nowhere Else

As briefly discussed in Chapter Two, students often provide the information that prompts a search. While searches are not supposed to be based on student rumor,[18] it is obvious that they often are. In fact, courts have previously held that it does not even matter if school officials are aware of the identity of the informant. Thus a crime fighting strategy becomes: Trust 'em when we can pit 'em against each other, demonize 'em all other times. Coupled with the fact that courts generally uphold searches when a student has some type of prior history of trouble,[19] it seems especially unlikely that anyone would be too concerned about tracking down and verifying a student source. Further, the courts have previously held that, "absent information that a particular student informant may be untrustworthy, school officials may ordinarily accept at face value the information they supply."[20]

Sometimes the school faculty even asks students to become informants. As school violence expert Ronnie Casella states in *At Zero Tolerance*; we have "come to believe that students can be controlled if they are convinced of the nearly omniscient power of the school to watch, to apprehend, and to quickly and severely punish."[21] In her 1999 *Time* magazine article, "A Week in the Life of a High School," Nancy Gibbs reports that some schools have teams of student spies, or "monitors," as they are called. At Webster Grove High School the principal chose sixty students for her "Principal's Student Leadership Group," charging them with the duty of "reporting any incidents or smoldering resentments that might lead to trouble. Kids who **look or act different** (emphasis added) at Webster know the walls have ears."[22] Hyman and Snook tell the story of fifth-grade student Lynn in their book, *Dangerous Schools*. Lynn was a well-behaved and bright girl who very much enjoyed school. That is, until she experienced something in fifth grade that deeply disturbed her. When the students were lining up for lunch one day, her teacher, Mrs. Smith, whispered to her that she should watch the other kids and tell her if any of them talked in line. Lynn's father, a lawyer, was initially amused, stating, "You mean that Mrs. Smith is setting up a system of spies. Maybe she is preparing you to work for the CIA."[23] But when Lynn discovered that some of her friends had been told to do the same, her parents decided that they should talk to Mrs. Smith. Lynn's father inquired as to why Mrs. Smith might ask her students to spy on one another. She responded that it was a pedagogically appropriate practice, although could not cite any support for that contention, and that she and others had been using the student-informant tactic effectively for years.[24]

Mrs. Smith decided to change her tactics after the meeting with Lynn's father, stating that she would announce the "monitor" each day, who would be responsible for spying on the other kids. Mrs. Smith clearly failed to appreciate the messages she was sending her students. According to Hyman and Snook, "pressure to tattle on friends strains relationships, fosters a climate of distrust, causes loyalty conflicts regarding teachers versus peers, and is anathema to both the spirit and letter of democracy."[25]

Well-Paid Narcs

Even more insidious than Mrs. Smith's lunch-line antics is the use of monetary rewards for students who inform on others. Crime Stoppers International (CSI), a private, non-profit organization, raises money for rewards to informants. CSI has chapters in several high schools called "Scholastic Crime Stoppers." The program offers rewards to students who narc out one another, with the biggest payoff going to those who share some dirt on crimes committed both on and off campus. However, rewards are also paid to informants who tell of students violating school rules. One principal reports that he paid student-tipsters approximately $3,000 between 1995 and 1999.[26] Similarly, the sheriff's department of a small town in Georgia pays students $20 each time they turn in their peers for suspected drug use or dealing. Some students must have struck it rich on this deal, as the sheriff's department received 224 tips.[27] In the course of four months a district in Antelope Valley, California paid out more than $1,000 to tipsters. The school board deemed their pay-for-information program so successful that they voted to increase the maximum reward to $1000 and added vandalism to the list of offenses.[28] So now a students wings wet toilet paper onto the bathroom ceiling and his buddy gets a payday. Supporters of such programs argue that it allows students a role in keeping their school safe. It's hard to imagine that this is the best way we can involve youth in school safety efforts. This might be comparable to say, East Germany, or other countries where everyone is (or were) encouraged to spy on everyone else, and the result is an acute corrosion of society.

Snitch Technology and Snitching For Pay

In the summer after Columbine, North Carolina governor James B. Hunt commissioned the development of WAVE AMERICA, a high-tech snitch system. "Built around a 24-hour anonymous telephone tip line and supported by a sophisticated multimedia advertising campaign, it is designed to take reports on any student suspected of acting even a little different, or holding unpopular political beliefs,"[29] according to James Redden. Students receive perks for their contributions; they get a WAVE AMERICA card that qualifies them for discounts at participating stores. The Los Angeles School District was considering a similar proposal, where students could earn up to $75 for valid tips redeemable for various merchandise.[30] Certainly the framers of the Constitution didn't envision that citizens would exchange their privacy rights and squeal on one another for discounted burgers and fries. Another program, Safe School Helpline, has employees who listen to and transcribe tips left on the hotline. The program operates to the tune of $1.80 per student at each participating school.[31]

Of course, payments to snitches are by no means exclusive to schools. In fact, schools seem to be merely adopting a tried and true method used by the government. The government does it, in the form of actual payments or, more frequently, in sentence reductions to felons, who constitute the largest portion of snitches. Eric Schlosser describes one way this works in *Reefer Madness*. Asset forfeiture laws have been written in such a way that "confidential informants" can be rewarded with up to one quarter of the assets seized as a result of their testimony.[32]

The use of student snitches, in conjunction with police officers and high-technology forms of surveillance, has proven effective in rooting out the "undesirables" from our schools. For instance, the number of suspensions nationwide nearly doubled between 1974 and 1998.[33] Expulsions in the Chicago Public Schools increased 3,000 percent over a three-year period in the mid-1990s.[34] Yet are the students being booted out of our schools really so bad? It's hard to imagine, as some of the "early warning signs" that students and parents are to watch for in the WAVE AMERICA program include "low interest in school."[35] That might describe almost all of the present school population at one time or another. The students may not be bad, but they do tend to fit a certain profile; they're disproportionately male and of a racial and/or ethnic minority.[36]

Everywhere a Narc

The increasing use of young people as snitches merely reflects a culture that supports perpetual surveillance at the cost of personal liberties. As Redden maintains in *Snitch Culture*, "the new school surveillance systems are the result of the same forces at play in the larger society."[37] There have always been informants. From the use of "delantors," paid informants in ancient Rome, to the McCarthy raids of the 1950s, governments have supported people ratting out one another. But Redden maintains that snitches are much more pervasive than ever. For instance, while it is impossible to tally all the expenditures on informants, federal spending on these "services" quadrupled between 1985 and 1993.[38] According to Robert Dreyfuss of *Mother Jones*, police are being trained not only to apprehend criminals, but it seems that they are also encouraged to **create** criminals. "Under a Justice Department training curriculum, police are taught to pay attention to citizens' political affiliations and to look out for 'enemies in our own backyard'."[39] What better means to garner this information than through the use of snitches?

Assuming that there truly is an increased use of snitches, it is not surprising that students are being recruited as spies. In fact, use of children as informants against their parents has become a concern in recent years. Allegedly "nothing is more offensive to the average citizen than the notion of children informing the authorities on their parents."[40] Young snitches are supposedly part of totalitarian regimes, not democratic governments. As Orwell warned in *1984*, such regimes would encourage children to inform on any transgressions made by their parents for the "good of the party."[41] But, in light of recent trends both in and out of schools, one must ask if the "democratic" U.S is heading down this road.

Children **do** sometimes inform on their parents. Some children who have "graduated" from the D.A.R.E program "have concluded from this training that becoming a government informant is the apex of virtue."[42] In a 1997 case a Maine court found that a D.A.R.E officer had lied to and threatened an eleven-year old girl in order to get her to incriminate her parents.[43] While the court found this particular case appalling, others have affirmed the use of children as snitches. In 1986 thirteen-year old Deana Young turned her parents in for drug use after hearing an anti-drug talk at church. Her parents were promptly arrested after she turned in a bag of marijuana, cocaine, and some unidentified pills. While the thirteen-year old clearly did not realize that her actions would lead to separation from her parents, she was praised by former First Lady Nancy Reagan, the queen of "Just Say No."[44] How about "Just Say No" to manipulation and exploitation of children, Nancy?

What is the impact of using kids as spies, on each other as well as on their parents? Orwell offers some frightening implications in his prophetic work *1984*:

> "Nearly all children nowadays were horrible. What was worst of all was that by means of such organizations as the Spies they were systematically turned into ungovernable little savages, and yet this produced in them no tendency whatever to rebel against the discipline of the Party. On the contrary, they adored the Party and everything connected with it."[45]

In both *1984* and current reality, youth come to embrace their role and their loyalty to the system before their own family and they are lionized for doing so. To that effect, kids become so accustomed to being asked to snitch that they may cease to question the practice. Of course, it helps to usher in a new area of child snitches when all Americans are being asked to keep an eye out for "anything suspicious" in the post-9-11 era. Orwell was sure that kids would eventually use their snooping skills within their own homes:

> "It was almost normal for people over thirty to be frightened of their own children. And with good reason, for hardly a week passed in which the *Times* did not carry a paragraph describing how some eavesdropping little sneak-'child hero' was the phrase generally used-had overheard some compromising remark and denounced his parents to the Thought Police."[46]

The aforementioned case indicates that Orwell was right. Kids can be manipulated against their own parents. And Nancy Reagan would likely be the first in line to pin a medal on the "child hero."

Outside sources also provide schools with tips to search. In *Martens v. District No. 220 Board of Education*, 620 F. Supp. 29; 1985 U.S Dist., the court upheld the use of an anonymous phone call from someone claiming to live in the area as reasonable suspi-

cion to search a student for drugs. Since the caller identified a spe-
cific student, Michael Martens, and provided some detail about the
allegation, the court felt that the tip was credible.[47] In addition,
Martens was coerced into complying with the search by a local
sheriff who was on school grounds for an entirely different matter.
Yet the court decided that the officer was not excessively involved
in the search nor was there a cooperative effort between the school
and police.[48]

Even stale information provided by anonymous tipsters is
often used. In *People v. Joseph G.*, 32 Cal. App. 4th 1735; 38 Cal.
Rptr. 2d 902; 1995 Cal. App., the court held that a search based
on information about an event that occurred five days prior was
not problematic.[49] Interesting circular logic follows from the use of
old information; schools can (and do) profile certain students as
troublemakers, watch them more closely, inevitably catch them
doing something, then cling onto that information as justification
to continue watching those same students with even greater zeal.

Bad TV Comes To Life

Schools do not just rely on their faculty and student body to
inform on others. On the contrary, many schools have enthusiasti-
cally embraced the use of police undercover agents, generally with
the goal of rooting out drug users and dealers. A survey of federal
agencies, local police, and school officials in 42 states revealed that
most are familiar with the practice, yet have collected little, if any,
data regarding whether it is effective.[50] Some private law enforce-
ment agencies even exist. These groups, like Professional Law
Enforcement (PLE), provide undercover services to high schools.
According to PLE's website, "superintendents and school board's
proactively employ undercover investigators to verify student and
parental complaints about drug abuse in the high schools."[51]

The *21 Jump Street* style infiltration is rife with problems, in
addition to the lack of data regarding whether it works. First, narcs
often walk perilously close to the line of entrapment, and in some
cases, cross over inadvertently or blatantly. Beginning in

September, 1995, two youthful-looking sheriff's deputies posed as high school students at Union High School in Redondo Beach, California. Their strategy was to show the suspected drug dealers that they had money. Some of the suspected dealers were approached more than five times. After three months of soliciting, the narcs made seventeen arrests. Of those arrested, few actually provided dope to the agents; most were busted for taking money in an "implied agreement" to sell drugs. Included in the bevy of arrests were several fourteen-year olds and a special education student. In describing the situation, Mike Males chronicles how this was not a unique case; since the 1980s L.A police have used young-looking narcs to make drug busts of high school students, especially targeting special education students.[52]

Kevin Davis, one of seventy-five students arrested and expelled in a 1995 sting at his North Carolina high school claimed an undercover agent had lured him into selling marijuana. This school had used a variety of undercover operatives, as had the other eleven schools in Wake County, for over twenty-years with little effect on reported marijuana use. According to the State Court of Appeals, the investigation, entrapment, and expulsion of Davis were all constitutionally permissible. The court "rendered the astonishing decision that expulsion is not punishment in the eyes of the law," but rather held that the expulsion is a "remedial measure."[53]

In addition to entrapment concerns, undercover agents in schools have been known to engage in unethical and often criminal behavior themselves. Kevin Carter, known to students as Craig Madsen, was working undercover in Lyman, a small rural community in Wyoming. He pretended that he was a disaffected druggie who was in constant strife with his father in order to connect with the school's most alienated youth. While playing student Carter was alleged to have been involved in a beer heist from the American Legion and was said to have thrown an oil drum off an interstate bridge. Despite his connections with the alleged drug culture, Carter's efforts yielded little in the way of criminal charges. He was, however, romantically involved with "Tammy," a fifteen-year old pregnant student. After failing to clean up the drugs at Lyman, Carter moved on to nearby Pinedale, where he used the same modus operandi, including seducing a vulnerable female student. This time the victim was "Pammy," an attractive seventeen-year old with low self-esteem. In 1993 Carter pleaded guilty to fondling the two girls, but denied that he had sex with either.[54]

"Tammy" and "Pammy" both went through bouts of depression and self-destructive behavior as a result of Carter's betrayal. Rumors about the two girls, either started by or at least exacerbated by Carter, injured not only the girls but also their families and friends.[55]

In another case, the covert operations at a high school in a Milwaukee suburb were headed by Clint Carson, who "targeted students he suspected of using drugs and turned them into dealers by encouraging them to sell him small quantities of marijuana."[56] It seems that Carson got a little too into his job, as he regularly drank with students and drove while drunk. Sixteen students were arrested after Carson's two-month charade, each for possessing minute amounts of marijuana. No dealers were uncovered.[57] According to Hyman and Snook, "the users who were caught could probably just as easily have been caught getting high at any party or place where they usually hung out."[58] Well-informed school officials can achieve the same if not better results without the need to wage covert warfare.

Another problem with Johnny Law going undercover in the schools is that, in his zeal to make a "big catch,' he may actually allow crimes to occur. If drugs are so bad for our youth, it is hard to see why allowing youth to use them would ever be considered a good thing. Yet, since large busts "impress the public, increase the political opportunities of prosecutors, and often enhance the reputation of the local police,"[59] the health and safety of our students becomes secondary. As Randy Beger notes in the journal *Social Justice*, school stings also put innocent students at risk of wrongful arrest based on faulty tips and overzealous police work.[60] Unfortunately, because everyone seems to rejoice when a big bust is made, it is next to impossible to estimate how frequently narcs allow crime to occur and/or target innocent kids.

School Stings and Severe Sentences

Consistent with the get-tough-on-crime mentality employed against youth, when kids are caught with drugs as a result of a sting operation we generally throw the book at them. Perhaps the most egregious example is that of Webster Alexander. Alexander was caught selling small amounts of marijuana to an undercover agent. He made sales on four different occasions, totally approximately $350. None of the sales actually occurred at school but because Alexander happened to live within three miles of the school building and a housing project, he was prosecuted with sentence enhancements, as per Alabama law. Most states have some type of drug-free school law that assigns extra penalties for sales made on or near school property, although most set the boundary at 1,000 feet.[61] For selling a couple of hundred dollars worth of pot spread over four occasions his sentence was…twenty-six years! And this was Alexander's first offense! Local authorities clearly decided to use Alexander's case to send a message. As Lawrence County District Attorney Ed Osborn stated, "Certainly it makes a point, a very big point, about accountability."[62] Alexander's sentence seemed especially harsh when compared to typical drug sentences for first time offenders. Terms of more than ten years are usually only assigned to repeat offenders and for gun-related crimes.[63]

The drug crackdown was a part of Principal Ricky Nichols' efforts to militarize the school. Nichols is an Army-Reservist who regularly target shoots with sheriff's deputies. He considers himself a "front-line soldier in the war on drugs."[64] He expressed elation at the request that an undercover agent be assigned to the school and wholeheartedly supported the effort, even creating situations to enhance the bad reputation of the "new student." The agent claims he was shown pictures of students suspected of drug involvement, and then was placed in classes with them. If this doesn't reek of profiling, nothing does. He sat behind Courtney Bush, another targeted student, and on his first day heard Bush's girlfriend say he was a drug dealer. The agent then tapped Bush on the shoulder and asked, "Hey, can you hook me up?"[65] On day two he made his first contact with Alexander and arranged to make a deal.

Principal Nichols was concerned, however, that the students might not believe the 26-year old agent was a student, especially after he turned in homework and received a good grade on a test. Of course only struggling students are involved with drugs, right? Nichols proceeded to stage a scene whereby the agent would get in trouble for being tardy to class. Nichols said, "I reamed him out. I tore him up. I ate him alive. He said a few choice words back to me and bingo, he's back in the pack."[66] There may not be a word to describe how reprehensible this situation is. As if the relationships between students and faculty aren't typically strained enough, resorting to shameless subterfuge to keep a stool pigeon firmly entrenched in the "bad" crowd has to take it to a new low. This begs the questions: Is this a principal or a hired gun, brought in to clean up town like in a Western? And exactly how much time does he spend on curriculum issues when he seems more interested in plotting slick entrapment schemes?

Thankfully, Circuit Judge Philip Reich showed some sense and determined that it was not necessary for Alexander to serve the entire twenty-six year sentence. After reviewing Alexander's accomplishments since his arrest, which include receiving his high school diploma, attending drug rehabilitation, enrolling in the local community college, and maintaining a job, the judge ordered Alexander to serve one year in the county jail, another year on probation, and then to return to court for an evaluation of his progress.[67]

No One Likes A Tattle-Tale?
It Seems That Many Do!

While of course some people do object to the use of narcs in schools, much of the general public is either unaware schools have been "bringing in the beef," as students call it, or is supportive of the practice. As Raines argues in *Attack On Privacy*, "what really gives pause is the degree to which the public acquiesces to and even welcomes this administrative invasion, this managerial takeover of our effectiveness as persons. We are grateful that others carry the burden of our lives!"[68] But this is not entirely surprising, considering the social and political climate we live in. At a time when citizens have offered little resistance to the invasions allowed by the Patriot Act and other recent legislation, why would we think they would care about the privacy rights of their children and teens? In fact, most families never "fight back" in the event of a questionable search. This could be due to several reasons, according to Hyman and Snook. Some parents may simply be deferential to all authority, some may feel that their kids are out of control at home so deserve some punishment at school, others may feel that if they complain their child will be further victimized, and still others may feel as though to complain would do no good.[69] A primary reason for the failure to question police tactics is that we have been inundated with pro-police messages.

Pro-Police Ideology

The pro-police hegemony is reflected not only in our legislation but also in the media, which is the primary source of information about anything related to criminal justice for most Americans. As Alexander Cockburn, writer for *The Nation*, explains, "for years now we've been subjected to a Niagara of pro-police propaganda on TV shows, 11 o'clock news reports and in the newspapers, such material providing the mulch for our present police culture."[70] Many scholars have documented that the average American receives 96% of their information about crime and criminal justice from the media, which is skewed in favor of law enforcement.[71]

The pro-policing messages that inundate television viewers are also common to shows that would be considered fairly highbrow. In describing an episode of the popular TV program *The Practice*, Alexander Cockburn illustrates how crime coverage often sends the message that police are hamstrung by civil liberties and that, if not for that darned Bill of Rights, we'd have little crime in this country. In the episode of this fictional show, one of the main defense attorneys is assigned to represent a nun-killer. In the course of preparing her defense she discovers that the police search, which uncovered the body, was unconstitutional and, despite her personal feelings, she demands in court that the evidence be suppressed and the defendant released. Even though he makes it clear that he also hates making this decision, the judge agrees and the charges are dismissed.[72] The effect of such a portrayal? According to Cockburn, "Across the nation, fans of *The Practice* wag their heads in dour agreement that the Bill of Rights and kindred protections should be shoved in the trash can."[73] Yet, in reality, few judges would make this decision in a case as ghastly as a nun being hacked apart. In fact, Cockburn quotes an award-winning defense attorney from the Bay area: "The only time you ever win those kinds of motions is on something like a case involving one rock of crack. A dead nun? No judge would ever suppress that. Anyway, when was the last time the Fourth Amendment counted? It's very, very rare that any major piece of evidence is excluded, based on violation of the Fourth Amendment."[74] Such depictions encourage citizens to support police at virtually any cost and undermine civil liberties for all.

The Consequences of a Spy Culture

The negative consequences of teachers, students, and undercover agents spying on one another are plenty. First, it sets up a climate of mistrust in schools, which undoubtedly has a negative effect on the learning atmosphere. Susie is probably not giving her full concentration to mastering algebra when she is also being asked to spy on Bobby who sits across from her, and can even make her weekly spending money by catching him in some wrongdoing.

Second, the blurring of boundaries between traditional police tactics and educational goals serves to undermine the democratic ideals our country was founded on and that we allegedly want our children to practice when they are older. Children learn what they see, not necessarily what they hear. So our lip service to democracy is likely negated by our totalitarian search and seizure tactics. As adults, will this generation of youth be more likely to support or condone privacy violations, as that is what they are accustomed to? As Webber notes in *Failure To Hold: The Politics of School Violence*, "without the necessary experience of freedom, students will be unable to function in American society without the false sense of security provided by the school's reaction to violence. Like prisoners, they will develop nonfunctional habits and become dependent on authorities to mediate their subjectivity for them, if it has not happened already."[75]

Third, all humans can and do learn from their mistakes. Yet when we push the siege mentality into schools, applying draconian punishments to as many students as possible, we do not allow for this to happen. This despite the fact that we know punishment is the **least** effective way to change behavior. Just look at our prison population; higher than anywhere else in the world, yet so too are our crime and recidivism rates. Additionally, use of actual cops and cop tactics in schools generally precludes any deeper understanding of **why** a student might turn to drugs or commit another offense. Police are not trained in dealing with kids and their emotional problems. In fact, their training might be antithetical toward this end.

Fourth, our privacy rights empower us as humans. As Raines asserts in *Attack On Privacy*, "privacy builds up a sense of personal significance, of individual power and effectiveness."[76] Privacy allows us to know ourselves. "Without privacy there is no individuality. There are only types. Who can know what he thinks and feels if he never has the opportunity to be alone with his thoughts and feelings?"[77]

In summary, the public has given schools the green light to treat their children with suspicion and to teach our progeny to do the same to others. They do this by distorting the constitution and the values of loyalty and duty. Redden explains that the best way to get people to snitch on one another is to appeal to their basic decency, "convincing them that snitching is the right thing to do. This is the Civics 101 approach, arguing that good citizens have an obligation to report wrongdoing to the authorities."[78] Teaching kids to spy and snitch would almost certainly be considered the antithesis of the vision shared by the founders of American compulsory education. As Neil Postman states in *The End Of Education*, "Thomas Jefferson, the moses of the great democracy-god, knew what schools were for-to ensure that citizens would know when and how to protect their liberty."[79]

QUESTIONS FOR REVIEW AND CRITICAL THINKING

Are there any cases in which a person's odor or dress should provide suspicion for a search in school? Outside of school?

Are you aware of other schools that have snitch policies? How do they operate?

Under what circumstances, if any, should police narcs be allowed in schools? How should their use be handled?

Why do many parents fail to advocate for their kids when students are wrongly searched or are asked to do something questionable, according to the authors?

EXTENSION QUESTIONS AND ACTIVITIES

Find out more about Crime Stoppers International. Who provides support for this non-profit organization?

Research other examples of kids being turned against their parents in court.

There is a fine line when using narcs between gaining useful information and entrapment. What is the definition of entrapment? Explore court cases where entrapment was used as a defense. Would such a defense be useful to students?

CHAPTER FIVE

Reefer in the Undies?
Strip Searches of Students

> Ours is a sick profession. [A profession marked by] incompetence, lack of training, misconduct, and bad manners. Ineptness, bungling, malpractice, and bad ethics can be observed in court houses all over this country every day."
>
> —Chief Justice Warren Burger

Strip Searches in Criminal Justice

Of all the heinous things that can legally be done to people suspected or accused of committing a crime, few can parallel strip searches. Unfortunately, strip searches occur more frequently than we would hope. In various arms of the criminal justice system, under the guise of efficiency and so-called need, thousands of these unnecessary intrusions have occurred throughout the country. Hundreds of females were subject to illegal strip-searches when they were admitted to the Marshfield lockup in Massachusetts between 1997 and 2000.[1] An attorney representing the women argued that the searches were conducted without any probable cause to believe the detainees were concealing weapons or drugs, and were even done to women charged with minor offenses. Some women were strip searched twice; first as part of the intake process and again when they were transferred for arraignment. In the second instance some were forced to undergo full body cavity searches.[2] Plymouth County officials have agreed to pay $1.35 million to over 700 inmates to settle the class-action suit.[3] In a similar suit, regarding people who had committed misdemeanors, a U.S District court judge approved a $50 million settlement to thousands of New Yorkers who were strip searched by corrections guards.[4] Such incidents are sadly similar to incidents that have occurred in schools.

Sometimes strip searches are conducted of people who have done nothing serious, evidently as a means of intimidation. Sixty-nine bicyclists who attended the 2000 Democratic National Convention in Los Angeles to champion more fuel-efficient transportation were arrested for allegedly blocking a thoroughfare, failing to stop at a stop sign, and riding the wrong way on a one-way street. Under California state law a person arrested for a misdemeanor cannot be strip searched unless the arrest involved drugs, weapons, or violence, or if officers believe the arrestee is hiding contraband. Must be these pro-environment cyclists were thought to be hiding handguns in their spandex shorts? The charges against the cyclists were dropped within weeks, as county officials found they had little merit.[5]

After a suit was brought against the county, the county agreed to pay $70,000 to each of 23 female cyclists who were strip-searched. Lead plaintiff Juliet Musso was not only strip-searched but endured a full body-cavity search as well. The arrested males were not strip-searched but will receive $5,000 apiece from their claim that they were denied medication, access to telephones, and timely arraignments.[6] Lest we think this is an isolated incident, perhaps an anti-Democrat political maneuver, the case is the third in a year in the area. A $150,000 settlement was awarded to a woman who was strip-searched at a jail while six months pregnant, and a month later another $150,000 settlement was awarded a different plaintiff.[7]

When visited on kids, the standards are even worse. In Connecticut, a thirteen-year-old girl filed suit after she was routinely strip-searched at a state juvenile center because she refused a judge's orders to attend her seventh grade classes.[8] Evidently this is standard procedure; it is unclear, however, how forcing a child to strip will inculcate a desire to hit the books. Children are strip searched whenever they enter the facility, even if they are just returning from court or have been moved from another supervised facility. Another female plaintiff in the suit, a fifteen-year-old, was sent to the detention center for running away. She had been treat-ed for depression and sexual abuse. Executive Director of Court Support Services for Connecticut's judicial branch William H. Carbone explained that the strip search policy was, "really for the overall security of detainees."[9] Clearly these two females feel "secure" as a result of having removed their clothing for detention center employees.

It was revealed in March of 2003 that juveniles at the Sacramento jail were not only being strip-searched, but that those strip searches were being videotaped. Supposedly this is necessary in order to keep a record in cases of alleged impropriety. The attor-ney who is pursuing a class-action suit on behalf of strip-searched minors cites California law, which prohibits the involvement of anyone in a strip search who is not carrying out an official duty. He stated, "By filming the searches, you lose control over the privacy of the detainees."[10]

Schools Don't Strip Search Kids, Do They?

Schools also strip search kids, of course always in "their best interest" or because of the school's "need" to maintain discipline. Although sometimes the courts have gotten it right and have ruled against forcing students to strip in school, sadly the "tough love" trend of the 1980s and 1990s has shifted both schools and courts increasingly in favor of the practice. While certainly there is no real "love" involved when school officials require semi or complete nudity of their students in order to check for drugs, money, or miss-ing property, we argue there **are** some quite discernible motives; displays of power, control and, like strip searches of misde-meanants, intimidation.

What IS a Strip Search?

The first issue of concern is exactly how schools and courts have defined "strip" searches. While definitions vary across states or jurisdictions, many definitions require that a strip search involve removal of some clothing. Revealing the student's underwear is generally included in the definitions of a strip search.[11] In an Alabama case, the state Supreme Court held that a fifth grade girl who was asked to remove her shoes while a teacher felt inside her socks for missing money was not a strip.[12] The state of Wisconsin defines strip searches more narrowly. A strip search in Wisconsin is "a search in which a detained person's genitals, pubic area, buttocks or anus, or a detained person's breast, is uncovered and either is exposed to view or is touched by a person conducting the search."[13] So in Wisconsin students can be asked to remove all of their clothing except their underwear and not have been strip-searched. While some may argue this is merely an issue of semantics, if a search is not deemed as one by the courts, the students who suffered from it lack any recourse because the courts won't even hear the case. Even if it **is** deemed an actual search students often have little or no recourse, as detailed later in the book.

When Can The School Remove A Kids' Clothes?

Another concern with strip searches is what type of evidence is needed to justify them. We argue that **no** amount or type of evidence is adequate for schools to treat students in this way, yet unfortunately some schools and courts do not agree. Until recently, courts have generally held that strip searches, because of their intrusiveness, require the highest standard of justification, and had found for the student in cases predicated on mere reasonable suspicion. The court in M.M v. Anker, 607 F. 2d 588, 589 (2nd Cir. 1979) went so far as to declare that reasonable suspicion could never justify a strip search, while other courts have suggested that probable cause, and perhaps even a search warrant, should be required in order for a strip search to be conducted.[14] Yet some courts have upheld searches as long as there were multiple sources of evidence to support reasonable suspicion. These courts have relied on a "totality of the circumstances" approach first articulated in T.L.O., and have held that even the "reasonable scope" standard passes muster in the event that school officials are looking for drugs in areas that they believe crafty students are likely to secret contraband, such as around the genitals.[15]

In *Williams v. Ellington*, 936 F. 2d 881 (6th Cir. 1991), the court held that a strip search of female high school student Angela Williams was constitutional because the school based their suspicion on a number of factors, including a tip from another student, an incriminating letter found in a classroom, a teacher's report of odd behavior, and her father's expressed concern about her drug use. She was forced to remove her t-shirt and lower her jeans to her knees.[16] Likewise, in *Cornfield v. Consolidated High School District No. 230*, 991 F. 2d 1316 (7th Cir. 1993), a case described in the Introduction, the court upheld the requirement that Brian Cornfield strip to his underwear and pull them tight across his genitals because of a teacher aide's report of an "unusual bulge" in Cornfield's genital region, reports that Cornfield had bragged about failing a drug test and crotching drugs previously, reports from the school bus driver and students on the bus that Cornfield smelled like and was smoking marijuana on the bus, and a tip from a local police officer.[17] In both cases the court was more concerned with the nature of the contraband than with the age and sex of the students involved or the intrusiveness of the searches. This "totality of circumstances" produced no drugs on either student.

Missing Cash is Adequate Cause

What is considered adequate cause to justify a strip search? Is missing property or money adequate justification? The courts seem to shift gears in this regard, with several recent decisions supporting the use of strip searches for as little as a missing $10. In the case of Stephanie and Raejean, two thirteen year-old students at King Intermediate School, strip searches were prompted when the girls noticed a wallet on the floor and returned it to the student to whom it belonged. He complained to the teacher that $10 was missing, and said that since Raejean picked the wallet up she must have taken the money. The girls were taken to the principal's office, but since neither the principal nor the vice-principal were around, the situation was turned over to the school's new security guard. She conducted a strip search of both girls. It is unclear whether she received any suggestion to do this from other school faculty or if she wanted to play Dirty Harry and crack the case solo.[18]

Their suit was settled out of court and for an undisclosed amount. In handling the case this way, the school received little reprimand for the atrocious actions, the students received little compensation for their trauma, and schools have the green light to continue using strip searches. Large settlements to students could potentially have a deterrent effect on administrators, but such settlements are virtually unheard of.

As Hyman and Snook express, "the imagery of strip-searching is one of hardened criminals being searched for contraband before incarceration. Are not strip searches used to find deadly weapons, drugs, and even valuable items such as diamonds that can be hidden in body cavities? Whoever heard of making someone take their clothes off to find a pittance such as $10?"[19] Surely to strip search pre-teens for an amount totaling less than what would purchase a pizza perverts the meaning of the Fourth Amendment beyond belief. Suppose they found $10. How do they know it belonged to the boy and not any other student?

In *Singleton v. Board of Education*, 894 F. Supp. 386 (D. Kan. 1995), the court again upheld a strip search for money. Singleton, a thirteen year old at the time, left gym class to meet with an assistant principal. He was, instead, met by a screaming adult woman, who accused him of stealing $150 from the front seat of her car. A second assistant principal observed the altercation and questioned the woman, who reiterated that the plaintiff took the money, before stating that his mother was a cocaine dealer. Singleton was taken into the office and questioned about whether he possessed money and/or cocaine. The assistant principal did all of the following to Singleton; reached into his pockets and turned them inside out; removed his socks and shoes and searched them, patted him down in the genital region; searched the inside of his waistband; forced him to hold up his arms while his shirt was removed and his shirt was shaken out; then searched his coat, books, and papers that were contained in his locker. No money or contraband was uncovered through any of the searches.[20] Surely such actions are over-the-top.

Sadly, no, according to the court. The court found that the prods and probes of Singleton were justified at their inception. The statement by the woman, in addition to the fact that Singleton had previously been in trouble with the police, satisfied the court. The court also held that the searches of Singleton were appropriate in scope, since the searches were conducted in the principal's office, Singleton was never required to remove his underwear, and he was not touched inappropriately.[21] As long as students aren't actually fondled by school officials, the reasoning seems to be they have nothing to complain about.

Never Too Young

In addition to concerns about what amount of money, if any, should justify a strip search, there are also questions about at what age, if any, it is appropriate for school officials to act this intrusively with students. In *Jenkins v. Talladega*, 115 F. 3d 821; 1997 U.S. App., the Eleventh Circuit declined to address the constitutionality of a strip search for a missing $7, but did suggest that theft could be considered a serious offense that might justify strip searching students. And the age of the alleged miscreants? Eight! Cassandra Jenkins and Oneika McKenzie were forced to completely remove their outer clothing and drop their panties to their ankles, based solely on another student's accusations.[22] The court copped out of making an important decision here by stating that the law regarding strip searches was not clearly established at the time "to the extent that these defendants should have known that their conduct violated constitutionally permissible norms."[23] "Without such practical, fact-based application, school officials in this circuit were left to interpret, balance and evaluate" the appropriateness of strip-searching.[24] Oh dear, that must require superior intellect. One would think educated professionals could handle evaluating the appropriateness of strip-searching eight-year-olds. The court also implied that they would have ruled that the scope of the searches was acceptable, because "it is apparent that the instant searches were reasonably related to the objective of uncovering the stolen $7.00." The court rejected the appellant's "attempt to trivialize the nature of the infraction; the stealing of $7.00 in an elementary classroom reasonably could be considered by the school officials to be a matter of serious concern."[25] In addition, the court felt that mandating the nudity of eight year olds was not a problem, as they were searched by same-sex teachers. Teachers also "frequently assist students of that age in the bathroom."[26]

One of the dissenters provided a much more reasonable interpretation of the situation. The dissenting judge first explained that the law was indeed clear on the matter, as per *T.L.O.* This judge felt there was no way that school officials met anything close to reasonable suspicion in conducting these searches. Especially problematic is the contention that failure to find evidence in the students' backpacks or shoes and socks warrants additional searching, because it "rests on the questionable premise that more intrusive searches can be predicated upon prior unrevealing searches. *T.L.O* makes clear that such bootstrapping is impermissible."[27] The dissenting judge also took issue with the contention that, because eight-year olds are prepubescent, they require assistance in the bathroom. "Physical maturity is an elusive and, in my view, unworkable constitutional standard and is by no means the only consideration relevant to intrusiveness."[28] Even if this was the case, a student asking for assistance buttoning her overalls after urinating is obviously worlds apart from demanding that she drop all of her clothes, panties included, in front of her teacher. Finally, the dissenting judge held that there were many reasonable and minimally intrusive measures available to school officials that could have replaced the strip searches. Here the judge cited *Mary Beth G. v. City of Chicago*, 723 F. 2d 1263, 1272 (7th Cir. 1983), in which the court deemed strip searches "demeaning, dehumanizing, undignified, humiliating, terrifying, unpleasant, embarrassing, repulsive, [and] signifying degradation and submission."[29] In fact, school officials even failed to question whether the money might simply have been misplaced. Hmmm.

There are also cases in which the court expressed concern about the age of the students being searched yet determined that school officials were immune from damages. In *Oliver v. McClung*, 919 F. Supp. 1206; 1995 U.S. Dist., two girls reported $4.50 missing from the locker room, prompting school officials to first search the girls' lockers and book bags, then remove and check their socks and shoes. The missing loot was not recovered, so an employee of the school (a substitute food service worker) suggested that perhaps the girls had the money in their bras. It's unclear why she thought this might be the case; perhaps students at this school had been hording items from the salad bar in their brassieres. The searches varied to some degree, with some girls being asked to completely remove their bras while others were required only to loosen them. The girls were all released to their next classes after they had been inspected and, as is typical, no money was found. In fact, the principal felt that he had erred in authorizing the searches, and spent that evening and part of the weekend contacting the girls who had been searched to apologize.[30]

The six girls argued that they should be allowed to recover damages from the school officials because strip searches had become a custom or accepted practice at the school. The Supreme Court had ruled on the issue of affording school officials qualified immunity from damages in *Wood v. Strickland*, 420 U.S. 308, 95 S. Ct. 992, 43 L. Ed. 2d 214 (1975). The justices held that, "in the specific context of school discipline...a school [official] is not immune from liability for damages under statute 1983 if he knew or reasonably should have known that the action he took within his sphere of official responsibility would violate the constitutional rights of the student affected, or if he took the action with the malicious intention to cause a deprivation of constitutional rights or other injury to the student."[31] Citing evidence that the school had conducted a similar strip search in the boys locker room three or four weeks prior (although the boys were only asked to remove their shoes and socks), the plaintiffs contended that this established a pattern, and thus school officials most certainly knew their actions were in violation of students' constitutional rights. Further, they argued that the search of each girl, as well as each boy in the earlier incident, should be considered separately, thus the school had really conducted 30-40 strip searches in less than four weeks. The court rejected this argument and treated each of the strip situations as one incident, not separate ones. Thus they determined that there was really only one prior incident of strip-searching, which did not constitute a pattern.[32]

The girls then argued that, since the principal has final decision-making authority over school policy, one incident is sufficient to establish a breach of authority and to disqualify the school from immunity. The defense contended that, while the principal did have a great deal of authority, especially over educational issues, any policy initiatives he proposed must be met with approval by the school's superintendent. The court agreed that either the superintendent or the school board had final authority, thus holding that the school was indeed immune from suit.[33]

The court did express concern about the age of the students who were searched, as well as the lack of suspicion and the use of intrusive means to search for non-dangerous items. The plaintiffs were all in the seventh grade and roughly 13 years old. Foreshadowing the "anything-goes-if-we're-searching-for-drugs" mentality, the court stated, "Perhaps even at that tender age, such a search might be argued to be reasonable if McClung (principal), Miller (teacher) and Stewart (substitute food service worker) had evidence that certain of the girls were in possession of illegal drugs or weapons."[34]

Missing property can also provide justification to strip search. In *Potts v. Wright*, 357 F. Supp. 215; 1973 U.S. Dist., a search of eight female junior high students for a missing ring was upheld. The principal called the police after requests that the missing ring be returned were fruitless. The police arrived and questioned the students. Over protests from the plaintiffs, one of the officers required the girls to strip to their bras and panties. The girls also stated that the female officer made threats to them if they did not comply, stating that she had a black belt in karate so they better not cause her any problems. So, in addition to violating their privacy rights, this officer felt it appropriate to badger young girls into submission.[35] Excellent policing. The ring was not found on any of the girls. Since police actually conducted the search, the courts refused to hold the school liable.[36]

In another search for missing property, a fourth grade student had brought to school a World War II medal for show-and-tell. When he claimed the medal was missing, the school's principal decided he should strip search the whole class. The medal was later found under a desk. At least the principal apologized and gave all the students sodas for their trouble.[37]

Targeting Minorities and Special Ed

There are legitimate concerns that certain students might be more likely to be forced to endure strip searches. As with other punitive measures in schools, minorities and special education students are often seen as easy targets for the most aggressive and authoritarian administrative styles. An African-American middle school student was strip searched in Little Rock, Arkansas after a Caucasian student accused her of stealing $11. Keisha Quince was forced to remove her shirt, dress, bra and even her underwear. She was instructed to "lift her arms and assume a spread eagle frisk position."[38] No money was found on Keisha.

In December of 1992, the principal of Ben Franklin Middle School in western Pennsylvania arranged for the school to have an undercover agent on campus. The agent reported that he had seen six African-American boys on the practice field smoking marijuana and that one of them also had a vial of crack. Legal advice from the school's solicitor assured Principal Amen Hassen that he could "legally search lockers, have students empty their pockets, and do 'other things of that nature'."[39] Ignored was the fact that there was no other evidence to suggest these boys had ever used drugs, nor were the boys questioned. The school could also have utilized their campus nurse to see if there were any signs of drug use, but did not.

The lockers and pockets of all six, who ranged from thirteen to six-teen years of age, were searched. Five hours after the initial tip, the boys were made to remove their shoes and socks, lower their pants to their knees, and raise their shirts. Two of the boys stated that the principal ran his thumb along the inside of their underwear and waistband, telling them to lower their pants. No contraband was found.[40]

During the search the boys inquired whether they could call their parents and were told that district policy required the school to notify the police if parents were called. Further, the boys were told that their parents would not be called until the search was over. One of the boys was also threatened during the search. He reported that a teacher said to him, "I'm not through with you yet, Darren."[41] When the boys' parents complained to the school dis-trict, one school official had the nerve to get belligerent, saying, "I will strip-search any child in this school if I want to, even kinder-garten children."[42] The boys and their parents felt that part of the problem was that they were African-American. They were espe-cially upset that an African-American administrator at the school had betrayed them through his involvement in the searches.[43] Thankfully, the court ruled the strip searches violated the students' Fourth Amendment rights, that the district's strip search policy was unconstitutional, and that the school needed to consult the ACLU to craft a constitutionally acceptable policy.[44]

Special Problems With Strip-Searching Females

Strip-searching of female students elicits some specific prob-lems. Menstruating females, for instance, are likely to be even more self-conscious about their bodies. Yet in at least one case, *Konop*, school officials pressed on with their privacy invasion despite the student's protestation that she was having her period.[45] Yet another concern involving females (although certainly males as well) is the similarities between strip searches by authority fig-ures and prior incidents of sexual abuse. One of the plaintiffs in the suit against Connecticut juvenile detention officials had been sexually abused; forcing her to endure a strip search brought those memories back.[46] It is not necessarily uncommon for females to be subject to a different standard than males; Alderman and Kennedy in *The Right To Privacy* chronicle the abusive and discriminatory search policy held by the City of Chicago since 1952. The federal district court thankfully found no justification for the policy, which required strip-searching of women brought into lockup for even trivial traffic violations. No exceptions were made; menstruating women were simply required to remove tampons or drop sanitary napkins. Men taken into city lockup were patted down, but not strip-searched as a matter of policy.[47] Remarkably, even a successful lawsuit did not bring an end to discriminatory strip-searching; Chicago's neighbor community, Calumet City, had a virtually identical policy into the 1990s. Even worse, at least twenty-seven of the women who filed suit in this case were searched by male officers.[48]

Mention Drugs and You've Got Justification to Strip Search

Consistent with other intrusive measures being used in and out of schools to fight the war on drugs, strip searches for drugs have generally been upheld in recent years. According to a school law textbook, "the pervasiveness of drugs in American society and their deleterious effects on the schools have led some courts to give school officials increasing latitude in the conduct of searches."[49] The atrocity that is the *Cornfield* case has already been described as an example of the drug war mentality gone awry. In *Picha v. Wielgos*, 410 F. Supp. 1214; 1976 U.S. Dist., the court upheld a strip search based on a phone tip regarding possible drug possession. After receiving the tip the principal called the police, who actually conducted the searches. No drugs were found. As in *Potts*, the court refused to hold the school liable because the police conducted the search.[50] In *Rudolph et al. v. Lowndes County Board of Education*, canines found drugs under a table where some students were sitting. One of the students sitting there pointed the finger at another, so the police officer present forced the student to remove all his clothes and drop his underwear to his knees. The court held that the dog's find as well as the student's accusation (it couldn't possibly have been him, attempting to shift the focus?) provided justification for the search.[51]

In all, the courts have been prone to interpret the constitutionality of strip searches based on the *in loco parentis* doctrine (where schools act as parents), especially when it comes to purported drug offenses. The court stated in *Rone v. Daviess County Board of Education*, 655 S. W. 2d 28: 1983 Ky. App. that, "the common view that school officials stand in the same relationship as parents during school hours is a compelling one so long as they do not act unreasonable."[52] In our eyes, strip searches of students are **always** unreasonable. It is difficult to imagine a parent strip-searching their child, yet the court seems to think that schools conducting strip searches are merely acting as a parent would.

People Actually Support This!

Scary as it is, many administrators have supported strip searches. Twenty-nine percent of respondents to a survey of administrators in Pennsylvania stated that their district allowed strip searches. The respondents reported a total of 89 strip searches in the prior school year. The main reasons cited were to find drugs, money, jewelry, and other missing items.[53] When asked what was an appropriate scope for strip searches, 52 percent of the respondents felt that requiring removal of socks and shoes was acceptable. Approval rates decreased as more clothes were removed, with three percent supporting complete clothing removal. Amazingly, only half of the respondents indicated they believed strip searches were emotionally damaging to students.[54]

But Thankfully Not Everyone!

Sometimes the courts have condemned strip searches. One early decision, *Doe v. Renfrew*, recognized the plethora of problems with this practice. Diane Doe was a thirteen-year old Junior High student when her school decided to bring in drug dogs. Shortly before first period was to end Diane's teacher requested that everyone stay put, and an assistant principal, a police officer, and a dog handler and dog entered the classroom. Students remained in the classroom for two and a half hours, forbidden to even use the restroom unless accompanied by a school or police official. The dogs were led up and down the aisles of each classroom, sniffing every desk and every student. When the dog reached Diane it repeatedly pushed its nose and muzzle into her legs, appearing to indicate at something. Doe was ordered by the officer to empty her pockets, which she did, revealing nothing. The dog alerted at Diane again, and she was taken to the principal's office to be strip-searched. There she removed all her clothing, while a female officer and another female inspected her body and clothes and touched her hair. Again, no drugs, and Diane was ushered back to class. Ten other students were subjected to bodily searches that day.[55]

The court issued a scathing indictment of the school.

> It does not require a constitutional scholar to conclude that a nude search of a thirteen-year-old child is an invasion of constitutional rights of some magnitude. More than that: it is a violation of any known principle of human decency. Apart from any constitutional readings and rulings, simple common sense would indicate that the conduct of the school officials in permitting such a nude search was not only unlawful but outrageous under 'settled indisputable principles of law'.[56]

Regarding the issue of immunity, the court stated that it should be accorded to school officials who "act in good faith and *within the bounds of reason*. We suggest as strongly as possible that the conduct herein described exceeded the 'bounds of reason' by two and a half country miles."[57]

In another case, this time about a missing $100, the court also allowed for students' to collect damages. In *State of West Virginia ex rel. Galford v. Mark Anthony B.*, 189 W. Va. 538; 433

S.E. 2d 41; 1993 W. Va., the court critiqued a strip search of a four-teen-year-old eighth grade student suspected of stealing $100 from a teacher. Another student was the initial suspect and was questioned and patted down, revealing nothing. It was then discovered that Mark Anthony worked with the school's janitors and that he likely had access to the classroom and the purse. He denied taking the money, and was taken to the bathroom where he was stripped. Surprisingly, the student actually did have the money, as these searches typically reveal nothing more than a child's bare skin.[58]

In deciding whether the search was justified at its inception, the court held that Mark Anthony's access to the room, coupled with the fact that he was serving a two-year probation term for attempted burglary, was adequate. However, the court felt the scope of the search was excessive. The primary concern expressed by the court was the lack of danger associated with the missing money. The court held that, "at some point a line must be drawn which imposes limits upon how intrusive a student search can be. We certainly cannot imagine ever condoning a search that is any more physically intrusive than the one now before us."[59] Judge Neely offered an interesting dissent. Stating "had the appellant been suspected of stealing an elephant, searching his underwear would have been 'unreasonable.' But where else would a guilty child hide $100?" Later, "if we wonder why our schools are going to hell in a hand basket, it's probably because of decisions like this one."[60] That an educated man can utter such complete gibberish is testament to the culture of meanness that has overtaken the U.S.

The District Court of South Dakota affirmed that not only is money inadequate justification to strip search students but also that the law is indeed established enough for school officials to know that their actions are subject to potential lawsuit. Eighth-grade students Amber Konop and Lacy Genzler were strip searched by a music teacher upon either order or suggestion by the school's principal. On the second to last day of school a student reported that approximately $200 from cheerleading candy sales was missing from her gym locker, which was unlocked. It was later found that the amount was actually between $57 and $59. The principal did nothing at the time of the report, but decided he better act after being confronted by the girl's mother, who was the school's head cook. He decided that the money was either in the lockers or on the girls who had been in the locker room that morning. He assembled all the girls and lectured them. He then stated that "he didn't care if it was legal or not, he was going to search the girls, including a strip search, and find the money." He also threatened that whoever was found with the money would be "going out the front door with the sheriff in hand cuffs."[61] Gotta love the ways these administrators connect with students.

Genzler and Konop were found to have $14 and $10, respectively, in a search of the contents of students' pockets. All other students were allowed to leave at this time. Genzler and Konop were forced to strip, even though the principal admitted that he did not think the money the girls had was the missing dough. Genzler refused to remove her pants but took them down to her knees, and both girls refused orders to remove their underwear. Both did pull their bras away from their bodies. Genzler's underwear, both in front and back, was pulled away from her body while Konop's were only in the back. Konop was actually touched while this occured. She was menstruating at the time and was especially humiliated, although neither girl felt as though they could say "no." No additional money was found.[62]

The court felt that the searches were not justified. There was no evidence of students at the school having hidden items in their clothes or underwear. There was no reason to believe that Konop and Genzler had the money; in fact, they were both good students, involved in extra-curricular activities. The court also held that there were far less intrusive means available, especially in that there was no imminent danger. It seems no one thought to consult legal counsel, police, or even the girls' parents. The strip searches were made in lieu of any locker or vehicle search, which would have been far less intrusive. Further, after failing to find the money in the pockets, shoes, and socks they searched, there was most certainly no reasonable suspicion to search the students' bodies.[63]

In denying the defendant's assertion that they should have

qualified immunity, the court held that to determine that the case law was unclear regarding strip searches would result in "'absolute immunity,' not 'qualified immunity.' In other words, any school official would receive one 'bite of the apple,' regardless of the nature of the conduct."[64] In this case the court felt that "Any reasonable school official should have known that strip searching students without a reasonable basis to believe they committed a crime violates their rights."[65] The court also cited *Cornfield* in expressing concern about the age of students being searched. "As children go through puberty, they become more conscious of their bodies and self-conscious about them. Consequently, the potential for a search to cause embarrassment and humiliation increases as children grow older."[66]

In *Kennedy v. Dexter Consolidated Schools*, the court ruled that strip-searches to find a missing ring were in violation of students' rights and that the school district was liable due to their failure to train personnel regarding strip search policy. A student in a second-period computer class reported to the teacher that her ring, which she **thought** she had removed and placed on her computer console, was missing. The student, the teacher and the remaining ten students in the class searched the room for the ring but did not find it. The teacher consulted with the principal, and the students were required to remain in the classroom after the hour had ended. Both the principal and the school counselor spoke to the students, with the counselor even leaving the room after telling the students that if the ring was returned when he was gone no questions would be asked. When no ring appeared he questioned each of the students, which also failed to uncover the ring. The students were then taken to the school restrooms and strip-searched.[67]

Chrystal Kennedy testified that, when asked, "Who wants to go first?" she thought she was finally getting permission to use the restroom, so she volunteered. She was accompanied by a female teacher and the principal's secretary and told to keep the stall door open. As she stood up, with her pants and underwear still down, she was made to remove her shoes, socks, pants, and shirt, and to pull her bra away from her body and shake it. The other appellant,

Randy Ford, was escorted to the boy's restroom by the principal and male athletic director. He also thought he was being allowed to use the restroom, not being subject to bodily intrusions by school faculty. After using the urinal he was instructed to remove his shoes, socks, shirt, and pants, and to pull his boxer shorts away from his waist. Ford, as well as several other students, testified during trial that he arrived late to class, after the ring was reported missing. The students informed the principal of this, but clearly he was hell-bent on stripping the students so he ignored the information.[68]

Evidently a similar incident occurred several years earlier at the same school, when the current superintendent was principal. That search was over some lost money. Rather than disallow strip searches, protests by parents at that time resulted in an addition to the school policy allowing for students to request the presence of a parent or guardian during a search.[69]

The court held that there was not individualized suspicion to justify the searches. Simply being part of a class of ten was inadequate means to make them any more suspect than the other students. Because the administration had the chance to address how to go about conducting strip searches of students with their faculty and failed to do so, policymakers were not immune from damages. The employees of the school, however, did have immunity because they were not policymakers.[70]

In perhaps the most egregious violation of students' rights, a middle school in Washington D.C. decided to have nine boys strip searched at the local jail in order to "scare them straight." The trip to the jail was arranged by the school's In-School Suspension (ISS) coordinator, who felt that these boys, all of whom had spent some time in ISS, could benefit from seeing what the "real world" would hold for them were they to ever be arrested.[71] One boy who was involved stated, "I felt scared. [The guards] were cussing and hollering at us. They said if we didn't take off our clothes, they were going to beat us and make us take them off."[72]

While the teachers as well as several jail employees will likely lose their jobs over the incident, some people have expressed

support for the move. Columnist William Raspberry, although con-
demning the actual practice of strip-searching, has expressed that
we should go easy on those involved, since they were trying to do
something positive. His anti-student perspective comes through in
this statement: "It appears more likely that the youngsters will col-
lect hefty damages from D.C's struggling school system and that it
is the teachers who'll be scared to try anything not pre-approved,
centrally ordained and certified action-proof to grab the attention
of children they fear may be headed the wrong way."[73] Raspberry
could well be correct that awarding such damages will deter further
strip searches—but that is what they are intended to do.

Little Recourse for the Wrongly Searched

Unfortunately, few courts have responded quite so vigorously
as some of these courts did. While others have sided with students
that strip searches are terrible violations of students' rights and dig-
nity, often they still accord school officials immunity, thus essen-
tially silencing the students. For instance, in *Thomas v. Clayton
County Board of Education*, fifth-grader Sergio Evans brought to
school an envelope containing $26 he had collected by selling
candy and placed it on a table near his teacher's desk. He discov-
ered shortly thereafter that the envelope was gone. He and his
teacher, Tracy Morgan, searched the room without success. By
coincidence an officer, Zannie Billingslea, was on school grounds
to hold a D.A.R.E session. Although there is some confusion about
who authorized the continuation, Morgan resumed searching. She
looked in desks, book bags, and purses, demanded that students
remove their shoes and socks and investigated those, and poured
through the contents of students' emptied pockets. She even pat-
ted the students down, to no avail, She then asked Billingslea to
assist in the search. Billingslea suggested that the students could be
wearing an extra set of pants, and thus the money was hidden in
another layer of clothing. The boys in the classroom were sent into
the bathroom with Billingslea, who unfastened his own pants and
belt and dropped his pants in order to demonstrate what he want-
ed the boys to do. Some boys even dropped their underwear as well.

Shockingly, a boy from another classroom entered the bathroom when this was happening and Billingslea demanded that he too cooperate. Some boys also alleged that Billingslea threatened them with arrest or school suspension if they did not comply, allegations Billingslea denied.[74]

The girls stripped in the girls' bathroom in front of teacher Morgan. They were mandated to lower their pants, raise their shirts or dresses, and "pop up" their bras to ensure the money was not hidden there. Some girls alleged that Morgan touched them, which she denied. The searches did not reveal the money.[75]

When parents received word of what happened they were understandably upset. The school was highly uncooperative, at first denying that any strip search took place. In a written report based on the school's in-house investigation of the matter one administrator stated that the searches were not "strip searches" and they were not "anything out of the ordinary."[76] How frightening.

Judge Carnes ruled that the strip searches violated the Fourth Amendment, arguing that while no bright-line rule governs the issue of strip searches, the nature of the item in question and the lack of individualized suspicion failed to justify an intrusive strip search. Again, she held that had the school been looking for weapons or drugs her decision might have differed.[77]

In a separate decision several months later, Judge Carnes ruled that the school employees as well as Officer Billingslea had qualified immunity against monetary liability, as existing case law was not clear in regard to strip searches. The school district was also not liable, since they had no policy regarding strip searches. The students had also sought an injunction requesting prohibition of mass strip searches for small amounts of money or requiring, at minimum, some training and a specific policy regarding strip searches. Carnes denied this as well, stating that she believed such decisions should be made on a case-by-case basis and that "school officials are better suited than judges to decide on the necessity for a policy and training."[78] By refusing to allow damages or require the school to address their strip search policy (or lack thereof), Judge Carnes might just as well have upheld the searches, as the students received no compensation and no changes were likely made at the school to prevent this from occurring again.

Likewise, in *Bellnier v. Lund*, 438 F. Supp. 47; 1977 U.S. Dist., the court struck down a strip search of fifth grade students for a missing $3.00, yet afforded qualified immunity to school officials. The classroom teacher and student teacher watched as students arrived at school and placed their coats in a coatroom located within and accessible only from the classroom. Some time that morning a student complained that he was missing $3.00. The teacher appealed to the class to return the money, which met with no success. There had been prior complaints about missing money, lunches and other items. In addition, no one had left the classroom that morning. These facts prompted school officials to first search the coats hanging in the coatroom, then the contents of the students' pockets and their shoes. The students were then taken to the restroom, where same-sex officials ordered them to strip to their underwear. Their clothes were inspected. All of this was futile. The students were returned to the room, where a search of their desks, books, and again of their coats, was conducted.[79]

The court decried the lack of individualized suspicion. While stating that, "the court is not unmindful of the dilemma which confronts school officials in a situation such as this," they held that the slight danger of the missing money (slight? How about **zero** danger?), the extent of the search and the age of the students involved did not warrant strip-searching. Yet, citing *Wood v. Strickland*, the court chose to essentially overlook the emotional damage caused by such a search in affirming qualified immunity for the school officials.[80]

The Strip Search And The Damage Done

Requiring students to strip naked, regardless of the reason, can be emotionally damaging. Hyman and Snook assert that the damages are the same as for someone suffering from Post-Traumatic Stress Disorder (PTSD). Students suffering from PTSD may become depressed, moody, and/or rebellious. The use of strip searches can also have a ripple effect throughout the school, as students quickly learn that those in whose care they are entrusted cannot actually be trusted not to violate them.[81] In addressing the damages to females forced to strip for minor traffic citations per Chicago city policy, Alderman and Kennedy maintain that the harm is almost always emotional, rather than physical, and thus hard to quantify. The women who testified in that suit described an abuse of basic trust; they felt they had been violated by the very same people to whom we are supposed to look for protection. All said they dreaded future contact with police. In addition, the strip search had lasting effects on their relationships with others. One woman testified that several relationships had broken up over this, as some men seemed incapable of understanding her anger, humiliation, and fear of intimacy. Another explained that she changed clothing in a closet for years following the search. Many others detailed how their jobs and/or schoolwork suffered, and that they had a period of nightmares and depressions, as well as times where they felt shame, panic, and rage.[82] Ironically, all those bringing a suit alleging a violation of privacy rights, for strip-searches or other forms of searches, must be ready for further invasions of their private lives in court, or at least must be ready to tell their stories repeatedly to attorneys.[83] All of these same concerns are also true of juveniles who have been strip-searched. It is our opinion that the effects are simply too distressing to continue to allow administrators ever to require the undress of students.

QUESTIONS FOR REVIEW AND CRITICAL THINKING

Are any students too young to be strip-searched under any conditions?

What types of evidence, if any, should justify a strip search?

Why do school officials have qualified immunity? Should they have it?

Who are the most likely targets for a strip-search, according to the authors? Why?

What are the gender issues related to strip-searches?

EXTENSION QUESTIONS AND ACTIVITIES

What other government agents have qualified immunity? Why? What are the problems with it? Weighing each side, should any government official have qualified immunity? Under what circumstances?

Research the history and application of the *in loco parentis* doctrine in schools. Has it generally been positive or negative for students?

What does research say on the effectiveness of "scared straight" type interventions?

Many argue, as do the authors, that victims of crime receive a second victimization by their treatment in court. In what cases is this most likely to be true? Is it more true of males or females? How does this play out when the victimizer is an arm of the government?

CHAPTER SIX

Whizzing In A Cup Because You're A Teen
Drug Testing of Students

> The court's ruling [in Earls] turns logic on its head, giving the insides of students' bodies less protection than the insides of their backpacks, the contents of their bodily fluids less protection than the contents of their telephone calls.
>
> —Richard Glen Boire, J.D.

> Should we believe the self-serving, ever-growing drug enforcement/drug treatment bureaucrats, whose pay and advancement depends on finding more and more people to arrest and 'treat'? More Americans die in just one day in prisons, penitentiaries, jails and stockades than have ever died from marijuana throughout history. Who are they protecting? From what?
>
> —Dr. Fred Oerther

Right off the bat let us assure the reader of one thing: Drug testing doesn't work. It never has and likely never will. Do drug tests sometimes catch people? Sure. But does it change behavior as intended? Absolutely not, and if behavior does change it is typically only for the worse as drug users pursue new drugs that will escape detection. Drug testing is a first strike in what quickly becomes an arms race between the testers and those interested in beating the test, with the cheats almost invariably staying a step ahead. This is true even when the testers are armed with the most recent and extravagant technology and extremely deep pockets. Schools are armed with neither. Understanding the drug testing issue as it applies to schools requires some examination of its use in other arenas.

The Origin of Sport Drug-Testing

The drive to eradicate sports of drug cheats through testing began at the 1968 Olympic Games in Mexico City,[1] but the history of sport doping goes back much further. Athletes in ancient Greece and Rome used potions to enhance performance and this behavior continues today. Through the 1800s many athletes relied on strychnine to get them "up" for events. Soon thereafter boxers began to use heroin as a painkiller. But eyes opened wide when young men felt the affects of amphetamines they were given during World War II. The applications to sport were immediately obvious.[2] At the same time, medical advances allowed hormones to be isolated that would soon be used to create a whole new class of international athlete. As weight lifting and conditioning programs developed in the 1950s, hormone use developed as well.[3] The International Olympic Committee and many sports' governing bodies knew they had a problem and attempted to use scientific counter-measures to stop it. They failed and have continued to lag behind the cheats for over thirty years.

In fact, many have suggested that drug testing of Olympians in the United States is about looking good, not actually making an impact. There is a growing body of evidence to suggest the U.S tests far fewer athletes than do other countries. At least 15,000 serious, national-level athletes compete in the United States, yet the U.S. Anti-Doping Agency tested only 4,700 athletes between late 2000 and 2002, most of them only one time.[4] And while experts all agree that the best way to catch dopers is through surprise testing, which should occur approximately 70 percent of the time, less than 40 percent of the U.S Anti-Doping Agency's tests have been given without warning.[5] Some sports do not actually conduct any surprise tests, thus giving the dopers a staggering advantage in the game of beat the test. For instance, USA Water Polo has over 30,000 athletes nationwide, with over

1000 of them competing at elite levels. Less than fifty of the elite athletes (4.7 percent) were even tested between 2000 and 2002.[6] American track and field, swimming, gymnastics, and figure-skating athletes won 66 medals in the 2001 World Championships; only 14 of those athletes had undergone surprise testing in the months prior to the event.[7] Over 100 athletes who were caught with banned substances were allowed to compete internationally between 1988 and 2000.[8]

When athletes receive warning that they will be drug tested, it is often quite easy for them to pass. Says Robert Kersey, an athletic trainer and health professor at California State University at Fullerton, "You can pass the drug test in almost any sport if you know what you're doing and you have time to prepare."[9] Even when athletes are given only a few hours they have time to drink pots of coffee and urinate repeatedly, enough to dilute their urine so as to prevent accurate results. It is estimated that this occurs 50 to 60 percent of the time.[10]

The Transition to Workplace Drug Testing

Drug testing in sports helped pave the way for drug testing in the workplace. As noted in the Introduction, President Reagan really fired up the drug war against workers when he issued an executive order in 1986 requiring federal agencies to conduct urine tests.[11] Of course, Reagan paid lip service to the notion that the tests would not be used to penalize workers but rather to target help to those with substance abuse problems.[12] Aside from the fact that the help generally comes in the form of a perpetual vacation (read: firing), this is also quite presumptive in that most people who **use** drugs do not have a substance abuse problem, per se. As Jacob Sullum aptly chronicles in *Saying No*, most drug users are not drug abusers.[13]

The Drug Free Workplace Act of 1998 even provided federal funds for those small businesses that wanted to monitor their employees' personal lives via their urine, yet could not afford to do so.[14] Of course, the use of drug testing in any venue, be it professional sport, the workplace, or amateur, collegiate, and school sport, is not a neutral process done solely for the betterment of the greater society. Rather, certain pharmaceutical companies make out quite well financially by pushing for increased use of drug testing. For instance, as Schlosser notes in *Reefer Madness*, two of the four companies on the Institute for a Drug Free Workplace board are pharmaceuticals that handle drug tests.[15] Yet when we hear the arguments regarding the "need" for drug tests in the workplace, few are aware this is the case. The industry has annual revenues of approximately $740 million.[16] Only one group seems to have completely evaded any proposal to check their possible drug consumption; those bastions of morality, the U.S Congress.[17] Yet it is not untrue to label Congress as one of the more criminal enterprises ever. As of 1999, twenty-nine members were guilty of spousal abuse, eight were convicted of shoplifting, and fourteen were involved in drug-related arrests.[18] And they have the nerve to advocate greater testing of kids?

Costs of Workplace Testing

Drug testing programs in the workplace are expensive. One study found that 38 federal agencies spent $11.7 million on drug testing in one year alone.[19] Texas Instruments, for example, spends approximately $100 per employee in order to make sure no one enjoyed a puff of weed on the weekend.[20] A study of the federal government's drug testing program estimated the cost of finding **one** user at a ridiculous $77,000.[21] Between 1993 and 1998, the federal government conducted over 250,000 random drug tests, turning up 1,345 positive results. This is a "catch" rate of half a percent. That calculates to a cost of $23,637 for each positive result.[22] According to the Web site 4cleanp.com, businesses spend $1.2 billion per year on drug testing, and 90% of companies now do pre-employment drug screening.[23]

Workplace Testing: Based on Faulty Logic, Ineffective, and Intrusive

In spite of the costs, drug testing must surely be an effective way to maintain a drug-free workplace, right? Wrong. First of all, assertions that drug users are absent more frequently, are more likely to be involved in workplace accidents and thus file workers compensation claims, and use more health benefits than do non-users have not held up when actual research is conducted. The primary reason why these assertions fail is that most people who admit to using drugs do not do so at work. When they use away from work, they generally do so in a casual way that does not impact their job performance.[24] In fact, the "residual effects" of drug use were found to be, at most, similar to those of employees who did not get adequate sleep.[25]

Second, workplace drug tests are actually quite unlikely to uncover incidents of drug use at work because they reveal drug metabolites, which are by-products of drugs excreted from the body days or sometimes weeks after a drug's ingestion.[26] And, when indications of drug use are clear, it is typically marijuana that is detected, not substances like cocaine or heroin. This is because marijuana stays in the urine longer than other drugs.[27] So urine tests typically only reveal that you enjoy pot on occasion, not that you ever have used it at work. Such evidence can be used to keep you from being employed, or to justify your firing. Conversely, people who obliterate themselves by drinking shots of whiskey on a nightly basis would not face the same risk, since drug testing is not about use of legal drugs. Yet a recent study of 14,000 employees at seven major U.S corporations found that eight percent of hourly workers and almost a quarter of managers actually consumed alcohol on the job.[28] Another study examined autopsy findings from 173 workers who died on the job and revealed that 23 had detectable blood alcohol contents, eleven had traces of prescription drugs, but only one had detectable traces of marijuana.[29]

In addition to the fact that workplace drug testing is founded on faulty premises, it is also prone to error and manipulation.

Sometimes drug tests fail to distinguish between legal and illegal substances. For instance, Depronil, a prescription drug used to treat Parkinson's disease, has shown up as an amphetamine, while over-the-counter products like Ibuprofen have been misinterpreted as marijuana.[30] Robitussin and diet pills can show up as amphetamines. Migraine medications and anti-depressants can mimic LSD in test results.[31] In a case involving a drug test of a firefighter, it was found that a skin lotion he used cross-reacted with the test, causing a positive reading.[32] We've probably all heard that poppy seeds on bagels or muffins can and sometimes do show up as evidence of opiate use. Some employers, including the New York City Police Department, have instituted policies prohibiting their workers from consuming or using any products that might trigger a positive result.[33] Obviously the motive behind such an edict is to maintain positive public relations; reports of drug use among cops are not likely to increase citizen support, even if it turns out such reports were due to flawed testing. Yet to ask workers to eliminate legal substances from their diets is an unwarranted invasion of privacy carried out simply because the drug test is not good enough to detect the difference. The fault is with the test, not the poppy seed bagel eater.

Employers have even been known to sneak in tests for other purposes under the guise of drug testing. For example, in 1988 the Washington D.C. police department admitted they were using urine samples collected for drug tests in order to test their female employees for pregnancy.[34] Lawrence Berkeley Labs was found to have tested samples for syphilis, pregnancy, and sickle cell disease for at least a decade.[35]

Consider the implications of this. First, such tests are an invasion of privacy—they have no right to know if an employee is pregnant, especially if they are finding out surreptitiously. Second, this puts the employer in the position of possibly knowing something about the employee that the employee doesn't yet know. Imagine hearing from your boss, for example, that you were pregnant, or worse, that you had some life threatening medical condition. Such information is at the heart of the sacred doctor-patient relationship and involves discussion of critical issues and choices between them and with family members. The entrance of an employer on these issues is wholly unwarranted.

Workplace Testing for Educators?

As drug testing has wormed its way into schools teachers have not been exempt from scrutiny. Fortunately, many of the policies school boards have enacted have been struck down as unconstitutional. However, In *Knox v. Knox*, 158 F. 3d 361 (6th Cir. 1999), the Sixth Circuit upheld the Knox County, Tennessee, Board of Education "Drug Free Workplace Policy."[36] The policy, passed in 1989, called for pre-employment drug and alcohol screening as well as reasonable-suspicion testing of current employees. The court held that the policy was constitutional only if there was a "special need." Since educators are in the unique position to keep students safe, this governmental interest constituted a special need.[37] The court then applied a balancing test to determine "the magnitude of harm" that could result from the use of illicit drugs by educators. Per previous decisions, such as *Skinner v. Railway*, 489 U.S. 602 (1989) and *Chandler v. Miller*, 521 U.S. 305 (1997), the court must find that there is a safety risk in order to mandate testing.[38] So, despite the failure to provide **any** evidence of a substance abuse problem at the Knox County schools, the majority held that the school board "did not have to wait for a tragedy to occur; it could adopt a pro-active measure to head off disaster."[39]

Because they work in a "highly regulated industry that involved the care of students," the court determined that educators have diminished privacy rights.[40] The court felt that educators entered the field knowing that there are many rules they must adhere to regarding certification, thus subjecting them to urine tests was no more intrusive. Once again, the logic breaks down as false analogies are revealed. Requiring teachers to demonstrate content knowledge absolutely does not equate to requiring them to demonstrate the content of their urine.

Testing in Schools: The Pot Patrol

While drug-testing teachers as a matter of routine is questionable, *Vernonia* opened the doors wide open to test student-athletes. In the process of expanding the uses of drug testing, the original intents have been ignored or subverted. Drug testing in sports has historically been about maintaining a level playing field and protecting the safety of the athletes. In contact sports it has been an agenda to protect both the drugged players and their opponents. It is believed that 'roided up players are likely to injure their under-sized opponents while jeopardizing their own health in the process. It is interesting to note that as drug testing has made its way into our public schools, the interest in protecting the opponent has taken a back seat. For the most part, schools are testing for marijuana and other recreational drugs but not for steroids or other performance enhancers. This is almost certainly due to the fact that it is far more expensive to test for sport related drugs than for pot. It might also be an extension of the stereotype of student drug users being crazed potheads rather than athletic stars bringing home state championships. Thirdly, testing is simply another means of control, which adults love to have (or say they do) over teens. But if schools are interested in protecting the athletes, and now students in all extra-curricular activities as well, shouldn't they be willing to flip the bill for more meaningful tests? Is it that they can only afford to try to ferret out the pot smokers while letting the steroid users go free? Or don't they care if their prized linebacker breaks a few opponents in half, as long as he doesn't get hurt himself? Of course, in the long run it doesn't matter what they are testing for, as the means are ineffective either way, as we will demonstrate.

Who Is Testing and How

Estimates of the percentage of schools with drug testing policies vary. Most studies place it at approximately 18-20%.[41] According to a recent study by the University of Michigan Institute for Social Research, the group of students most commonly tested are those "for cause," or based on some suspicion. Fourteen percent of the reporting schools reported testing for cause. Athletes are the next group most frequently tested, followed by students who volunteer for testing and students who are on school probation. Approximately two percent of the responding schools test students involved in extracurriculars besides athletics. Most testing programs are instituted in high schools, although some middle schools have them as well.[42] While only 200 schools currently randomly test their entire student body, Drug Czar John Walters is on tour stumping for greater use as we write this book.[43]

The Pro-Testing Position

The primary reason cited for drug testing has shifted from the protection argument to deterrence. Drug Czar John Walters has proclaimed, "As a deterrent, few methods work better or deliver clearer results."[44] Likewise, former New Orleans District Attorney Harry Connick has gone on the record stating, "There is one method that stands out as the most effective prevention method today, and that is student drug testing. (It is) the most effective demand-reduction tool, I believe, that this country has ever known..."[45] President Bush has even pledged $24 million to drug testing. In the slippery-slope argument so often made by the drug warriors and anti-teen conservatives, Walters asserts that, if we do **not** drug test our students, we are failing to protect them from drug use and addiction. So if we don't test we must be doing nothing? Worse, we're supporting teen drug use? Not surprising, given the source, the claim that schools can either test students or fail to protect them reeks of being short-sighted political rhetoric intended to label any who oppose the new drug testing culture.

NOT a Deterrent!

Like drug testing in professional sports and the workplace, drug testing of students has not proven effective. Most studies to date have addressed the efficacy of drug testing athletes, as testing policies for students involved in other activities are relatively new and thus have yet to be evaluated thoroughly. Results of the largest-scale national study on school drug testing, released in May of 2003, show that screenings in school do not discourage kids from using drugs. Simply put: The deterrence argument is bunk. The study, which involved 76,000 students nationwide and spanned several years, found drug use to be just as prevalent in schools with testing as in those without. According to the study, 37 percent of 12th grade students in schools with testing had smoked marijuana in the previous year, compared with 36 percent in schools without testing. Similar results were found for every grade level and for every illegal substance considered.[46] The study measured prevalence, or percent reporting any use in the last 12 months, and frequency of use in the last year. Additional analyses addressed specific sub-groups of students. It was found that use of any illicit substances by male athletes was not significantly different in schools that tested compared to those that did not. The investigation even looked specifically at self-reported marijuana users (defined as those students who reported smoking more than twenty times in their lifetime) to assess whether drug testing would decrease numbers of heavy users. Results again did not differ significantly, indicating there was the same percentage of serious pot smokers in schools whether they test or not. The study also addressed whether policies allowing random testing of the entire student body were any more effective than not testing at all. While only seven of the 891 schools surveyed reported having such a policy, no statistically significant differences were found between these schools and those that do not test their student body.[47]

Proponents of drug testing suggest the rate of usage possibly would have been even higher had the districts not imposed drug testing. Yet the researchers feel this is extremely unlikely, as they controlled for behavioral factors typically associated with substance abuse, including truancy.[48] One of the researchers, Dr. Lloyd D. Johnston, said, "It's the kind of intervention that doesn't win the hearts and minds of children. I don't think it brings about any constructive changes in their attitudes about drugs or their belief in the dangers associated with using them."[49]

Another study found that athletes in schools with drug testing programs reported more negative attitudes towards testing and more positive attitudes about drugs. When compared to students from schools without drug testing, the tested students were less likely to believe that there are negative consequences of drug use and more likely to believe that there are benefits of drug use. They believed their peers used more drugs, and believed their peers and authority figures were more tolerant of drug use. They also held less positive attitudes toward drug testing, less belief in its' efficacy, and less belief in its' potential benefits. Finally, the athletes in schools with drug testing reported less fear of the consequences of testing positive.[50] So, not only does testing fail to decrease drug use but it also seems to foster dangerous attitudes about drugs amongst the tested population. University of Michigan researcher Johnston admitted that, "one could imagine situations where drug testing could be effective, if you impose it in a sufficiently draconian manner...that is, testing most kids and doing it frequently."[51] However, the researchers, as well as the authors, do not advocate such a measure.

Not Even the Right Targets

Drug testing in schools is also based on flawed premises regarding who uses drugs. As in the workplace, hard-core users are not evenly distributed. Students with serious drug abuse problems are not likely to last long in school and are thus not detected by school-based drug testing. Schools therefore run the risk of testing groups of students who are unlikely to use drugs and alienating some of the most involved students at the school. For instance, Lindsay Earls, one of the plaintiffs in 2002 *Earls* case was involved in several service-related clubs and organizations and is now a successful college student at Dartmouth.[52]

The flawed assumptions regarding drug use are especially true in the case of athletes. Micah White, a student at Grand Blanc High School in Michigan, was a member of the National Honor Society, a National Merit Commended Scholar, and a National

Achievement Finalist who had never been suspended, expelled, or even disciplined for a behavioral problem while in school. Yet he was going to be forced to submit to a urinalysis when he wanted to be a part of the wrestling team. Rather than simply sign the agreement to be tested, he sued the school, indicating that drug testing policies are forcing battle lines to be drawn between our schools and our finest students.[53] No resolution to this case was found at the time of this book's writing, but the authors were happy to hear that Micah White was being honored by the ACLU of Flint, Michigan for his resistance efforts.

In a study of 1515 high school students in Massachusetts, it was found that significantly more non-athletes smoked cigarettes, used cocaine, and psychedelics. Athletes were also slightly less likely to use marijuana, amphetamines, and barbiturates. The only substance used more frequently by athletes was creatine, a nutritional supplement available at any local General Nutrition Center.[54] According to the studies' authors, "the significantly lower use of cocaine and psychedelics by athletes can possibly be explained by the commitment necessary to participate in high school athletics."[55] It seems that participation in sports is a protective factor against drug use, so schools should think long and hard before implementing policies that alienate this group.

In addition to being costly and failing to be a deterrent, drug testing typically produces few positive test results. Of the 1,400 middle and high school students tested at the Olentangy district in Ohio, only three positive tests were found.[56] At the Pottawatomie District Schools, of which appellant Lindsay Earls attended, the school had only three or four positive results in over 500 tests.[57]

Cheating Is Hardly A Challenge

As schools consider enacting drug-testing policies, they should also consider that the accepted testing format makes cheating the tests laughably simple. In order to be completely effective, drug tests must be monitored at **all** times by a neutral adult. Thus a monitor would have to watch the urine leave the student's body and enter the cup, which is clearly even more invasive than standing outside of a stall and listening while the sample is procured. Hopefully no court will ever allow a program in which adults actually watch kids tinkle. As it is, a student who is out of sight in a stall has ample opportunity to alter the sample.

Students report beating the tests by faking a "bashful bladder," adding salt, Visine, bleach, and vinegar to their samples, and drinking excess amounts of water to dilute the sample.[58] Students have been known to leave samples for other students within stalls or to purchase pre-screened urine from online pee-purveyors. One such group is Privacy Protection Services. President Kenneth Curtis procures each sample himself and seals it in a bag that can be concealed under a student's clothing, heating it to body temperature. Curtis refers to his business as "an appropriate response to an inappropriate system."[59] It is also not difficult to purchase masking agents. For instance, at the Waterbeds 'n Stuff Emporium in Franklin County, Ohio, a display counter holds a variety of products designed to hide the presence of THC. Tommy Chong, of Cheech and Chong fame, has his own line of such products with the amusing name of "Urine Luck."[60] Passitkit.com advertises that they have the "finest synthetic urine" for sale.[61] Sixty-nine dollars can purchase a desperate student (or employee, for that matter) a drug masking kit from 4cleanp.com.[62] Since schools have not taken testing to the level where they actually observe students' genitals (finally some good news), nor can they generally afford to analyze the samples for masking agents, school drug tests to date may be absolutely pointless. Some schools have, however, begun to test for common adulterants. One school even compounded the privacy rights violations by strip-searching students to ensure that they were providing a clean sample. Amy Valdez says she was forced to strip to her underwear, lift up her hair, and twirl around as her principal examined her. "I felt like I was on display. It was devastating," said Valdez.[63]

The High Price of Testing

As with drug testing in other locations, use of screenings in schools is costly. In October 1997 the Dade County School Board in Florida set aside $200,000 to pilot a random drug test program.[64] During his 1998 campaign for governor, Gray Davis of California proposed that all California schools institute random drug testing and was willing to allocate $1 million to a private firm to pilot the idea in five schools.[65] At $70,000 a year for weekly random test of 75 students, only the wealthiest districts can afford drug testing.[66] One way to get around the high cost is to use cheaper tests. Most schools use a low-cost immunoassay urine test, which generally runs between $20 and $40 per sample tested. These tests typically can only screen for one substance at a time. While being one of the cheapest tests, it is also one of the least accurate, showing false positives as well as failing to be sensitive enough to detect the substances students may be using. For instance, one high school student, an admitted marijuana user, reported that he was required to take a drug test nine times and tested negative in all of them. The cheaper tests can get it wrong between five and sixty percent of the time.[67] Tonic water can show up as cocaine, and Nyquil has been misinterpreted as an opiate or amphetamine.[68] These false positives are not just hypothetical situations or extremely rare cases. They do happen and they do seriously disrupt the lives of real people. For example, an honor-roll student, regional debate champion, and star athlete in high school, Travis Robinett tested positive for THC in 1996. His mother believed him when he denied that he smoked pot and had him re-tested at two clinics, both with negative results. Nonetheless, Travis was kicked off the school's baseball team, losing any hope for an athletic scholarship.[69]

Further, some of the most popular drugs used by students, especially nicotine and alcohol, are generally not included in the testing because to do so would be cost prohibitive.[70] These substances are also widely regarded as exempt because they are legal, but in fact are not legal at high school age, generally. More accurate tests, such as those used by the NCAA, cost approximately

$200 per sample tested.[71] Hair tests, while shown to be more accurate, have also been proven to be discriminatory, as some studies show that drug traces may stay in black hair up to fifty times longer than in blond hair.[72] Despite the fact that hair tests discriminate, Hyman and Snook report that Psychemedics Corporation in Massachusetts will conduct a hair analysis revealing students' drug use for a modest fee.[73] This service first became available to schools in 1995.[74] A new, supposedly more accurate, cheaper, and more efficient technology has been developed that may also weave it's way insidiously into schools. Ron Rutherford, of InTeliSource, Inc., has developed a "drug test wipe" that can test for illegal substances on skin, most surfaces, and even on the sweat of a uniform. Those interested must purchase separate wipes for different substances. A single wipe costs $12.95, while a double set, which can test for two different substances, can be purchased for $19.95. According to one report "It's not uncommon for Rutherford to drag his drug-testing wipes across a seemingly innocent piece of your computer keyboard."[75] Such Pearl Harbor tactics are clearly anathema to any provisions of privacy rights and due process and would represent a dangerous tool in the hands of school administrators hell bent on cleaning up drug use at any cost. While this type of test clears up some of the issues of invasive monitoring, it opens up another nasty can of worms to which we are also opposed: the notion that one can be under surveillance of some highly personal sort **without even knowing it.**

Another way to get around the cost issue is to receive some kind of assistance. While some federal funds are available for drug testing, they do not amount to enough to cover all of the costs. This is, big surprise, expanding under the Bush administration. The Department of Education approved $2 million in grants for local educational agencies and public and private entities to develop or enhance, implement, and evaluate student drug testing programs.[76] Absent adequate federal funds, enter private companies. In a rural school in Ohio, the local Coca-Cola bottling company is sponsoring drug testing in exchange for a ten-year contract as the school's exclusive soft drink vendor.[77] Super, not only can we fid-

dle with kids' urine but we can also contribute to and profit from
soft drink addiction at the same time. Another source of funds
comes from the drug testing industry itself. Roche Diagnostic
Systems, a leader in workplace drug testing, contributed $100,000
to drug testing in schools in the hopes of building future cus-
tomers.[78]

One way that schools have sold students on the idea of drug
testing is to offer them some type of financial incentive. In
Autauga County, Alabama, students who volunteer to be tested
and whose test results are negative receive discounts and perks
from several local businesses. Kids take a urine test for nicotine,
cocaine, amphetamines, opiates, PCP, and marijuana. After a neg-
ative test the student receives a picture ID that gives them special
deals at 55 area locations. Students keep the ID as long as they
continue to test negative. Tests are conducted randomly two times
during the school year.[79] Given the test is voluntary, it is almost
certain that it will not identify any current users, although it will
not likely be as invasive as other tests. Further, are we so naïve as
to believe that fifty cents off an order of French fries will really dis-
suade a student from experimenting with the herb if they feel so
inclined? Likely the only benefit of this program is that it looks
good for all involved. The school has created a voluntary program,
local businesses are chipping in and students are queuing up to
show they are drug free. Perhaps an even greater problem is that
students who decline to submit a sample will likely be viewed as
drug users by their peers and the faculty, regardless of whether
there is any merit to the accusation. These tests create two classes
of students: those who test clean and those who don't test, auto-
matically casting undeserved aspersions on those who refuse to
test.

Peeing in a Cup Gives Kids a Way to Say No

Schools that use testing also try to convince students, and
even more so, their parents, that drug testing provides students a
reason to say "no." Said Representative John Peterson, a
Republican from Pennsylvania and the foremost supporter of drug

testing in Congress, "By helping our schools and communities implement random drug testing, we can give kids a reason to say no to drugs and provide parents with a report card that may help them save their child's life."[80] Yet, as described in this chapter, drug testing often targets the wrong kids and it alienates all students. Further, the insinuation that students need a cheap excuse to say "no" is problematic at best. First, we are not convinced that students are using the potential of drug testing, just as they do not use a visit from the local police with Spot in tow, as an excuse not to imbibe. Second, even if a student should use this excuse they send a terrible message to the drug pusher. Saying, "No, I'm in sports and might get tested," sends the message that the student would be interested in drugs under other circumstances and should be approached when the season ends. It also fails to send a message that pushing drugs is unacceptable. We would prefer that children be taught to say, "No. And don't ask again." Claiming that our students are somehow incapable of taking such a strong position underestimates the character of most teenagers.

Wise use of recreational drugs both legal and illegal ultimately depends on the development of good judgment. Is this good for me? Is this how I want to spend my time? How often do I want to take these? In what contexts? If the constraint on using drugs is always external—fear of getting caught, tested or strip searched—then students may feel no need to develop their own judgment, which could lead to problems once the external constraints are lifted.

What The Courts Have Said

As described in Chapter One, the two main Supreme Court cases dealing with drug testing in schools are *Vernonia*, which upheld the constitutionality of testing of athletes only, and *Earls*, which expanded testing to cover students involved in extra-curricular activities. In addition to these cases, there have been a variety of lower court decisions that deal with various issues regarding drug tests in schools. In 1997 the 7th Circuit Court of Appeals heard *Todd et al. v. Rush County Schools*, 139 F. 3d 571; 1998 U.S App. In

August of 1996 the Rush County School Board approved a policy
that prohibited students from involvement in extra-curricular
activities as well as driving to and from schools unless they con-
sented to a random, unannounced urinalysis check for drugs, alco-
hol, and tobacco. In the event of a positive test, the student and
family were informed and allowed the opportunity to explain pos-
sible reasons for the test result, such as taking of a prescription
medication. Barring a satisfactory explanation, the student would
be banned from participation or driving until the time he or she
could provide a negative sample. The school also reserved the right
to test any student if they had reasonable suspicion of drug, alco-
hol, or tobacco use. If a student tested positive twice, the school
assumed that to be reasonable suspicion to commence with further
testing, even though the student would no longer be able to par-
ticipate in extra-curricular activities or drive to school. Positive
results from the random tests were not used in disciplinary pro-
ceedings, but positive results from suspicion-based tests were.[81]

The plaintiff, William Todd, refused to provide consent for
the test and was therefore not allowed to videotape football
games.[82] Apparently we need to make sure that a kid isn't suffering
from the munchies when he tapes games. Heaven forbid he might
have a shaky hand or use the zoom erratically. The three other
plaintiffs who refused to sign were barred from involvement in the
Library Club and in the Future Farmers of America.[83] The court
held that the school's policy is consistent with the Fourth
Amendment. Since the program was designed to deter drug use
and not catch and punish users, the court felt it was in line with
the *Vernonia* decision. The court was not bothered by the testing
for nicotine and alcohol because they felt those substances also
affect students' mental and physical condition.[84] But what about
excessive abuse of caffeine? Sugar? Fat? These also affect students'
mental and physical condition, but the court is unconcerned.
Perhaps that is because schools have a history of pushing these
onto students every day at lunch at a great profit. Since the plain-
tiffs did not bring forth the issue of driving to and from the school,
the court refused to consider it.[85] So let's get this straight: the state

compels students to attend school, but then when they try to get themselves there they may be subject to a search of their vehicle (as described in an earlier chapter) as well as of their bodily fluids?

In another case, *Joy v. Penn-Harris-Madison School Corporation*, 212 F. 3d 1052; 2000 U.S. App., the Seventh Circuit let stand a school district's policy to test all extra-curricular participants, as well as students who drove to school and those suspended for three days or more. Despite absence of any indication that a student suspended for, say, swearing, is likely to be using any type of drug, the court upheld the policy. Rather than applying the standards set by *Vernonia*, the court simply affirmed because the Seventh Circuit Court had previously done so in the *Todd* case.[86] Thanks for your time and consideration, judges. A job well done.

In one school in Arkansas, students must sign up for random testing if they want to go on school field trips or attend the prom. This policy was upheld by the United States Court of Appeals for the Eighth Circuit.[87] In May of 2000 the ACLU of Maryland filed a suit against the Talbot County school system because they required, upon threat of expulsion, students to submit to drug testing based solely on other students' allegations. Because it was rumored that the plaintiffs attended a party where some people were allegedly using drugs, these students were being forced to undergo drug screening. The eighteen students who were tested were removed from classes during their review for final exams and sent to the school auditorium with little explanation. Once there they were directed to sit apart from one another. Their parents were summoned to the school over the next four to five hours. Most of the parents eventually permitted the testing, as the district threatened to expel their children if they did not. In addition, rather than send the samples out for screening at a certified laboratory, which is mandated by the school's policy, administrators evaluated the samples themselves on school grounds. None of the samples were positive, although one was initially misinterpreted. That student was immediately suspended from participation in school and sport activities, was publicly chastised by school officials, and was paraded through the halls by security guards. An independent test conducted the next day revealed that the initial interpretation was wrong.[88]

In May of 1998, school officials in Sayville, Long Island, concocted a plan to conduct Breathalyzer tests for alcohol at the beginning of each school day. Tests would be performed on those students whose breath or behavior "raised suspicion."[89] As Hyman and Snook remark, "An obvious advantage for merchants is that mouthwash and mint sales would soar in Sayville."[90]

Those Who Disagree

The trend toward expanding who will be tested and what they will be tested for continues, although some relief may be in sight. The Associated Press reported in October of 2002 that a number of schools have begun using urinalysis tests to see if students are smoking cigarettes or using other nicotine products. Supporters argue that drug use begins with smoking, and thus such testing can nip it in the bud.[91] In Indiana such testing was, until recently, permitted of students involved in extra-curricular activities as well as those who take driver's education and apply for parking permits.[92] However, a state Court of Appeals decision in 2003 invalidated the use of testing for nicotine as a violation of students' Fourth Amendment rights.[93]

There have, thankfully, been a number of successful challenges to the array of drug testing procedures schools have drummed up. In a state court decision, *Linke v. Northwestern School Corporation*, 2000 Ind. App., the school had required every student who drove to school or who participated in certain activities to be randomly tested. More than half of the student body was included, as the activities ranged from varsity sports to a variety of student clubs and organizations. The Indiana court focused only on whether the policy violated the state constitution, not the U.S constitution. They held that it did. At minimum, the state constitution requires some individualized suspicion in order to search a child at school. The overly broad policy instituted by the school "was a dangerous step toward mass and random drug testing of all school students."[94]

Another state court decision also invalidated the use of drug testing for those who are in extracurriculars, who drive to campus, or who obtain parking permits. The Pennsylvania court was also critical of the lack of individualized suspicion, as well as the fact that the school failed to demonstrate any special need for the policy. Importantly, the court recognized that a student's privacy interests should not be lessened simply because he or she exercised the privilege of participating in school-sanctioned activities.[95] These lower court decisions dealing with testing of students in extracurriculars have been invalidated, however, by the 2002 Supreme Court decision in *Earls*. The Supreme Court did not address the other portions of these policies, testing students who drive to school or who obtain parking permits, leaving those to stand as precedent in the areas where the respective circuit courts have jurisdiction.

As of now, drug testing for all truant or suspended students has not been upheld. In this case, *Willis v. Anderson Community School*, 158 F. 3d 415; 1998 U.S. App., the school could not justify why the same purpose could not be attained via a suspicion-based search, nor was the voluntary nature of the activity or communal undress issues cited in *Vernonia* present.[96] When freshman James Willis was suspended for fighting a fellow student he was informed that he must submit to a urine test upon his return to school, and that he would continue to be suspended until he consented to the test. The policy also mandated testing for students who possessed or used tobacco products, who were suspended for three or more days or suspended for fighting, or who were truant habitually. Allegedly the goal of the policy was to "help identify and intervene with those students who are using drugs as soon as possible and to involve the parent immediately."[97] Results of positive tests were only disclosed to parents and designated school officials and did not lead to additional punishment. However, students who tested positive were required to participate in a drug education program; failure could lead to expulsion from school.[98]

The court questioned whether there was any evidence to substantiate that students who get into fights are more likely to use drugs or alcohol. A deposition with the school's Dean of Students, Philip Nikirk, revealed that he had no such evidence in regard to Willis. The court was introduced to some literature that showed a relationship between fighting and use of illegal substances, yet also noted that the same literature lists 31 other indications of substance abuse, including "sleeping more than usual," and "playing parents against each other."[99] Further, the literature cautions that the list of possible signs of substance abuse "could be endless," and that many of the indicators "are to some extent normal in many adolescents at certain times."[100]

The court cautioned that schools must consider the group(s) to which their testing policy applies. The judges stated,

> "For one insidious means toward blanket testing is to divide students into several broad categories ('extracurricular-ites,' troublemakers, etc.) and then sanction drug testing on a category-by category basis. Eventually all but the most withdrawn and uninvolved students will fall within a category that is subject to testing."[101] These insightful judges recognized that "simply invoking the importance of deterrence is insufficient."[102]

In *Tannahill v. Lockney Independent School District*, 133 F. Supp. 2d 919; 2001, the court refused to permit the random drug testing of an entire student body. Again, the court found that the school did not have a compelling interest that outweighed the students' privacy rights. In fact, there was no demonstrable increase in drug use prompting the policy; the school actually had lower usage rates than many others in the state. The court determined that "general concerns about maintaining drug-free schools or desires to detect illegal conduct are insufficient to demonstrate the existence of special needs."[103]

The "Other" Costs

As with drug testing in the workplace, there are several concerns with school drug testing that often go unconsidered. One is that students are forced to reveal any physical or emotional difficulties they may be having that require them to take medication. The point in requiring this admission is that the metabolites produced by some legal medications are identical to those of illegal drugs, so testers must be made aware in advance so as not to falsely accuse a student. Yet, since most students being tested are completely unaware of which substances could be misinterpreted, they have no choice but to list everything they take.[104] One student objected to the requirement to list the prescription drugs she takes, but eventually submitted because she wanted to participate in extracurriculars in order to get into a good college.[105]

In addition to the fact that students must disclose personal information, the privacy of the test results remains in question. This was an issue in both *Earls* and *Vernonia*. While most policies of late mandate that urinalysis results are only provided to appropriate school officials, the student, and his or her parent or guardian, there are instances where results are given to police. Further, exactly what measures schools take to ensure that no other students or unnecessary faculty members will see the results is unclear. While it's bad enough that your school principal knows you're taking Prozac, it would be much worse if the student body or faculty became aware of your prescription against your will. The confidentiality problem is only likely to worsen. Addressing complaints about the immodest testing conditions being used by Olentangy Middle School in Ohio, the coordinator of the district's program, Joseph Franz, explains that, judging by the success of his company Sport Safe Testing Services, new schools will be constructed with built in testing facilities.[106] Well, it seems that chemistry class experiments are going to get a whole new twist but we have to wonder, do prisons even have their own drug testing facilities?

The treatment of people who object to drug testing is yet another concern. The Tannahills objected to a mandatory drug test for their son, who was being targeted for testing along with his entire sixth grade class. They received threats from the community for their stance. Parents were told if they refused to sign the form allowing their child to be tested, it would be presumed that he or she was using drugs. In this case, students would be punished with in-school suspension and banned temporarily from participation in extra-curricular activities. One of the nicer community members simply berated the Tannahill's parenting: "If either one of my children were doing drugs, I'd want them to get help. I don't see what the big deal is," said Pat Garza.[107] Others reacted even less maturely to the Tannahill's exercising their right to object; someone shot their dog with a paintball and a note was left on their door saying, "You're messing with our kids." Letters to the editor published in the local paper suggested that the family move.[108] Mighty neighborly behavior with some frightening implications. It's no longer just school administrators pushing these tests in violation of constitutional rights—its other parents. This should ring an alarm bell for anyone concerned with civil liberties.

Barring kids who test positive, or, even worse, those who are constitutionally-aware and refuse to consent to a drug test, from participation in extra curricular activities simply serves to increase students' disdain for school and prevents them from benefiting from all the positives associated with participation. In addition to the fact that participation in something additional to the regular school day is virtually required for college admittance, activities like the Debate club and National Honor Society can build citizenship skills.[109] According to Richard Glen Boire, counsel for the Center for Cognitive Liberty and Ethics, "A policy that deters students or bans them outright from participating in extra curricular activities isn't just bad for students, it's bad for society."[110] Screening may simply decrease involvement in extracurriculars among students who have used drugs or even tried them once. Since the literature on juvenile delinquency clearly shows that the bulk of incidents occur between 3:00 and 6:00 p.m., we're simply decreasing the likelihood that students will engage in healthy activities and increasing the chance that they will do something less-good for them. Research has linked lack of participation in school activities to higher drop out rates, higher teen pregnancy rates, more likelihood of gang membership, and, who would have thought it-substance abuse![111]

Further, labeling kids as "druggies" or as "delinquents" can easily become a self-fulfilling prophecy. As Ronnie Casella explains in At Zero Tolerance, "the labels adults affix to students, including those denoting deviance, do more to justify maltreatment of young people than they do to treat students with the care and respect that they deserve."[112] Since we know that it is extremely important to youth that they be respected by their peers as well as adults, labeling students based on the results of a highly flawed drug testing procedure may serve only to alienate and anger them.

Studies have shown that adolescent drug addiction is a developmental disorder. As adolescents develop, the motivational circuitry of their brains is changing, making them more vulnerable to the effects of alcohol and addictive drugs, according to Yale University School of Medicine researchers.[113] This is not to say that we necessarily need to allow students to use drugs and alcohol, but we do need to try understanding, rather than alienating, in order to have any positive impact on their behavior.

The continued use of intimidation tactics to ferret out drug users in schools is clearly not working and may be detrimental to kids. Even so-called educational programs like D.A.R.E are taught by police officers, not trained drug educators, and tend to be grounded in a threat-based approach; "if you use drugs, you will be a loser...have no friends...go to jail...blah, blah, blah" Such methods of social control may lead us further down the road toward people simply assuming they have no privacy rights, as that is what they have become accustomed to. According to Boire "Raised with the ever-present specter of coercion and control where urine testing is as common as standardized testing, today's students will have little if any privacy expectations when they reach adulthood."[114] The real goal of drug testing and other school surveillance techniques may be just that; to desensitize future generations to civil rights abuses that prior generations would not have tolerated.

Particularly troubling is that drug testing, as with all the types of searches discussed in this book, sends the wrong message to students. Said one father at a school just beginning to drug test their athletes, "From my perspective, it's an insult. I find it very invasive and symptomatic of a social trend in this country where you are assumed guilty until you are proven innocent."[115] Drug prevention efforts would likely be more effective if we were to try harder to base it on realistic information, rather than fear tactics. As Dr. Kent Holtorf, author of *Ur-Ine Trouble*, notes, all our efforts are based on the faulty "drug use equals drug abuse" premise. This is in contrast to what students actually see; they often know of many people who have used drugs, especially marijuana, without a problem. Since they know that nobody applies the same logic to alcohol use in our "alcohol-swilling society," the message that drug use equals abuse "is regarded as further evidence that the entire anti-drug message is a pack of lies."[116]

In Sum, Why Drug Testing Fails

While alienating students, drug testing fails to serve any practical purpose in schools. First, it is terribly expensive, especially when the cost-per-catch is considered. Second, contrary to claims by politicians, it fails to deter use among any student group. Third, the format of the testing, which is unlikely to change, allows the students ample opportunity to cheat the test in myriad ways. Fourth, established drug testing policies, approved by the Supreme Court, target a group that is the least likely to be using drugs. Fifth, it produces alarming rates of false results that can do irreparable harm to students. Finally, students in schools with testing report less belief that drug use has negative consequences and greater belief that it has benefits than do non-tested students. The bottom line: Drug testing in schools is a mess that can't be cleaned up.

QUESTIONS FOR REVIEW
AND CRITICAL THINKING

Should school faculty be drug tested?
What are the potential costs or consequences of using the

new types of drug tests, such as drug wipes?

Why has drug testing failed to have a deterrent effect?

Should schools test for tobacco, nicotine, and/or alcohol?

What are the pros and cons of voluntary drug tests?

Do you believe students are pressured by other teens to take drugs?

Should students be required to take a drug test in order to drive to school? To attend prom? As part of their punishment for fighting?

EXTENSION QUESTIONS AND ACTIVITIES

How effective has drug testing in collegiate athletics been? In professional or Olympic-level sports? Find out more about the recent scandal involving Dr. Victor Conte and the Bay Area Laboratory Cooperative (BALCO).

Some states are considering making it illegal to sell masking agents. What do you think? Should it be a felony to cheat on a drug tests, as other states are considering?

What are some good alternatives to the threat-based drug programs, such as testing and D.A.R.E.?

CHAPTER SEVEN

Money Well Spent?

Deterrence, Cost-Effectiveness, and School Searches

> Laws to suppress tend to strengthen what they would prohibit. This is the fine point on which all legal professions of history have based their job security.
>
> —Frank Herbert

As noted throughout the previous chapters, the primary logic behind most school searches is based on notions of deterrence or prevention. Regarding drug testing, the following claims have been bandied about: "Drug testing has been shown to be extremely effective at reducing drug use in schools...all over the country. As a deterrent, few methods work better of deliver clearer results," claims the Drug Czar for the George W. Bush Administration, John P. Walters.[1] According to former NIDA Director and Nixon/Ford Drug Czar Robert L. Dupont, M.D, "The key to...dramatically reducing the number of young people who start to use illegal drugs each year is school-based drug testing."[2] Lay people have also adopted the deterrence parlance. "If we can save just one kid from being maimed or killed by drugs it's worth the infringement on their rights," said Ohio's Olentangy High School Principal Bob Thompson.[3] Even if these claims were true, they come at the expense of constitutional rights, a horrible lesson to teach the next generation.

Is there any merit to these claims? In short, the answer is a resounding no. There is no credible evidence that security hardware or personnel have any impact on reducing violent or deviant behavior; they might, however, foster student alienation. Alienation: there's a quality educational mission. Yet similar deterrence claims have been made of searches other than drug testing, as politicians and parents search for some simple panacea for the perceived problem of teen drug use and violence. This chapter explores the origin of and assumptions behind deterrence theory, as well as research regarding it's utility in general and in regard to youth delinquency. The chapter also addresses the failure of school search procedures to be cost-effective.

The Roots of Deterrence Theory

The notion that punishment can deter or prevent someone from committing a crime or act of deviance originates in classical criminology. First promoted by Cesare Beccaria in the 1700s, crime was seen as a rational choice made by offenders who would always seek to maximize pleasure and minimize pain. While certainly an improvement over previous theories that postulated crime or deviance was the result of demonic possession, classical school/rational choice explanations for crime are rife with problems, especially when applied to youth. Deterrence can be of two types, either specific or general. Specific deterrence refers to those who have already offended and been sanctioned; the sanction is supposed to stop the person from re-offending because this presumably rational person will want to avoid punishment. General deterrence impacts the rest of the populace; the idea is that if we see others being punished for certain infractions we will seek to avoid that consequence by not offending. Beccaria's original theorizing of deterrence stressed that, in order to operate efficiently, punishment must be certain, swift, and only slightly more severe than the pleasure that would be obtained by offending. Thus there was no reason to believe that people would be deterred if punishment were not virtually guaranteed (for those found guilty, of course), if it did not occur shortly after the offense, and if it was **too** severe. A basic assumption of classical criminology is that deviants are no different than other people. Deviance is not a problem of "bad people" but of bad or inadequate laws and punishment.[4]

It's Back!

Recently the U.S. has witnessed a resurgence in classical school thinking. Faith in rehabilitative treatment has waned, since it "failed" when we tried it in the 1960s, at least that is what we are told. Forget that we never truly implemented any rehabilitative efforts as designed. The American public is encouraged not to think about the nature of deviance and not to concern ourselves with treating its causes; we need merely to devise a fixed and certain system of punishment and to warn everyone that offenders who are caught will be punished without exception.[5] "We need to send a message" is one of the more commonly heard refrains. Left in the hands of George Bush and his henchmen this mentality manifests in such civil rights atrocities as the Patriot Act. Too few people have considered the original deterrence theory and subsequent research which shows that excessive punishment does not typically deter people from offending. The death penalty provides a case in point; virtually all studies comparing states that have the death penalty with those that do not have found no evidence of a deterrent effect and some have actually found a "brutalization effect," or an increase in homicide rates in the months following an execution. The efficacy of deterrence theory in general is rarely questioned today, it is simply accepted as common sense. Failing to question whether deterrence truly works and, even if it does, whether it works with all demographic groups assumes, rather than challenges, the status quo.[6]

Does Deterrence Work?

Some scholars have, however, explored whether deterrence actually works and have found, at best, minimal support. Specific deterrence is difficult to study, as it would require comparing recidivism rates of offenders who are punished with similarly situated offenders who are caught but **not** punished. Not punishing offenders is likely to be frowned upon, especially in the current war-on-anything political climate. Given this limitation, studies addressing the efficacy of specific deterrence have generally compared the subsequent offenses of similarly situated persons assigned to various levels and types of punishment. So, for example, a study might compare whether offenders who shoplift are more likely to re-offend if they are given community service or if they are assigned probation. Criminologists generally agree that such studies are flawed, in that one offender's recidivism rate is being used to predict another's. Other studies, seeking to get around this methodological problem, have utilized self-reports of deviance. Of course there are limitations with this methodology as well, namely the degree to which people respond truthfully.[7] One study used self-reports from 35 matched pairs of adolescent delinquents. Each pair was similar to the other in terms of prior history. Members of one group had been apprehended and sanctioned, while the others admitted offending but were never caught by authorities. Results contradicted deterrence theory in that the majority of the apprehended delinquent pairs had higher rates of subsequent offending.[8] In fact, so few studies have found support for specific deterrence that some have said, "an equally good case may be made for the opposite conclusion: punishment **increases** future law violations (emphasis added)."[9] The impact of severe punishment on offenders in general and on youth specifically will be discussed more thoroughly later in the chapter.

Research regarding general deterrence is more mixed. Most studies that have found support for general deterrence have found certainty of punishment to be much more important than severity, in stark contrast to the tough on crime movement and it's fry-the-bastard mentality. A study of the deterrent effects of "getting tough on juvenile crime" in Texas found that harsher sanctions do not produce positive net benefits. Benefits were calculated financially, including benefits to victims, which were assigned a monetary value. Incarcerating juveniles for $2,565,000 was found to prevent only two felonies. Had they occurred, the cost to victims and others was calculated at $114,000, thus no savings from the tough sanctions.[10]

In addition, studies seem to suggest that the perception of punishment plays an important role. That is, some people **perceive** they are more likely to be punished than others, and are thus more likely to be deterred.[11] Others hold the "it can't happen to me" attitude, and consequently pose a challenge to the basic assumption that offenders reach a rational choice to commit a crime after weighing the potential costs and benefits. These folks are perhaps weighing the costs and benefits, but are assigning them skewed values. Some criminologists have posed what they call the resetting explanation for why some are seemingly not deterred. This explanation posits that sanctioned offenders believe punishment helps insulate them from future apprehension. Once they are caught and sanctioned, they "reset" their estimate of the certainty of being caught and punished again. It's much like the gambler's fallacy that, because they were dished out eight shitty hands in a row, they are somehow "due" to win the next one.[12]

A 1998 study by Criminologists Piquero and Paternoster utilized telephone surveys of 1,686 licensed drivers, inquiring about their perception of the likelihood that they would be caught and punished for driving while intoxicated. Those who had already been punished for DUI were more likely to offend, according to their self-reports, because they believed the certainty of punishment to be lower than those who were unpunished or who received less severe sanctions.[13] In essence, they felt that luck would be on their side, a sort of lightning never strikes twice mechanism. Pogarsky and Piquero also found support for the resetting explanation. They used a hypothetical scenario with college students regarding making the decision to drive home drunk and found that those who had previously been sanctioned were less likely to believe they would be caught and punished again.[14]

Another arguably flawed assumption made by deterrence theorists is that all people are equally likely to be deterred. Bentham, Beccaria and the like gave no weight to the fact that punishment may impact different types of people differently. All people may not be the rational cost-benefit calculators that were envisioned when these theories were being developed; in fact, some entire demographic groups might differ in their ability or simply lack the ability to rationally calculate, like mental patients and, perhaps, juveniles.[15] Criminologists Robert Schwartz and Len Rieser maintain that, "There is nothing in what we know about child and adolescent development to suggest that adult penal theories have relevance to children. Deterrence has limited applicability to them..."[16] Criminologists Nagin and Pogarsky contend that those with a present-orientation, rather than a future-orientation, are less likely to be deterred from offending. The thinking is that these people are not considering what might happen if they are caught, as they are too busy living in the now.[17] Youth tend to be somewhat egocentric, so this explanation makes sense. Another personality factor that might impact deterrability is whether an individual has a self-serving bias, or tends to skew judgments in favor of themselves. Such individuals may offend because they lack the ability to perceive punishment as ever applying to them personally.[18] Sounds like just about every juvenile we know.

Classical deterrence theory ignored the issue of intent. There was, at the time, no distinction made between intentional murder and manslaughter. Neoclassical reformers who used classical school theories to craft French penal codes began to tweak with the theory, adding such gradations, but still intent remained an unimportant piece of criminal justice.[19] This premise remains, in large part, in American criminal justice. Take for example the fact that prosecutors are not required to show motive in order to win a case. Yet, according to Jennifer Sughrue, nowhere is it more important to consider the intent of someone's actions than in public schools, "with their dynamic mix of children and adults. Not unexpectedly, the multitude of expectations, interactions, and ages can result in misunderstandings, misbehavior, and poor judgment."[20] Knowing this, it seems simply asinine to apply a theory of punishment to juveniles that does not consider intent. Yet that is the key to the zero tolerance approach; treat all offenders the same, no matter what.

Finally, there is quite a bit of support for the idea that social context matters, and that individuals are often more concerned with the social stigma they will face as a result of punishment than from the punishment itself. So, if there is anything to the notion of deterrence, it is linked to people's choices not to offend so as to avoid stigmatization by those close to them, not to avoid punishment. This assumption provides the central tenet for the work of criminologist John Braithwaite, author of *Crime, Shame, and Reintegration.* He contends that the reason people choose not to offend is that they are shamed. Thus those who are sanctioned do not want to be shamed again, and those in the general populace do not want to face a similar shaming.[21] He argues that, "repute in the eyes of close acquaintances matters more to people than the opinions or actions of criminal justice officials."[22] Yet in order to be productive, shaming must be re-integrative, not disintegrative. Disintegrative shaming is at the heart of the American law-and-order approach, and is not only ineffective, but serves to push offenders into criminal or deviant subcultures. Such subcultures supply offenders with opportunities to reject their rejecters, thereby maintaining self-respect. According to criminology's labeling theory, once a criminal or deviant label is assigned to someone, that stigmatization results in a self-fulfilling prophecy, whereby the role of deviant takes on master status. Social control efforts that are moralizing are much more effective than those that are repressive, according to Braithwaite, because they treat people as responsible actors, yet recognize the impact of broader societal forces. Retributive punishment denies the conscience of the offender "by reducing norm compliance to a crude cost-benefit calculation."[23]

Deterrence Theory and Juveniles

So how does deterrence theory apply to juveniles? While few have studied this, the implications are certainly clear from the above research. Mike Males, author of *Scapegoat Generation* and *Framing Youth,* chronicled the impact of increased surveillance on youth by addressing the effectiveness of curfew policies. The affluent city of Monrovia, California, population 40,000, had instituted an oh-so-popular "zero tolerance" policy, broadly crafted to include all possible juvenile "crime." Part of the policy, and a point of pride for the anti-teen legislators, was the curfew policy, which was couched as an anti-truancy measure, despite the fact that tru-

ancy was already outlawed by the state. According to local author-
ities, the policy was necessary because there had been a disturbing
trend of truant students, between 75-100 per day. The suggestion
was that, while playing hooky, these evildoers were out reeking
criminal carnage on the city. Yet police records show Monrovia
had dramatically lower levels of **all** types of crime in 1994 when
compared to the previous year. In brief, Monrovia had a low juve-
nile crime rate that was continuing to decline.[24] Nonetheless, zero
tolerance prevailed.

Between October 1994, when the policy took effect, and July
1997, police records show that 800 teens were each given $135
citations. Parents were forced to pay $62 per hour "custodial
charges" if they were unable to pick their kid up within the hour.[25]
Who cares if it's necessary or effective, it's a great moneymaker for
the state. So Roscoe P. Coltrane gets paid to play cards in the sta-
tion while Billy cowers in his cell.

So, did it work? The answer is, of course, no. After adopting
the curfew policy, Monrovia experienced a 53 percent increase in
juveniles arrested for non-curfew crimes during the school months,
when the policy was enforced. In contrast, juvenile crime declined
12 percent during the summer months when the policy was not
enforced.[26] Not a lot of support for the general deterrent effect of
curfews. But who cares, it sounds good.

An additional concern brought up by the Monrovia case is
who is being targeted, or in this case, curfewed. Males found that
in Monrovia curfew citations were disproportionately given to
non-white teens.[27] So being caught and punished for a curfew vio-
lation was by no means certain, as classical criminologists recom-
mended. That is, unless you were non-white, which seemed to vir-
tually guarantee your apprehension for skipping. Attorney
Bernardine Dohrn asserts that a similar racially biased effect
occurred with Chicago's youth curfew laws.[28]

That a punitive intervention would have a disproportionate
impact is not surprising, in fact, it has become a standard of crimi-
nal justice and, increasingly, education. For instance, A.A. Akom,
On-Campus Suspension supervisor at Berkeley High School,

reports that black students were 40 percent of the school population but 68% of the off-campus suspensions and approximately that same percentage of on-campus suspensions.[29] Bernardine Dohrn points out that, in Massachusetts, African-Americans made up 8.4% of the school population in 1996-7 but were 23% of the expulsions; Latinos were 10% of the population but 33.8% of the expulsions.[30] In regard to searches, studies conducted in Rhode Island show that police are as much as five times more likely to stop and search vehicles driven by Blacks and Hispanics than those driven by whites. This is despite the fact that police find contraband more often when they search the vehicles of **whites**. While some of the variance could be due to reasons other than racism, it is likely that racism is a factor.[31] The Rhode Island findings are consistent with those of nationwide studies, according to Jack McDevitt, associate dean of Northeastern University's College of Criminal Justice.[32] Dennis Langley, executive director of the Urban League, claims that police searches of vehicles is "a means of intimidation and harassment."[33]

Why School Searches Do Not Deter

Since no one has studied whether school search policies, with their subsequent sanctions, serve as either specific or general deterrents (except drug testing which research has shown **does not** deter), the following arguments are speculative but are based on the literature cited above as well as personal experiences. The first issue to be considered is whether students are even aware of their school's search policies and the punishments they carry. This is not to suggest that students lack the intelligence to understand the policies or consequences, rather that they may perform a cost-benefit analysis and elect not to read this information. Anecdotal evidence certainly suggests that teens are not, for the most part, aware of the specifics of school policies. The authors' own experiences support that students pay little attention to school policies. Schools generally brief students on school policies via student handbooks that are distributed at the beginning of the year. Rather than even going over the policies, administrators shove the handbook at kids and tell them to read it, assuming this direction will be followed. Right, that's what kids are likely to do in their free time. Some schools demand that students bring back a parental signature saying that the policy was read and allegedly understood. Obviously this is done to absolve them from legal liability, not because they care about the civil rights and general welfare of their students, as anyone knows most students will do one of two things: stick it in mom's face on the way out the door and demand she sign it, or fake the signature. Again, our point is not that kids lack a general notion that they are prohibited from bringing drugs or weapons to school, but that a condition of deterrence theory is that they both know and consider the **specific** consequences of their actions.

Further, in order to be deterred, students must know precisely how an offense is defined, who will enforce it, what the punishment they might face is, and the certainty to which they are likely to receive that punishment. Again, our personal experience as well as reviews of school handbooks indicate that students cannot possibly have all this information, as the handbooks are generally written with a broad stroke. For instance, the policy at one school reads, "Principals and teachers may search students and their personal belongings if they have a reasonable suspicion, based on the totality of circumstances, for suspecting the search will turn up evidence that the student has violated or is violating either the law or school rules." Another part of the student handbook stipulates that lockers are the property of the school and that students may not expect privacy in them nor in contents within them. Readers are warned that the principal can search the lockers at any time or can authorize school officials or law enforcement agents to do so.[34]

Assuming we face the first hurdle and students are actually aware of their school's search policies, how likely is it that they weigh the potential consequences of say, drug possession, when deciding whether to bring a joint to school? Do adolescents think these things through in the same manner as adults? Literature from adolescent psychology indicates that they do not. This is not to suggest that teens are irrational. On the contrary, we believe they are not given enough credit in this regard. Perhaps, though, adolescents do make rational choices to be delinquent, but what is rational to them differs significantly from what adults consider deviant. Adolescents and adults may consider different options, may differently identify possible consequences, may place different value on particular consequences, may assess the likelihood of consequences differently, and may use different decision making rules, according to psychologists studying adolescent behavior.[35] Whichever is the case, it is unlikely these teens are thinking through what might happen to them in the same way an adult would if an administrator observes them with the goods, gets a tip from another student or an undercover snitch, decides to randomly search lockers or call in drug dogs, or even feels as though they have a specially endowed genital region. They might be thinking it through, but thinking a) who cares; b) it won't happen to me.

While schools are increasingly turning to canines and metal detectors to present a façade of safety, there are still few enough that these measures will not deter the bulk of kids. Further, schools bring in canines on limited occasions, which are generally randomly chosen. Allegedly the random nature of the dogs' arrival makes kids think twice about using, dealing, or packing. Yet there is no suggestion that kids think "I better not bring my bud, the canines haven't been to the school in a month so today's the day." And, as noted in the chapter on canine searches, the dogs are not allowed to sniff a student's person, which kids quickly learn the first time the dogs come through. So doobies, pills, weapons and the like make their way into students pockets instead of lockers or vehicles. Like many adults who want to do something, juveniles seek ways to mitigate the deterring punishments or circumvent them. Again, rational thinkers, all-right, just not in the sense that deterrence theory assumes.

Metal detectors have proven to be an ineffective means to keep weapons off school campuses. Metal detectors were installed in several of the schools where students opened fire on their peers, so clearly were not an effective deterrent. In an interview shortly after the fall, 2003 shooting at Rocori High School in Minnesota, St. Cloud State Criminal Justice professor Richard Lawrence stated, "I'm here to tell you, based on all the information we have from across the United States, metal detectors do not make schools safer. Cannot. There's limits to them—guns still get in."[36] While certainly some weapons that were headed for the school halls have been confiscated after detection, many others have made their way in via flawed search strategy or student ingenuity. Since most schools use handheld detectors, they must also use a pseudo-random search schedule that students can and do easily decipher. Students can also rely on arriving to school late as a detection-avoidance mechanism. In addition, they can sneak items through unmanned entrances.

Strip searches are horrendous, but still (thankfully) happen way too infrequently to provide any kind of deterrent effect. Most students we have spoken to were not even aware that strip searches ever occur in schools and, while appalled at the notion, had a hard time envisioning faculty at their school doing so. The perception of punishment, then, is not supportive of either general or specific deterrence.

Finally, as detailed earlier, drug testing has proven an utter failure in deterring drug use among the tested populations. Students report similar rates of use, more belief in the benefits of using drugs, and a stronger belief that more students indeed use. Further, drug testing rarely catches anyone and there are myriad ways to beat the tests. It is easy to see how kids might use the resetting effect here too; if they are caught once they may convince themselves that they will not be selected for testing again or, if they do, their use will not be detected.

Part of the problem with school-searches as a deterrent is that they don't meet the criteria essential to deterrence. It is true that punishments for violators occur relatively swiftly, but they are not by any means certain. They typically are also too severe for the problem, and thus are more likely to have the reverse effect. In regard to the certainty of punishment, there is a great deal of literature to support that certain types of students are much more likely to be watched by school officials, and are thus more likely to be searched. Of course if you increase surveillance of a particular group you are more likely to find something, just as heavier police presence in poor and minority communities will inevitably detect more crime there, regardless of whether the gated Big-Bucks Acres communities actually have a similar or even worse problem. Special education students have been targeted for years.[37] In Kentucky students with disabilities make up 14 percent of the population but are 20% of the school suspensions.[38] In fact, the problem was so bad that legislators were forced to create a law, the Individuals with Disabilities Education Act (IDEA) that proscribes a maximum punishment for special education students unless their behavior is not a manifestation of their disorder. As always, minority students and those deemed different are much more likely to be searched than are Cathy Class-President or Quiet and Cooperative Cal.

The School Climate

There is a growing body of literature to support the fact that, rather than making schools safe and drug free, the overly punitive approach that searches are a part of is negatively impacting the school climate and perhaps making drug use and violence more, not less, likely. A negative school climate shows students the expectations the faculty have for them. If all that students see is that administrators feel they are drugged out losers or gun-wielding misfits, students may simply meet that expectation.[39] Further, increased use of punitive measures has a cyclical effect. That is, students come to take on the role that is expected of them, and teachers continue to expect students to behave in those ways. As school violence expert educator Mari McLean explains, people are more likely to interpret others' actions as threatening or problematic in a climate of fear. She states, "In a climate of fear, teachers are more likely to see students who are uninterested, uncooperative, or disrespectful as posing a potential physical threat and, consequently, are unlikely to see promise in those students."[40] And, as described by Braithwaite, the negative climate and low expectations may only push kids into deviant subcultures where they feel as though they receive a modicum of respect.[41] It is well-documented that the hostile climate at Columbine high left shooters Klebold and Harris searching for respect, respect they felt they could only find behind the barrel of a gun.

It seems logical that the very kids who even want to bring drugs or weapons to school are the least likely to be deterred, largely because they likely are all present-nature oriented. Of course, teens are known to have a me-first attitude anyway, simply as part of their moral and psychological development. Compared to the number of kids who admit to using drugs, relatively few elect to bring them to school. Those that do, then, may be quite different in personality type from those who would never dream of bringing their weekend stash to school. Those that do may be simply thinking of the immediate pleasure of use, and may be calculating the risks and rewards differently. Part of the egocentrism of adolescents is the "it will never happen to me" mentality. Coupled with the "blame the man" attitude many teens have, this self-serving bias precludes most teens from being deterred.

We know that for most people social stigma is more feared than punishment. This is true of adults, and is even more true of teens, who merely want to feel as though they are worthy of respect by their peers and adults.[42] Many experts as well as lay people have held that school search and surveillance policies give students a reason to say no. Even the Supreme Court bought this argument in the *Earls* case. This is predicated on the assumption that other teens are pushers; that is, they are trying hard to peddle their drugs on others or goad others into using dangerous weapons. Yet research suggests that the peer pressure argument is largely a farce. The latest State of the Our Nation's Youth survey found that most teens do not feel pressured to use drugs and, contrary to the image presented by politicians and the media, actually enjoy spending time with their families.[43]

The implications of the importance of school climate are numerous. Above all, it suggests that the best way to deal with student drug use and to prevent school violence problems is to create a climate where students do not want to do either thing. According to Social Psychologist Elliot Aronson,

> It is reasonably clear that a major root cause of the recent school shootings is a school atmosphere that ignores, or implicitly condones, the taunting, rejection, and verbal abuse to which a great many students are sub-jected. A school that ignores the values of empathy, toler-ance and compassion-or, worse still, pays lip service to these values while doing nothing concrete and effective to promote these values-creates an atmosphere that is not only unpleasant for the 'losers,' but one that short changes the 'winners' as well.[44]

Yet none of the school search methods do anything to address the overall climate of the school, nor do they address the mixed messages students receive about drugs and violence. On one hand we tell kids that drugs are bad, but then if they struggle in the often stifling atmosphere of a public school we push pills on them. We tell students it is naughty to beat up and bully others, yet we show-er the football team in glory when they pound their opponents. According to DiGuilio, author of *Educate, Medicate or Litigate?*, research has shown that the best deterrent to school-based vio-lence is...surprise, the presence of a supportive teacher.[45]

By failing to address structural causes for violence and drug use, like a negative school climate, we leave untouched the status quo. As the satire news source *The Onion* details in their story, "Columbine jocks safely resume bullying," when we look to "bad kids" for explanations we absolve others of responsibility. "Others" includes the faculty and administration who look to hardware options rather than humanistic ones to make their school a sup-posedly safer place. "Thanks to stern new measures, a militarized school environment and a massive public-relations effort designed to obscure all memory of the murderous event, members of Columbine's popular crowd are once again safe to reassert their social dominance and resume their proud, longstanding tradition of excluding those who do not fit in."[46] Not only is the climate that fostered the violence in the first place left unchanged, but it is more restrictive. As Jon Katz documented in *Geeks*, the police tactics put in place post-Columbine, rather than helping those students who were being bullied, were often used to profile and target them.[47]

Searches Aren't Cost Effective, Either

Perhaps school-based searches, while not necessarily having the deterrent effect they are touted as having, are still the best way to deal with drug and violence problems. Perhaps they are, compared to other methods, more cost-effective. It would be nice for politicians and those in the drug-testing and student surveillance industries, but it is simply not true. Only a few examples are needed to illustrate why none but searches based on, at minimum, reasonable suspicion, are cost effective in the long run. 1400 students were drug tested at Olentangy middle and high schools during the 1998-99 school year. Each test, performed at a federally certified lab, cost $25. So the school spent $35,000. They found three positive results.[48] Assuming that other schools spend a similar amount on their drug testing procedure, the Pottawatomie School District spent $12,500 to catch four kids.[49] The Shaler Area Schools figure that their drug testing policy costs between $35,000 and $40,000 per year.[50] Of course these figures also only include one test. Since virtually all of the schools that use drug testing have policies dictating that each positive sample will be re-tested to ensure accuracy, the costs are slightly higher than those listed above. Further, when a policy is challenged, as was Pottawatamie's, the attorney fees and all that they entail (costs for expert testimony, for example) significantly up the overall price for catching a few recreational pot-smokers. Additionally, most schools use immunoassay tests, which can only test for one substance at a time, so to test for more drugs they must pay more. One way to offset the cost of drug testing is to require those being tested to pay. Yes, that's right-we'll even charge you to invade your privacy. Shaler Area Schools got the idea from nearby Seneca Valley, which tested 2,164 students in five months at a cost of approximately $26 per student.[51] Total cost to yield eight positives: $56, 264.

Metal detectors are also costly. While the hand-held variety can be purchased for approximately $100, the walk through variety runs around $5000. If a district has multiple schools in which they want to place the detectors, of course the cost is double or more. Even elementary schools are getting metal detectors nowadays, with the first installed in an Indiana elementary in April of 1998.[52] Even more important, though, is the cost of personnel to man the detectors. Typically a district does not have personnel already in place that it can spare for this purpose, so many end up hiring some type of security guard who fills the role. Bill Bond was principal at Heath High School in West Paducah, Kentucky when a 14 year-old shot eight students, killing three, in 1997. Bond does not think metal detectors would have prevented that shooting nor others. Heath considered installing metal detectors after the shooting but opted against it, largely due to the costs to train security personnel.[53] Unless that person is a police officer whose salary is covered by the department, the school must pay them. Even if all they make is minimum wage, which is unlikely, the district has now committed to another major expenditure.

Snitch policies are also costly if the school offers rewards to the informers. One school spent over $1000 in four months and has elected to increase the per-incident pay out.[54] Clearly it would be much cheaper and less invasive were teachers simply to interact with students at times when information about drugs and violence is likely to be exchanged, such as lunch time, immediately before and after school, and during passing times, rather than hole up in their rooms and ignore their charges. Or, worse yet, leave all non-instructional interaction up to security guards, police, and administrators, as John Devine documents in the New York City public schools.

Canine searches range in cost, depending on how frequently they are conducted and the number of dogs used per visit. Using figures from Interquest, one dog costs $600 per day. Most schools use between one and eight dogs. It is recommended that the dogs root around twice per month for the ten months of the school year.[55] So a district using only one dog in the prescribed way would pay $12,000 and a district using eight dogs would pay an exorbinate $96,000. When the authors were high school teachers in Michigan we made approximately $40,000 per year. Granted the cost to a district of hiring a new employee is higher due to health benefits, etc. (although in many locations teachers are being forced to pay for part or even all of these themselves nowadays), it seems as though reducing class size by hiring more teachers, known to help students both educationally as well as help reduce school-violence, would be a better use of such funds. And, as with drug testing, the costs look even worse when the results yielded are factored in.

Stripping a kid of their clothes and their dignity is free of cost (financial ones, anyway), but since many times such practices are legally challenged, a district deciding whether they want to have a strip policy should factor in potential court and attorney fees. For instance, the Greene County School Board in Virginia had to pay $30,000 to six students they wrongly strip-searched, in addition to the costs of litigating the case.[56]

The costs of implementing the privacy violating measures described in this book are exacerbated by the woeful state of educational funding. Many schools felt a regression in the reforms they had previously made in class size and teacher training post 9-11, as they could no longer afford them. Federal funds promised in 2002 by George Bush were, not surprisingly, earmarked for testing and vouchers.[57] The New York City Board of Education, facing a $400 million gap, cut after-school reading programs and middle school sports, while schools in Central Florida scaled back their summer school programs and dipped into emergency reserves to get by.[58] Forty-five states have budget deficits for the 2003 year.[59] Alabama's budgetary crisis is so severe that 38 of the state's 129 school systems are on the verge of bankruptcy.[60] Many states cut their education budgets between 5-10%.[61] As noted in an earlier chapter, Oregon's schools are in such dire straits they actually had to cut days from the school year to reduce operating costs. In North Carolina cuts have largely been made to administrative and support positions, which Governor Easley claims has not hurt the classroom one bit, a contention that seems unlikely.[62] Never fear, though, Secretary of Education Rod Paige has assured the public that, "We won't spend a dime on programs that won't work. If it's not working, we won't spend money on it."[63] Guess they better read this book!

Kids Sometimes Believe the Hype

Sadly, many students have glommed on to deterrence philosophy, as it has been pushed on them for so long. Hence we hear some students say things like this about canine searches: "Some in the stoner crowd are apprehensive, but the majority think it's a good idea or they don't care."[64] This is part of the hegemony perpetrated by the law and order folks. As Sociologist David Garland points out, "So long as the existing sanctions appear to convey a punitive effect in a manner which is broadly in keeping with current sensibilities, there tends to be limited moral interest in the details of how punishments are actually carried out."[65] According to Marxist penal theorists Rusche and Kirchheimer, the use of such ideology allows punishment, and we can add surveillance, to be perceived as something that benefits society, when in actual fact it's real function is to dichotomize and stigmatize whole portions of the population whom are feared or deemed less worthy, like teens.[66] According to Akom, focusing on individual responsibility perpetuates this ideology. He says that by focusing on individual responsibility, discipline systems,

> Divert our attention away from the ways in which the school itself may exploit and violate the rights of individuals, as well as of entire racioethnic groups. By virtue of its presumed neutrality, the discipline system transforms the established social order from one that is open to critical comparison with another into a supposedly normal social order immune from criticism. This is an extremely important bit of ideological alchemy.[67]

Even though searches in schools are more and more commonplace, the vast majority of public school students rarely, if ever, face an intrusive search. Similarly, policies have shifted so much in recent years that their parents cannot relate; canines, metal detectors and drug tests, for instance, were not used in their day. Thus a good bulk of the population, and all those who have any political power (read: Adults), are largely kept out of the loop regarding what is going on in schools. Even those who may question whether all the school searches described herein are necessary can be snowed by the propaganda. As Jim Redden asserts in *Snitch Culture,* "Tying an unpopular activity to a popular cause is good propaganda, and one of the most effective tools for recruiting new informants and justifying more surveillance programs."[68] Few are comfortable arguing that drugs or weapons in schools are good, so even if they are not enamored by the methods, they accept them because they accept the goal. Garland maintains that,

> In being kept at a distance from the penal process, and being unfamiliar-and often unconcerned-with its detailed operation, clientele and effects, the public may become susceptible to misinformation about punishment. Sensational headlines, emotive political appeals, or particularly heinous cases may lead to outbreaks of popular emotion which lack the counterweight of extensive knowledge and moral commitment.[69]

In sum, as Dostoevsky claimed, "the standards of a nation's civilization can be judged by opening the doors of its prisons." Although there is an apt comparison between schools and prisons, more importantly this quote instructs us to be wary of how we handle those we dub deviant, as the punishment may have a more serious effect than the offense.

QUESTIONS FOR REVIEW AND CRITICAL THINKING

Why is deterrence not effective with juveniles? What requirements were included in the original idea of deterrence?

Do you believe a person's intent for wrongdoing should matter? In what cases?

What are some problems with the individual focus we have tended to take with criminals or deviants?

EXTENSION QUESTIONS AND ACTIVITIES

What other areas or institutions in the United States have been influenced by classical criminological theory? In what ways? What has been the impact?

Research more about how teen courts have been used in schools. How do these courts apply Braithwaite's work?

CHAPTER EIGHT

Bringing In The Beef and Dropping the Hammer On Kids

> I realized there is tremendous anger toward America's youth…[We are] gutting the education infrastructure and replacing it with the police…
>
> —Reverend Jesse Jackson

In Virginia, a high school boy took a knife away from a classmate who he thought to be suicidal. He innocently placed the knife in his locker, inaccessible to the suicidal girl. Rather than applauding him for assisting someone in need, he was suspended for having a weapon on campus. The knife, which he obviously had no intention of using, was found as a result of a school-wide surprise locker search.[1] Brooke Olsen was suspended from Riverwood Middle School in 1996 for inadvertently bringing a bottle of Advil to school in her backpack. A drug-sniffing dog detected the Advil. When Brooke explained that she simply forgot the bottle was in her bag, school trustee Al Moore responded, "Nothing is more important than keeping drugs off campus."[2] These cases of school-regulations- gone-crazy are not unique. They are also both examples of something called "net widening." They are illustrative of the nexus between school search policies and zero tolerance, one-size-fits-all punishments. Each also demonstrates the micro-level impact of the search-and-destroy policies in schools. It's far too easy to advocate school searches in the abstract and lose sight of the fact that these are actual children and young adults being treated so shoddily, human beings whom we require to attend school.

Schools Help Keep Police in Business

Net widening is a term criminologists use to describe when the effect of an intervention increases the involvement of police or criminal justice. Sometimes this is an unfortunate by-product of a seemingly positive policy, such as diversion programs for youth in minor legal troubles. Other times, though, net widening seems to have been built into a policy almost purposely, as it is so obvious and its impact so potentially devastating. This is the case with school search policies and the disciplinary actions that follow. As illustrated from the cases described above, school searches can and do result in good kids losing educational opportunities, and sometimes even becoming embroiled in the criminal justice system. Most people are aware that once a person has a criminal record life becomes much more difficult; it is harder to get a job, harder to earn people's trust, and harder to be taken seriously. Although most schools claim their goal in instituting pee tests or bringing in the hounds is preventative, not punitive, many turn the students they catch with drugs over to police, and most states require that they do so when kids are caught with weapons. For instance, in the case *In re Patrick* 124 Md. App. 604; 723 A. 2d 523; 1999 Md. App., a search revealed the plaintiff had a knife and rolling papers in a book bag in his locker. Despite paying lip service to dealing with school problems "in-house," Patrick was promptly handed over to Johnny Law.[3]

Increased surveillance of teens in schools no doubt results in a greater number of deviant acts being caught, championed by conservatives as a triumph of both safety and morality. While it is true in all cases that more intense scrutiny results in more crime being discovered, it is especially so in those schools employing officers on campus; obviously even the most inept of the Keystone Cops is more likely to catch kids in their misdeeds than would no surveillance. Some would argue that it does not matter if more students become involved with the law as a result of school policies; they say that if search policies lead to catching more kids with something illegal, so be it. The response is really quite simple; these students are U.S. citizens with constitutionally guaranteed rights that are being trampled on in our thirst to **say** our schools are safe places, rather than deal with root issues and actually make them be safer. As Randall Beger writes in *Social Justice*, "Instead of safeguarding the rights of students against arbitrary police power, our nation's courts are granting police and school officials *more* authority to conduct searches of students."[4] And, with one-size-fits-all punishments stemming from zero tolerance policies in place, being caught virtually assures that some fashion of callous anti-teen treatment will ensue. It is impossible to divorce the surveillance culture from the punishment push endemic in schools as well as in broader society, so the impact of both on individuals will be addressed in this chapter.

Removal of Teacher Discretion

Incidents that once would have been handled informally at school are now turned over to police. While not all net-widening involves police-the term can also refer to increasing the scope of social services agencies-the involvement of officers is made easier by the prevalence of officers in and around schools. For instance, Brian Werries thought he was quite the jokester when he left a note in his locker stating, "Bomb's in other locker, sorry for the trouble." He expected that his friends who regularly accessed the locker would be the only one's to see his jab at what they all had been discussing; their school's overreaction to Columbine. Unfortunately for Brian he played his prank precisely when the administration instituted a school-wide locker search. Administrators were not amused; Brian was expelled and faced one to three years in prison when the later was turned over to the police. Thankfully he had a good attorney and a judge who ruled the search unconstitutional, but the fact remains that the school's involvement of the police served to widen the net.[5] And, had Brian been poor, or god forbid, a poor minority, he would likely have served some time due to less able counsel. It's like a one-two punch: first students are hit with unfair and invasive searches, then while they're reeling from that, we nail them with a punishment Godzilla.

In fact, some school boards have elected to turn control of "student safety," a.k.a student surveillance and punishment, completely over to local police.[6] This virtually ensures that both invasive searches and net widening will be the result; it's not as though the local police are trained and encouraged to teach students about civil liberties or to institute conflict resolution programs. Once instituted in schools, police will likely search more, find more, and punish more. While school-based arrest rates may assure the fearful citizenry that the teen devils are under control, reality is that most of the arrests are an example of net widening, not controlling those that truly present a threat to fellow students and staff. A 1997 study found that zero tolerance policies often target the wrong behaviors and punish the wrong students. It was found that only about 20% of the students disciplined as a result of zero tolerance policies were actually those that teachers identified as posing a real threat.[7] In *Another Planet* author Elinor Burkett describes how the school officer, Goldy, did not even try to hide the fact that he followed around the "alternative" kids, despite the fact that none of them ever made any type of threat.[8] Further, approximately one quarter of those recommended for expulsion had disabilities that did or should have qualified them for special education services, a rate twice that of the special education student population.[9] Clearly no school-based search or punishment practices were effective in preventing Andy Williams from shooting fellow students at Santana High. In fact, he never impressed school officials as the kind of "alienated loner who bore watching."[10]

Lest the reader think we are advocating that teachers profile "scary" students, we are not. Unfortunately, as is clear from these examples, school officials already **do** profile students, they're just not doing a great job of it. School surveillance tactics such as metal detectors and armed officers aid in the separation of teaching from truly **knowing** students, as teachers become only the providers of content knowledge. What we would prefer to see, idealistic fools that we are, is teachers and administrators who have a connection with their students and can offer assistance if they seem to be struggling.

But the courts clearly do not care if search procedures or punishments are addressing real problems. In *T.L.O* the court provided for school officials to search for violations of school rules, not just for evidence of illegal or safety-threatening items. At the New Jersey school that T.L.O attended this involved evidence of membership in a secret society (this was a big problem?!), use of profanity, and misdirection of hallway traffic.[11] As Bernardine Dohrn points out, of the 158 arrests made by police at one Chicago high school in 1996-7, the largest number, well over one third, were for pager possession. Having redefined pager possession as "drug paraphernalia," they effectively transformed a "technological convenience into a crime."[12] Pagers are obviously legal for adults and in other settings, so this is an issue of a status offense and/or a school rule, not necessarily a law. While these examples may not specifically deal with searches, it is obvious that much of the evidence of illegal substances or of weapons is garnered by school-based searches.

Most of the categories of activity that students are being searched and punished for are subjectively determined. "Disorderly conduct" and "persistent disobedience" are two good examples. Our first question should be: What the hell are these? Aside from, of course, a license to selectively enforce harsh punishments. As Dohrn notes, "the decision to call a shouting match a crime, to arrest rather than intervene and instruct, to prosecute rather than resolve the dispute-is turning schools into policed territory."[13] The result of these school-based versions of Shock and Awe are clear at the micro and macro level.

> When school sanctioning is handed over to law enforcement in the first instance for the vast majority of minor school infractions, not only the offender and the victim fail to learn from the incident, and not only is the consequence more likely to be crushing rather than illuminating, but the entire community fails to take hold of the problem as a school community matter.[14]

Perhaps students will be refreshed to know that teachers too can be punished for silly reasons based on zero-tolerance mentality. A substitute teacher in a Chicago school district was fired for discharging a cap gun in class in order to get the attention of students. Students were scared and reported the incident to school officials.[15] Fair enough. But to fire someone the principal admits is an "experienced" teacher for a lapse in judgment seems to be overkill.

Why This Isn't Supposed to Happen But Does

There are, allegedly, several bright line laws, or legal standards, created by courts to guide police involvement in searches, thus supposedly minimizing the net widening effect. First, police (who are subject to probable cause standards) are never to use school officials (who need only reasonable suspicion) to search students and turn over information, called the "silver platter" doctrine. This was a concern at the time of the T.L.O case, as several states, including New Jersey, had laws mandating school officials report any crime committed at school.[16] Nothing has changed, except perhaps to get worse. Arizona law requires that school officials report any crimes or security threats involving students to local police.[17] Exactly what is deemed a security threat is open to interpretation, but is likely to be defined in a way that is increasingly broad, in light of our climate of fear of kids and the war-mongers in the White House the last several terms. Michigan law requires police presence in searches of student lockers, cars, and personal belongings.[18] Additionally, the law specifically states that items obtained in a search cannot be excluded in either court or disciplinary proceedings.[19] Other states have enacted laws requiring school officials to share personal information, including that obtained by school counselors and therapists, with police, which can then be used to justify a search.[20] Thus, despite the prohibition against the silver platter approach, it would be very easy for police to abuse school official's lesser search standard, making their job much easier. Unfortunately, that concern has only worsened with the increased militarization of schools. Does it really happen, though? Do schools **really** hand over their pupils for police and prosecutors to do their damage? Hell yes it happens. In one study it was found that in cases where evidence was found through a school-based search, fifteen of eighteen resulted in criminal proceedings.[21]

Of course, police do not always arrest these derelicts immediately. Many are sent to Juvenile Intake and Assessment Centers where they are grilled by social workers about their behavior and their family, information generally shared with police. In one county in Kansas elected officials established this type of center to evaluate whether students who have committed any act of violence at school pose a threat to themselves or others. Sounds good, but is really much more surreptitious. Families are required to bring their bothersome children to these centers, but are then promptly separated from them while the children complete a lengthy form called POSIT (Problem Oriented Screening Instrument for Teenagers) which features 139 potentially incriminating questions about themselves as well as their friends and family. If the responding student is deemed a problem, he or she may be sent to a diversion program, which often requires a urinalysis for drugs, regardless of whether there was any suggestion the kid ever even experimented. Children who do not comply are returned to the loving care of the police. So, "failure to produce an 'observed' urine sample can lead to incarceration in a juvenile detention center."[22]

The second guideline for school searches involving police is that whichever standard is appropriate for a school search will be determined by who is considered the agent of the search. That is, which party initiated the action supposedly dictates whether the reasonable suspicion or probable cause standard will be applied. This sounds simple enough, but has become a complex issue. The Ninth Circuit court attempted to establish a test in order to determine agency. It is a two-prong test. Part one addresses whether the government knew of and acquiesced in the intrusive conduct, while part two assesses whether the party (school employee) intended to assist law enforcement effort or to further his/her own ends.[23] Notice that neither part addresses the student, yet they are the affected party. So even when the courts do consider whether the appropriate search standard has been applied, the decision is largely irrelevant, as the impact of the search on the student is the same either way. It also seems that few schools and courts actually care about this guideline. In several cases police have clearly been the impetus and leaders in a search, yet the courts have held them to the reasonable suspicion standard. For instance, the court upheld a police-initiated search of the plaintiff's locker in *People v. Overton* 24 N.Y. 2d 522; 249 N.E. 2d 366; 301 N.Y.S. 2d 479; 1969.[24] And really, does it matter? Either way the student is likely to suffer the effects of net widening.

How The Exclusionary Rule Could Help

One way to limit the potential that police or school officials will abuse their power is to apply the exclusionary rule. There are three main elements of the exclusionary rule: an illegal search is committed by law enforcement or someone acting as an agent of the state; evidence is secured; and there is a causal connection between the evidence obtained and the illegal action. There are some exceptions created by the courts to the exclusionary rule, but none of them include school searches. Absent an exception, evidence obtained by school officials or police during a school-based search **should** be subject to the exclusionary rule.[25] The purpose of the exclusionary rule is obvious; to deter law enforcement from violating people's rights in order to obtain evidence against suspects. In addition to hopefully preventing abuse, applying the exclusionary rule to cases at school would simply be fair. Yet conservatives in Congress have been trying to abolish the exclusionary rule for over thirty years, claiming it ties the hands of law enforcement.[26] They tried hard in 1995, and the House even passed the Exclusionary Rule Reform Act, but it never, thankfully, became law.[27]

There is much evidence that the exclusionary rule does not significantly impact the chances of catching and punishing criminals. A 1978 study found that prosecutors declined to bring cases based on Fourth Amendment concerns in only 0.4% of cases and only 1.3% had evidence excluded at trial. A 1982 National Institute of Justice study found that only 0.79% of felony complaints in California over a three-year period were rejected for prosecution because critical evidence was obtained via some type of flawed search. Police officers testifying before Congress have even said they believed the exclusionary rule to be the most effective deterrent to police misconduct.[28]

As it stands now, the exclusionary rule generally does not apply to evidence obtained during a school-based search that is used for school punishments, and often does not apply to criminal proceedings either.[29] So it would be possible to use evidence in court obtained as a result of a search for violation of school rules. Nice. The tardy police feel that Joey has been late too much, use that to justify searching his locker (he must be tardy because he is pushing drugs on innocent classmates), find a joint or a pocket knife, and Joey looks at a possible criminal record. The argument is that allowing the exclusionary rule to apply for school punishments would cause harm to the school environment, deterring school officials from undertaking disciplinary proceedings.[30] Huh…hasn't this argument been disproved by the research cited above? Again, policy makers are not concerned with research, only what sounds good. The drivel seeping out of the mouths of some educators, lawmakers, law enforcers and politicians could make even the most gullible second guess.

In addition to police on campus, metal detectors and canine searches also offer an easy way for schools to coordinate their efforts to find, charge, and convict students with those of police. The detectors are often manned by security personnel or officers. Once something is detected by the scanner, the officer is in a perfect position to use that information against the student.[31] And, according to lower court decisions, as long as all students are treated the same during the scanning (wink, wink, nudge nudge), students' rights were not violated by the search. For instance, the hand-held metal detector in question in *People v. Dukes* 580 N.Y.S. 2d 850 (N.Y. Crim. Ct. 1992), which were manned by police officers at the request of the school, were deemed acceptable because, in the event that lines to be scanned became too long, officers instituted a "random" search of every few students.[32] Evidently it's OK as long as we violate **everyone's** rights. Schools are supposed to be about equal opportunity, which they rarely are, so perhaps being equal opportunity rights offenders is a major coup.

Unless the district employs a private company like Interquest, police canine-handlers will be used. In fact, most locker searches involving police also involve canines.[33] Of course, schools and police get around this violation of privacy rights by utilizing the questionable decision from *U.S v. Place* 462 U. S. 696 (1983) that canine sniffs are not searches. The same holds true of canine sniffs of privately owned vehicles. Please. Rover snouting through my stuff may be called an "indication," but the effect is my stuff is searched. Students caught with contraband will not only be punished for violating school rules, but will likely be charged criminally as well, effectively widening the net. Everybody has not been snowed by this logic, however. Justice Zappala issued a scathing dissent in *Commonwealth v, Cass* 466 Pa. Super 66 (1994), where the majority of the Pennsylvania Supreme court upheld a mass locker search that was requested by school officials but conducted by state police. He said, "To characterize the locker search in this case as a search by school officials is to engage in subterfuge. Appellee's school locker was searched by police officers and the contraband seized as a result thereof formed the basis of a criminal prosecution…".[34]

Sting operations, increasingly popular in schools, are another means of widening the net. What better way for police to infiltrate schools than to pose as students? Said one undercover officer who conducted a drug probe in a high school near Atlanta, "I knew I had to fit in, make the kids trust me and then turn around and take them to jail".[35]

No More Friendly Neighborhood Officer

It wouldn't be quite as bad to widen the net if all that happened was a slap on the wrist and a firm "no-no" by friendly Officer Joe. Or, better yet, if Officer Joe was trained to treat youthful indiscretions as learning opportunities. Unfortunately, states have been upping their penalties for having contraband on or even near school campuses. For instance, Louisiana law proscribes that any person caught with a firearm on school grounds "shall be imprisoned at hard labor for not more than five years."[36] Illinois, New Hampshire and Michigan have increased the penalties for possession or distribution of drugs in or near schools and have also lowered the age for prosecution of juveniles.[37] Alabama was able to sentence first-time offender Webster Alexander to 26 years based on their definition of selling drugs in a school zone.[38] Granted this sentence was reduced significantly, but the scary fact remains that the law allowed for such a sentence for a first offense.

Schools Can Even Monitor Behavior Off-Campus

Another way that the net has been widened is through school discipline policies that attempt to police what students do **outside** of school. Courts have generally held that students are not deprived of their constitutional rights when they are disciplined for behavior "detrimental to the school," even if that behavior occurred off school property. The court stated in *Blackwell v. Issaquena City Board of Education* 363 F. 2d 764 (Ca 5th Cir. 1966), "A reasonable suspicion school regulation is one which is essential in maintaining order and discipline on school property and which measurably contributes to the maintenance of order and decorum within the educational system."[39] Dealing drugs off campus impacts the safety and welfare of students, according to *Howard v. Colonial School District* 615 A. 2d 531; 1992 Del., so schools can pile their own punishments on top of those mandated by law.[40] Of course drug dealers are not considered **good** for any community, but it's unclear exactly how a student selling joints to his buddies on a Saturday night, miles away from campus, is something the school should be involved with. Drug testing by its very nature attempts to police behavior occurring outside of the school's parameters.

While legislators and judges are eviscerating Fourth Amendment rights of students, their attitude seems to be that they might as well work their way through other portions of the Bill of Rights. Next up for destruction: the Fifth and Fourteen Amendments.

The Fifth and Fourteenth Amendments

The Fifth and Fourteenth Amendments guarantee all citizens due process rights. The Fifth Amendment protects against actions by the federal government, while the Fourteenth applies to states. The courts have defined two types of due process; procedural and substantive. Procedural due process assures citizens the right to receive proper notice of charges against them, to be heard, and to have a fair hearing. Substantive due process means the state cannot arbitrarily deprive citizens of their right to life, liberty, and property. The courts have deemed education a property interest when the state establishes a public school system. Yet more and more frequently kids are searched then suspended or expelled based on possession of some small amount of illegal drug (or sometimes even legal ones), depriving them of this established property right. Liberty has been determined to include an individual's good name, reputation, honor or integrity.[41] To be targeted for a search and perhaps even kicked out of school or off of an athletic team surely sullies a student's name, yet the courts have been slow to interpret this as a Due Process violation.

To be constitutional it must be clear that a school search was reasonable and appropriate for accomplishing the objective.[42] In addition, due process has generally required that neither life, liberty, nor property be taken away unless the accused is aware that he or she did something wrong. This is the antithesis of zero tolerance, which does not generally consider intent. Here's how this might play out: A student forgets that she is to check her ibuprofen at the school office, instead leaving it in her purse, which is secured in her locker. Her school decides to bring in drug dogs that day, and a dog indicates at her locker. School administrators search her locker and find nothing illegal but do discover that awful ibuprofen. Rather than hear her explanation, which is entirely legitimate, or perhaps even institute some minor punishment for her error, the administration determines that they must expel her for 180 days because the state has a zero tolerance law.

Until 1975 students had no due process rights whatsoever. In *Goss v. Lopez* 419 U.S 565, the Supreme Court held that students cannot be suspended without a hearing, establishing minimal due process in schools. According to the court, "Having chosen to extend the right to an education to public school students, a state may not withdraw that right on grounds of misconduct absent fundamentally fair procedures to determine whether the misconduct has occurred."[43] Accordingly, students must be informed about matters pending, the court determined, in order to choose whether to contest them.[44]

Yet many school search policies are inherently unfair and often deny students both procedural and substantive due process. According to Jennifer Sughrue, a professor of Educational Leadership and Policy Studies, "there is firm reluctance in the courts to mediate questionable disciplinary action in schools".[45] *Tinker v. DesMoines* 393 U.S 503 established that courts will defer to the judgment of schools in matters of discipline, even when "the decisions of school administrators…[are] lacking a basis in wisdom or compassion".[46] What?! So we're admitting that administrators might make decisions that are neither wise nor compassionate, but we'll just roll with it?

A primary element of procedural due process is that the individuals presiding over any hearing are impartial. It is questionable whether administrators can be both accuser and unbiased arbiter of justice.[47] While the Supreme Court has not addressed the issue, lower courts have, no surprise, determined that there is no problem with administrators being judge, jury and executioner.[48] Amazingly, teachers and administrators are astounded at the gall of students and their parents who attempt to challenge school officials when due process rights are denied.[49] Today an incident at school, or an alleged one, can significantly impact a student's future, as students now face much more severe consequences for what would have once been treated as adolescent misbehavior.[50]

Who can blame a student or parent for challenging the school? In Texas, not surprisingly, state law requires that districts expel first, ask questions later in cases when they are applying their zero tolerance law.[51] George Bush taught the crew to cowboy up and nail them punks.

In another example of denial of due process and of a situation that once would have been treated with a short suspension but instead was "zero toleranced," six African-American students from Decatur, Illinois were expelled for fighting at a football game in 1999. Although the fight involved no weapons and there were no sustained injuries as a result, the school board chose to define the incident as an "extreme act of violence" and called the boys' actions "gang-like activities," allowing them to utilize the most severe sanction at their disposal. The zero tolerance mandate the school board cited was arbitrarily applied. Other students who had been in fights were not treated similarly. The district's discipline code made no mention of any zero tolerance resolution. Further, while the boys had different levels of involvement and different prior records, all were treated the same. This is a clear violation of the concept of due process. In fact, even the victim of the fight was subject to two-year expulsion. While he was later given the opportunity to withdraw from school, the result was the same, as he could not be enrolled in any public or private school in Decatur.[52] While this case did not involve a search, things tend to be even worse when there is one. "We got you" seems to be the attitude of school officials, and courts tend to support the actions of the schools at any cost. In fact, courts have elected to narrow the application of substantive due process rights in recent years to cover only those actions that are arbitrary or capricious, or "shocking to the conscience."[53]

The American Bar Association has recommended ending zero tolerance policies. In a 2001 report the 400,000 member group critiqued zero tolerance as having "redefined students as criminals, with unfortunate consequences."[54] These consequences, as we have seen, are often the result of privacy-invading search policies and include denials of due process and net-widening. And, according to Schwartz and Reiser,

> Our modern version of 'zero tolerance' is not only about expulsion. More insidiously, it involves the referral of misbehaving youth to juvenile or criminal court. Few would quarrel with a school that sent a gun-toting high school student to the justice system. But referrals for gun violations represent a small percentage of those students who end up in the nation's juvenile and criminal courts. School quarrels that once ended in after-school detention now result in referrals to juvenile detention centers.[55]

Mass school search policies and policies and zero tolerance laws necessarily break down due process because they do not consider intent. Attorney George Macdonald comments, "Our founding fathers would spin in their graves if they could hear a public official mindlessly parrot a slogan ("zero tolerance") as reason for dispensing with the due process which has been part of our Bill of Rights since 1790".[56]

Due Process Under Attack Everywhere

The trend toward reducing due process expectations in schools merely parallels that which is occurring under the Bush administration. As *The Onion*, a satire news-source, parodies in the article, "Bill of Rights pared down to a manageable six," the Bill of Rights is rapidly being eviscerated by George and his cronies. Paring the ten amendments down to a "tight, no-nonsense six" will supposedly allow democracy to flourish without those nasty bureaucratic impediments, like privacy rights. In an apt jab at surveillance guru Attorney General John Ashcroft, the article jokingly has him saying, "The Bill of Rights was written more than 200 years ago, long before anyone could even fathom the existence of wiretapping technology or surveillance cameras. Yet through a bizarre fluke, it was still somehow worded in such a way as to restrict use of these devices. Clearly, it had to go before it could do more serious damage in the future.î[57] The perception that we must give up all our civil liberties in order to be safe is pervasive in the

United States, especially post-9/11. Small wonder that schools too have reduced the rights of students.

Police officers are often trained to believe that providing due process to citizens unnecessarily constrains their ability to conduct investigations and make arrests. As Criminologist Lawrence Sherman notes, a somewhat consistent set of police values emerges from the interplay of academy training, stories from other officers, and first impressions with the public. This includes the fact that "due process is only a means of protecting criminals at the expense of the law-abiding and should be ignored whenever it is safe to do so."[58] It is hard to imagine that they think differently when conducting searches of students in schools. In fact, police officers assigned to schools may be evaluated on the number of arrests they make, clearly not an incentive to obey students' privacy and due process rights.[59]

As we've seen time and again, the loss of due process rights does not impact all students equally. While all student do suffer from less due process than they should be given and generally less than those of adults, the impact is disproportionally on those who are different; special education students, minorities, and students who dress and behave outside of the mainstream. This is not accidental or simply some deficiency on the part of these socially marginal populations. Schools employ a number of tools in order to shaft these groups. One of these is the use of technology to profile students. MOSAIC 2000, designed by the Bureau of Alcohol, Tobacco and Firearms with "safety and privacy" consulting firm Gavin de Becker, Inc., is designed to identify "troubled students" who have an "elevated risk of violence." Said one participant in an e-mail discussion list, "It's a scheme to detect the nonconformists and stigmatize them early on. This will lead to brainwashing, drugging, social ostracism (nobody will want to associate with a potential criminal), juvenile jail, adult jail."[60] Students are asked a series of questions that ensure they will rat on one another regarding drug use and potential for violence. Rather than rating actual behaviors for their threat potential, MOSAIC rates the students on a scale of 1-10.[61]

Once a student is red-flagged as a potential threat, what happens? According to Tiggre, the most likely response is that law enforcement will act as they do with drug courier profiles: "harass enough people, innocent and guilty alike, to eventually catch a criminal and get brownie points for the agency responsible."[62] As with other profiling endeavors, the results are likely to show some identification of true threats, but a whole lot of false arrests, civil rights violations, and law enforcement corruption.

> This is not just an accident caused by bad administration, but a necessary result of placing 'catching law-breakers' above 'protecting individual rights (the people),' which inevitably happens when any policy is implemented that subjects everyone to the same treatment. Violating everyone's rights because the few alleged criminals deserve it does nothing more than show that the nation-state truly does view all of its subjects as pawns, to be played as it pleases, regardless of whether or not they are 'criminals'.[63]

In addition, as Tiggre points out, MOSAIC was designed and is being implemented by non-elected officials who will not, and because of qualified immunity often can not, be held personally responsible for the violations of privacy and due process wrought by it's use.[64] We have a piece of technology designed to help schools search and punish students, and we simply assume because it is scientific it must be better than human knowledge.

So what we have is a Kafkaesque situation whereby certain students are identified and targeted for persecution (and often prosecution), often unbeknownst to them and typically without adequate justification. And, as has become clear, once a student gets snared in the trap layed by schools and police, it is often difficult if not impossible to break free. Schools can use this to their advantage, as they have received the nod to push out students who for whatever reason they dislike. "Schools are using these policies to get rid of kids they don't want. It's brutal, but that's what we're seeing," said William V. Huntington, coordinator for the Oklahoma Criminal Justice Resource Center.[65] According to a parent whose son was unfairly accused of stealing a substitute teacher's sunglasses, "School is the only place where the due process of law doesn't apply. If administrators decide to make an example of your child they can unilaterally do whatever they want. Even in the military, suspects have more rights."[66] If Dave in the Goth-garb and plethora of piercings is contributing to low standardized test scores, drum up some threat that Dave poses, invade his privacy, and it just might be possible to get that pesky Dave into the alternative school or to drop out altogether. In a textbook example of net widening, Dave may become a criminal justice statistic after dropping out, as it generally is not long before kids with nothing to do are arrested for some petty offense, often loitering.[67] As noted earlier, this situation has been dramatically worsened by the No Child Left Behind legislation which seems to demand, and definitely rewards, schools that rid themselves of trouble-makers.

What the Students' Think

As we've already addressed in previous chapters, too few people are aware of the things schools are doing. Consequently, few have offered challenges to school search and punishment practices. While even some students have been convinced that privacy invasions and harsh punishments are necessary to control their unruly peers, many others are angry at the assaults on their liberties. Some student comments are instructive. A 15-year old "A" student who was forced to submit to a drug test because another student alleged that she attended a party where **someone** (there was no specific allegation against this student) might have used drugs had this to say: "I did not appreciate that the school took away time during one of the most important school days of the year, when we were having review for final exams, in order to wrongfully accuse us and make us feel guilty."[68] Frustrating and alienating the school's finest scholars hardly seems a strategy for educational success. It may also backfire terribly. As Webber points out in *Failure To Hold: The Politics Of School Violence*, when students are forced to comply with policies they see as irrational and ineffective, they will react negatively, perhaps even violently.[69]

Of course, some students simply see the school search policies and zero tolerance punishments as a joke. The students at suburban Minnesota's Prior Lake High School that Elinor Burkett talked to in researching for *Another Planet* did not see the necessity of the surveillance and "disaster drills" their school had implemented post-Columbine, and spent a great deal of time ridiculing them and the administrators that came up with them. "What if you're taking a dump?" inquired one student upon being instructed to rearrange furniture as part of a security drill.[70] One effect of these ludicrous practices, it seems, is to provide students with further evidence that teachers, administrators, and essentially all adults, are overreacting imbeciles who could and should be spending their time worrying about bigger things.[71]

Other students are more than just angry; some victims of invasive school suffer from post-traumatic stress disorder. Recall the words of a female student who was scanned with a hand-held metal detector by a male security guard in a New York City Public School: "It's very uncomfortable, I feel embarrassed amongst everybody else." She went on to describe how guards use the scanners as a pretext to ogle and sometimes grope female students.[72] Hyman and Snook cite several examples in their book *Dangerous Schools*. Hyman evaluated Stephanie two years after she was strip-searched in an effort to find $10, which she did not take. Stephanie suffered symptoms "not unlike those of students who had been physically and psychologically maltreated in other ways."[73] She was depressed, moody, resistant, and avoidant, none of which were characteristics of her prior to the search. Similarly, six African American boys who were strip-searched because a narc accused them of having drugs (they did not) all had stress symptoms and felt angry and alienated from school officials. [74]

Once Again, Little Recourse

If students and their parents do challenge a school search and/or disciplinary action, what recourse are they likely to get?

Little to none is the pathetic answer. Under 42 U. S Section 1983, students can collect damages for violations of fundamental freedoms, like Fourth or Fifth Amendment violations.[75] However, courts have established that school officials are only liable if they acted with actual malice in denying a student's rights; in all other cases they have qualified immunity.[76] So simply stripping a student is not enough, **additional** invasions are required? Supposedly school officials need immunity in order to be comfortable disciplining students without constant fear of legal action.[77] The law regarding the issue in question, for example, school strip searches, must be clearly established at the time of the alleged violation. The question is what constitutes "clearly established"? If there must be prior case law about the exact issue, for instance, strip-searching eight year old second-graders for missing seven dollars, then no doubt many schools will be able to hide behind the clearly established requirement. Further, school employees are only liable for what a "reasonable person" would have known was a rights violation. School officials have immunity in cases where "reasonable public officials could differ in the lawfulness of [the] actions."[78] So a bunch of largely white, upper-class middle-agers get to decide whether the actions of their peers are acceptable. If anything will help preserve the conservative status quo there's the recipe. What about whether the student felt the action was reasonable? Sure don't want to give adolescents any kind of voice. So what we have is a situation where school officials can do pretty much anything short of wanton disregard for a student's rights and the courts will protect them. For instance, in the case of *Jenkins v. Talladega* 115 F. 3d 821; 1997 U.S App., where eight-year old second graders actually were strip-searched for a missing $7, school officials were immune because the law was not clearly established.[79] Please! A "reasonable person" isn't likely to have much trouble grappling with that one.

In sum, schools are locations where students are to learn about civic rights, duties, and responsibilities. This should be included in the curriculum, but it must also be taught by example. Despite much research showing that teaching about and for democracy is far more effective than using authoritarian tactics, schools "treat students as the enemy, to be controlled and contained at every turn. Despite the toxic climate it creates, such schools find it all too easy to set aside their obligation to be bastions of democracy, and to introduce police tactics into their routine administration."[80] These police tactics not only impact students at school, but, as we have shown, they increasingly stay with kids after their time in high school is over through net-widening.

QUESTIONS FOR REVIEW AND CRITICAL THINKING

Under what circumstance should school provide information about their students to police?

In what ways do schools attempt to monitor students' behavior off-campus? Should they do so?

What rights are guaranteed by the Fifth and Fourteenth amendments? How do they apply to school-based searches?

Which of the various student perspectives outlined in this chapter do you recall?

EXTENSION QUESTIONS AND ACTIVITIES

In what other ways are students profiled in schools? Howabout outside of schools-how do adults profile teens?

What are the exceptions to the exclusionary rule outside of a school setting? Do you agree with them?

Research more about Zero Tolerance laws. What do they say? What has been their impact? Should we keep them?

CHAPTER NINE

The Big Picture
A War on Kids

Wow-a war without end. If you get the people to believe this, they'll let you do anything, just as long as it's in the name of protecting them.

—Michael Moore,
Dude, Where's My Country, p. 12.

In order to understand why we have reduced the privacy rights of teens in schools, we must assess the social structures and social forces that have shaped the attitudes of the politicians and administrators who created these invasive policies. As Thomas McDaniel, author of "Demilitarizing public education: School reform in the era of George Bush" (Senior) notes, "American education has often looked to other areas of our national life for concepts, principles, and organizational models on which to base the design of schooling."[1] The culture of surveillance both in and out of schools is part of a wide-scale militarization of virtually all the social institutions in the United States. President Eisenhower cautioned of the military-industrial-complex in the1950s; as McDaniel maintains, perhaps we should also be concerned with the military-education-complex.[2] Military theorist Brian Fogarty explains, "The United States continues to be a society organized for war, as exemplified by the permeation of military values into many of its central institutions."[3] Criminologist Peter Kraska has argued that the war against internal enemies has become a central focus with the end of the cold war.[4] Unfortunately, teenagers have become this enemy.[5] Part of the "war on" mentality is the sense that society is united behind the effort to eradicate or at least subdue the enemy, and the enemy generally has no one to speak for them.[6] In regard to the war against teens, this could not be more true. The militarization of the United States has numerous negative macro-level effects that are discussed in the second half of this chapter.

Militarism Defined

Militarization is the readying of society for a constant state of war. Militarism is the ideology that supports it.[7] Further, good citizenship is about obeying authority, while to dissent considered unpatriotic, if not treasonous.[8] Another scholar offers a description of what she calls the war-thinking paradigm. War-thinking is dualistic, antagonistic and confrontational, and it causes us to think in terms of ends, not processes.[9] Feminist scholar Riane Eisler is describing militarism when she contrasts the ideological approach she calls the dominator model with the partnership model. These are "systems of belief and social structures that either nurture and support-or inhibit and undermine-equitable, democratic, nonviolent, and caring relations."[10] Militaristic values include those of hierarchy, centralization of authority, discipline, and obedience.[11] Another key component of militaristic ideology is a tendency toward revenge.[12] Other American values that help promote militarism include an emphasis on pragmatism, efficiency, rationality, faith in technology, capitalism and free markets, ethnocentrism, and American exceptionalism.[13] Militarization and its' effects are not new; Sherry has shown how the U.S government has demonized and rallied against common enemies or the threat thereof throughout history.[14] The problem now is that "the line between waging actual war against external enemies and metaphorical wars waged against internal enemies is becoming increasingly blurred"[15]

In a militaristic society, children are socialized in ways that promote war-like answers to problems. Criminologist and educator Susan Caulfield maintains that, "in order for the public to be persuaded of the importance of militarism, the values of militarism must be rooted in the political and social life of the state."[16] Militarism makes aggression and violence appear to be the only way to deal with things. Caulfield explains that we do not look to militarism to explain social phenomenon because "it is so pervasive that we lack awareness of its presence."[17] Feminist bell hooks argues that, "Ideologically, most of us have been raised to believe that war is necessary and inevitable. In our daily lives, individuals who have passively accepted this socialization reinforce value systems that support, encourage, and accept violence as a means of social control."[18] Peace studies scholar Betty Reardon states, "The war system is not only organized warfare and armed conflict-it is all the practices, institutions, and interrelationships that are essentially violent, that destroy relationships, that impede social development and fulfillment. It is at the very core of our thinking and our relationships."[19]

The Importance of Language

Specific terminology is part of the ideology. For example, the "war on drugs" exemplifies the militaristic tendency toward revenge in that we get back at small-time couriers and dealers with lengthy sentences of incarceration.[20] Although we are generally unaware that our language influences our thinking and behavior, it nonetheless does. As Kraska maintains, if we see social problems, such as crime control or drug abuse, through the lens of militarism, our thoughts and actions will be militaristic.[21] Temple University Criminal Justice Professor and former New York City policeman James Fyfe nicely sums up the consequence of using a militaristic lens: "The more a police officer thinks of himself as a soldier, the more likely he views the citizen as the enemy."[22]

U.S Presidents Are On Board

Presidents Reagan, Bush, and Clinton, supported by the mainstream media, all furthered the militarization of crime control and related issues. Even President Nixon equated drug abuse to "foreign troops on our shores," sowing the seeds for later militaristic rhetoric.[23] President Reagan heaped praise upon police chiefs who "command the front lines in America's battle for public order," and regularly equated the evils of communism with the threat of crime and drugs.[24] It was under the Reagan administration that drugs became an "official threat" to national security. President Bush the elder continued in the same vein, characterizing the U.S as a "nation under siege."[25] Even so-called liberal Clinton utilized militaristic language, although less toward drugs and more on crime and violence. Drug war discourse hardly disappeared during his administration, though. Rather it was conjured up whenever politically expedient, as exemplified by Clinton's comments during the appointment ceremony of Barry McCaffrey, himself an Army General, to the position of drug czar. "McCaffrey has faced down many threats to America's national security, from guerilla warfare in the jungles of Vietnam to the unprecedented ground war in the sands of Desert Storm. Now he faces a more insidious but no less formidable enemy in illegal drugs".[26]

Clearly the administration of Bush-the-unelected has no problem with the militarization of society, as exemplified by his zeal to engage in warfare with as many "evildoers" as possible and to spend over $80 million to do it.[27] In fact, George W. fashions himself a military leader, as illustrated by his arrival for a speech regarding Gulf War II on an aircraft carrier, decked out in military garb. Even worse, that sad moment is being commemorated with an action figure. His henchman John Ashcroft is the poster boy for militarization, demanding those pesky federal judges quit being so damned lenient and issue the most severe sanctions.[28]

Examples of the militarization of U.S institutions clearly abound. These include greater surveillance, an ideology which stresses that problem-solving requires "technology, armament, intelligence gathering, aggressive suppression efforts, and other assorted activities commensurate with modern military thinking and operations," a developing collaboration between government, the corporate world, and the defense industry, and the use of militaristic discourse.[29] Simon explains that, "concepts such as loyalty, duty, and obedience to rank describe mental attributes that the military does not presume; rather recruits must internalize them and officers must excel in them. All three concepts have been widely borrowed by other institutions seeking to establish discipline and motivate performance".[30] One such institution is public schools.

Militaristic Language Is Everywhere, Even Schools

Most concerning to some linguistic researchers is the use of military metaphors. For instance, we conceive of argument as war. "Your claims are indefensible"; ""He attacked every point of my argument"; and "He shot me down" are all examples. Military metaphors have also been used to describe love, health, and in politics.[31] As Orwell pointed out in *1984*, governments use doublethink to convince the populace of the rightness of the militaristic approach.[32] An example of militaristic language is used by some districts to describe herding students into hallways for "weapons inspection": "blitz operations."[33] Similarly, New York City schools now have "scan days," "holding pens," and "corridor sweeps," terms reminiscent of some total institution, either prisons, the military, or both.[34] Unlike the use of militaristic language in health or love, when it is used to describe our approach to crime control it also has the backing of state-sanctioned force.[35]

Schools are a place where, not surprisingly, militarism has been institutionalized in a number of ways. This has occurred on three levels; the school structure, processes, and content. School structure refers to the way that schools are set up, including their authority structure, their physical layout, their academic structure, and their rules and policies. For instance, the authority structure of most schools is hierarchical. It is akin to a military structure in that each person higher in command has more authority over the next. It thus reflects the militaristic value of centralization and efficiency over humanism.

Militaristic School Structures

The physical structure of schools, as noted in an earlier chapter, has oft been equated with prisons. According to one student cited in Patricia Hersch's ethnography *A Tribe Apart*, "When I go there [to high school], I was astonished by how much it was like a prison. They painted all the walls white and there were no windows in any of the classes except the art class."[36] This might just as well describe military barracks. "Poor fluorescent lighting, drab and often bare walls, minimalist restroom features, hard cement floors and many other standard features of schools are decidedly uncomfortable, and they are that way for a reason; because schools, like the military, have an agenda, and physical comfort is of minimal or no importance."[37] The comparison between schools and prisons has only grown in recent years, as most districts seem to jump on board the techno-security bandwagon. According to Crews and Tipton, who have identified many features that schools and prisons have in common, "An overly controlled environment may stifle individual creativity, individualism, and possibly intellectual development".[38] Last we checked those were supposedly the goals of schooling. Yet, like the military, creativity and individualism are not rewarded in most schools. But standardization is a militaristic value and clearly the school environment supports it.

The academic structure in schools also supports the militarization of society. Virtually all schools are based on a competitive model, which by their very nature excludes a focus on empathic cooperation. Standardized tests, every politician's idea of the best measure of a quality education, like in the military, emphasize ends over means.

In Our Teaching Methods

Process refers to the methods used to teach students, in the classroom, through disciplinary tactics, and in extra-curricular activities. According to Eisler, "many of our teaching methods also stem from much more authoritarian, inequitable, male-dominated, and violent times. Like childrearing methods based on mottoes such as 'spare the rod and spoil the child,' these teaching methods were designed to prepare people to accept their place in rigid hierarchies of domination and unquestioningly obey orders from above, whether from their teachers in school, supervisors at work, or rulers in government."[39] Like the military practice of breaking someone down in order to build him or her up (as a model soldier, of course), many of these teaching and discipline methods rely heavily on fear, guilt and shame.[40] Many of our teaching techniques require repetition and rote memorization. According to Eisler, much of our drive to think and explore "has been thwarted by pedagogies that suppress independent thought and emphasize rote conformity and obedience to orders."[41] Those who fail to comply with the militarism in schools are considered troublesome, while those who do are praised and rewarded. This emphasis on compliance echoes the military's focus on obedience. Dissent is not tolerated; in fact, under the Bush regime it is flat-out unpatriotic. According to Education scholars Sizer and Sizer, since not all kids are alike, "standardization of such routines is as inefficient as it is often cruel."[42] But it does provide a huge payoff in other settings, such as the factory, the office, and...the military.[43]

Our discipline strategies too rely heavily on militaristic and rhetoric and practice. According to Smith, "language unquestioningly promotes values, sustains attitudes and encourages actions that create conditions that can lead to war."[44] Disciplinary terms such as "Zero Tolerance" clearly reflect the military mindset. In fact, the idea of zero tolerance originated in the military.[45] According to school violence expert Ronnie Casella, "some reasons for the persistence of systemic violence can be found in national rhetoric that sanctions forms of discriminatory punishment and policing. These policies create in our society a general feeling that teenagers are no good, out of control, and morally void. They bolster punishment in favor of pedagogy, control in favor of understanding."[46] Casella notes in At Zero Tolerance,

> School security forces are in many ways the peace-keeping troops of schools. They make a militaristic response to school violence seem normal, which, along with tracking and expulsion, further distances school staff from the emotional lives of children, since it ends up being the guards, not the teachers, who intervene when students are troubled or in trouble.[47]

Our disciplinary approaches, including the searches that often lead to their implementation, are confrontational, as in the military. They emphasize efficiency and ends over means. As with the militarization of criminal justice, revenge seems to be a key focus. Whole categories are deemed potential criminals, as in drug testing of all participants in extra curricular activities, and are thus subject to suspicion and heightened scrutiny.

War-Making Content

Content, of course, refers to the material that is taught, either overtly or as part of the hidden curriculum. Most of history curriculum is devoted to the glorification of war, for instance. It is important to interrogate the ways that schools and other institutions reinforce militaristic values, for if we do not, we risk reproducing them.[48] Media scholar Linda Holtzman elaborates: "Hegemony is not secured through force but rather through the way that values get taught in religious, educational, and media institutions-through socialization."[49] According to James Loewen author of *Lies My Teacher Told Me*, "Education as socialization tells people what to think and how to act and requires them to conform. Education as socialization influences students simply to accept the rightness of our society. The more schooling, the more socialization, and the more likely the individual will conclude that America is good."[50]

Militarism Leads to Moral Panic About Youth

The ideology of militarism has helped to create a moral panic about school violence and drug use among students. A moral panic can be described as an irrational fear about a particular problem. Use of the term moral is not accidental; it "implies that the perceived threat is not something mundane, but is a threat to the social order itself or an idealized conception of it."[51] There is a long history of moral panics against youth, as no group is more associated with risk than adolescents.[52] No group scares the shit out of middleclass adults more than a pack of teens. There are five key elements or stages of a moral panic. First, something or someone is defined as a threat to "our" values or interests. This concern is generally measurable in concrete ways, such as by public opinion polls or media commentary. It is characterized by disproportionality, meaning that people perceive the threat to be greater than it really is.[53] Second, this threat is depicted in an easily recognizable form by the media so that everyone can readily identify it and direct their hostility toward it. "Us v. them" judgments and decisions are the result.[54] Third, there follows a rapid buildup of public concern. The population now believes there is a real and serious threat that is the result of the identified group's behavior. Fourth, a response of some sorts occurs. Fifth, the panic recedes or results in social change.[55] The typical response to a moral panic is a demand for greater regulation or control of the threatening group and/or a return to "traditional" values.[56]

The main actors in a moral panic are the press, who give it exaggerated attention, the public, law enforcement, who generally broaden the scope and intensity of their actions, politicians and legislators, who lead the call for stiffer penalties, and action groups.[57] According to Kappeler, Blumberg, and Potter, the media selects and presents crime-relates problems, such as school violence or teen drug use, based on competition, not necessarily based on the degree that there is a legitimate concern.[58] The myths that come from this presentation are often built around unpopular groups, such as teens.

The media have done a stellar job of whipping up concern about school violence and teen drug use and making teens a feared class. According to Mike Males, "faithful to the public ire they helped inflame, experts and the media combed the country for sensational teenage murder, drunken driving crash, heroin overdose welfare mother, devil cult, just plain badness. Most in media demand are evil young wastoids, preferably white and suburban, from 'good families' to prove that all kids everywhere fit the 'satanic' label…"[59] Headlines such as "KIDS without a conscience," from *People* and "Teenage Time Bombs!" from *Time* scream off of the pages and elicit the desired effect among parents; paranoia, and a call for action.[60]

The coverage of incidents such as Columbine are reported ad nauseam (contributing to a wide array of incidents nationwide), yet adult rage killings, which are much more frequent, are rarely covered.[61] In 1999 *Newsweek* presented a special report called "America Under The Gun." The lead story "In The Line Of Fire" began by suggesting that teen gunmen are all too familiar. It then provided a fold-out picture of sixteen gunmen as well as a large picture of an uzi, despite the fact that only one of the people depicted had used that kind of weapon.[62] Truth –be-damned. It's much more fun to exaggerate than to tell the sometimes boring truth. Popular culture too supports the school violence moral panic, through such films as *187*, which shows an urban school as the site of rape, frequent rumbles and general degeneracy, and *Light It Up*, which relies on every possible stereotype about urban schools in its rendition of school violence. Even films that do not specifically depict kids freaking out at school with their AK's tend to portray them as brain dead, at best. Referring to such films as *Dumb and Dumber* (1994), *Clueless* (1995), and *Kids* (1996), cultural critic Henry Giroux states, "these films and others portray kids either as vulgar, disengaged pleasure-seekers or as over-the-edge violent sociopaths."[63] According to Barry Glassner, author of *The Culture Of Fear*, one study found that 40% of the news stories about kids in major newspapers were about crime and violence. These stories tend to depict criminal or violent acts in vivid language and generally show type of dramatic increase in their occurrence, whether truly accurate or not.[64]

As Males explains, it is not just conservatives who seem to hate kids. Liberals, too, are on board to decry the current generation as the worst ever. So-called liberal President Clinton was quick to fuel the fire about school violence after the Springfield shooting, blaming violent video games and television as well as decrying the easy access and quickness with which today's youth turn to weapons to solve their problems. Pretty hypocritical from a president who, merely weeks before, threatened Iraq with the "severest consequences" for not complying with U.N weapons inspections. To claim that today's youth deal with everyday conflicts "not with words but with weapons" shows an amazing lack of introspection from the same man who sent troops to engage in multiple world affairs.[65] As Michael Moore points out in *Bowling For Columbine*, the day of the Columbine massacre was also the day of the heaviest bombing in Bosnia. Clinton also said, "The threat of violence hangs over children's heads and closes their minds to learning. We cannot let violence, guns, and drugs stand between our children and the education they need."[66] Never fear, though, we'll still use violence when we need to assert our global dominance and secure our access to oil. As Males explains, "the president [Clinton] is most definitely representative of an adult generation that refuses to take responsibility for the violent part of American culture typified by militarism, adult rage killings, household violence, and a grownup citizenry eight to 100 times more likely to murder with guns than adults in other Western nations."[67]

It is clear that many parents are indeed concerned about school violence and drugs in schools, the first element of the moral panic. While actual incidents of school violence are quite rare, one poll found that 85% of Oklahomans, in both rural and urban areas, were "very concerned about school violence."[68] A poll of 1004 adults taken after the Jonesboro shooting found that 71% felt it was "likely" or "very likely" that a similar incident would happen in their town[69], despite the fact that kids are much more likely to be killed outside of school.[70] According to Vincent Schiraldi of the Justice Policy Institute, kids are three times more likely to be killed by lightning than by a gunman at school.[71] The media are perpetually preoccupied with random violence, and school shootings fit this mold perfectly. Even one month after Columbine the three main networks were spending no less than half their time on it.[72]

In regard to drugs, we have such bunk as "Parents Have A Right To Be Scared" from *Newsweek*, and "Kids and Heroin: The New Epidemic" from *Time*.[73] President Clinton offered this incorrect gem: "Drug use is down all across America, but unfortunately it is still rising among young people."[74] His administration's manipulation of statistics, use of anecdotes as generalizeable evidence, and flat out lies about kids "escalated in late 1994 with a renewed 'just say no' assault on an imaginary 'epidemic' of teen drug abuse." The source of the problem, according to Clintonites? Nasty rap artists who glorify cannabis.[75] As Males explains, "the teenage drug crisis is a myth. It was concocted and maintained for political convenience."[76] Kids have been singled out for drug-war attention, despite the fact that the majority of the problem is with adults, an issue which we explored earlier. Further, as has been noted in this text, when kids do have real problems with drugs, it is more frequently with over-the-counter, legal medicines than with the illegal drugs so concerning to the school officials-cum-drug warriors. Males rightfully lays the sarcasm on awfully thick when he says "in the mean streets of the Nineties, the drug causing the most injuries to youth is dispensed not by a leering middle-school dropout or a Mr. T-sized alley pusher, but a Safeway checker?"[77] Hence we spend a lot of time, money, and energy "fighting" illegal drug use by students when legal drug **abuse** may be a greater concern.

The Result of the Moral Panic?
A Teen-Bashing Party

The response from authorities has also been consistent with that of a moral panic and reflects the militarized approach so common in dealing with deviance and crime today. Despite the fact that schools are safer than all other places where teens congregate, tax-payers continue to support increases in order to pay for surveillance cameras, metal detectors, and the like. Charleton Heston thinks arming teachers would be an excellent deterrent, while Texas State Representative Jim Pitts advocates that we try ten-year-olds as adults and permit the execution of eleven year-olds.[78] These punitive responses may be explained in part by what Barry Glassner calls the availability heuristic. We judge how common or important a phenomenon is by how readily it comes to mind. For instance, surveys asking people to rank the importance of certain social problems will typically select whatever the media is emphasizing at the moment.[79] Thus when the press goes nuts about school violence, the public inevitably believes the hype.

The result of the moral panic about school violence and drugs, according to Donna Killingbeck, is that "misdirected public policy is being generated to safeguard the schools, even though the real threat may lie elsewhere."[80] Focusing on school violence and teen drug abuse, despite their relative rarity, defocuses attention on the violence and drug problems of adults. It also diverts attention from the scary social control occurring in schools. For instance, teens may be searched, kicked out of school, and criminally prosecuted if they are suspected of having drugs. That is, unless their teachers find them difficult to control. Then their drug use is encouraged and even facilitated, like when high school secretaries dole out piles of Ritalin at lunchtime. Richard DeGrandpre cites a psychologist in *Ritalin Nation*: "There is something odd, if not downright ironic, about the picture of millions of American school children filing out of 'drug awareness' classes to line up for their midday does of amphetamine."[81]

Our focus on the badness of teens shifts attention from what might be the root causes of school violence and drug abuse. A recent analysis of 37 school shootings between 1974 and 2000 found that, while there are multiple causes, the primary motivation in over half the cases was revenge. Students who are teased may act like it does not bother them for quite a long time before they retaliate. Part of the issue is that they are electing to retaliate violently, as violence is considered the best way to show that they too have power.[82] Clearly this is evidence of a cultural problem. It's really not surprising that kids deal with problems in a violent manner, as that is what they've been taught to do in our society ever ready for war. But, rather than trying to understand them on a deeper level, our militarized revenge-focused policies in schools tell us to search and destroy the culprits, just as they do in criminal justice. As Kappeler, Blumberg and Potter maintain, "crime control bureaucracies consume an ever-expanding amount of social resources as they widen their sphere of influence and modify their missions to fit organizational and political goals. Such enforcement policies burden an already overtaxed criminal justice system and mask other social problems."[83]

Not only does the over-exaggerated panic about violence and drugs misdirect policy, but false information about drugs itself has been shown to **harm** kids. For instance, a recent study has refuted claims that even one dose of the drug Ecstasy causes brain damage. It seems as though the initial research was highly flawed, yet spawned a $54 million educational campaign, including several of the now famous "this is your brain on drugs" ad campaigns. As one young adult put it, "Now I'm convinced that any information about drugs coming out of the government is automatically suspect."[84] The Ecstasy study is merely one example of how the government manipulates science to support their agenda. After investigating the current administration's use of scientific information, ranking member of the House Committee on Government Reform Henry Waxman (D-Calif.) stated, "The Bush administration has manipulated, distorted, or interfered with science on health, environmental, and other key issues."[85] So what we have is a moral panic about teen drug use that is driven by flawed research and, because militarism is our driving force in schools, has led to repressive attitudes and policies.

Another effect of the militarization of schooling and the moral panic about violence and drugs is that teachers have been distanced from their students. Increasing specialization has allowed for teachers to be merely the purveyors of knowledge, while security personnel are in charge of discipline. In the words of one New York City principal, "I have no control over security guards, they don't report to me."[86] Zero tolerance policies exacerbate the division. Casella concurs: "The irony of zero tolerance is that it incorporates greater surveillance of students at the same time as it results in less surveillance. It pulls teachers away from the emotional life of students and relegates emotional and behavioral problems to guards, police, and the courts."[87] And the impression is that the security duties are more important than the educational ones, as the security personnel are the first thing one sees upon entering the school. According to Devine, "The really important knowledge in the school becomes not the binomial theorem but the report about the latest fight on the fourth floor."[88] Teachers often know only the academic side of their students' lives, and are even encouraged by administrators to keep it that way. When a legitimate authority, a teacher, fails to exert its true power to protect students in a mean-ingful way, kids have no choice but to rely on the code of the streets.[89] According to Boire, "the values of trust and respect have been chased from the schoolyards and replaced with baseless suspi-cion and omnipresent policing."[90] The implementation of mili-taristic surveillance and punishment becomes a nasty cycle, where-by each time another "incident" occurs, more is added and teach-ers are further distanced from their students, increasing the likeli-hood of yet another incident.[91]

Sociologist Max Weber discussed the increasing rationaliza-tion of the modern world. A key component of rationalization is the bureaucratization of major institutions, a notion quite consis-tent with militarism. As David Garland explains, from the late eighteenth century on, punishment has been increasingly monop-olized and administered by central governing agencies. This is part of a broader process of state expansion into private lives.[92] Militarism, too, increases the involvement of the state in personal affairs. Hierarchical chains of command were established and a measure of uniformity and alleged objectivity characterize modern punishment. As Garland explains, "it is a characteristic of bureau-cratic organizations that they operate in a passionless, routinized, matter of fact kinds of way."[93] The role of the public in assigning and implementing punishment has been diminished and the role of the so-called expert increased. In being kept at a distance, the public becomes unfamiliar, and often unconcerned about the details of punishment and, consequently, susceptible to misinfor-mation via sensational headlines and political appeals.[94]

The militarization of schools has increased their bureaucrati-zation as well. As the state has expanded into the private lives of adult citizens through criminal justice tactics, schools too have delved into the private lives of students through drug testing, strip searching and the like. As Weber suggested, school search and punishment policies are supposedly objective and uniform. In real-ity, as we have shown, this is merely an illusion, yet it is an impor-tant one, as to claim that metal detector scans or the application of zero tolerance laws are neutral and non-discriminatory has convinced the courts and much of the populace that they must also then be OK. The fooling of the public is consistent with Garland's description of modern punishment. Most are disinterested in what happens to students at school, as long as they hear the buzzwords "safe and drug free." As Albert Memmi describes in *The Colonizer and the Colonized*, the colonizers must constantly justify their system of oppression so that people do not challenge them[95]; in schools, militaristic ideology has done this job for them.

All people have a basic need for belonging and to be connected to others. As educator Alfie Kohn notes, "American high schools not only fail to meet those needs but make a mockery of them."[96] It's not that teachers themselves are evil or sadistic, "it's that something is seriously dysfunctional about the structure of high school."[97] Masses are thrown together for full days without any meaningful contact. Students are lectured at by one teacher then move on to the next for the same treatment. If any sense of community does begin to develop, it is promptly thwarted by those militaristic practices that pit students against one another and against the faculty. Students are coerced into complying with the whims of adults all day, yet we wonder why they are unprepared to make "good" decisions about drugs and violence. As Kohn explains, "The average high school is terrific preparation for adult life-as long as that life is led in a totalitarian society."[98]

Further, "when students predictably respond to all this by tuning out, or acting out, or dropping out, we promptly blame *them* for not working hard enough."[99] Memmi suggests, in his classic work on the relationship between colonizers and the colonized, that oppressed peoples will often respond in one of two ways. Some may become subservient and fearful, what he calls "defensive cowering," while others may put up a tough front, or "hostile bravado."[100] As Memmi explains, school faculty are in a paradoxical situation; while they disown "the colonized" (the students), the existence of the students is critical to their own. They often resort to the "mark of the plural," or characterize students only on group characteristics, not as individuals. Students are "entitled only to drown in an anonymous collectivity."[101] Sound familiar? He might as well have been describing the various types of profiling that occur under the guise of safe and drug-free schools.

If students do not feel as though they belong in the school community, they will get involved with something that provides that sense of belonging, be it a violent gang or a group of drug using peers. "Make students feel powerless, and the need for autonomy might express itself in antisocial ways. Treat students as interchangeable and anonymous, and occasionally someone will do dreadful things to attract attention and make his mark."[102] Follow this up with the assumption that **all** students are then bad, and we come to the equation currently being used in schools. Instead of challenging our militaristic practices, most schools and policy makers add fuel to the fire. "If punishment proves ineffective, then it is assumed that *more* punishment-along with tighter regulations and less trust-will certainly do the trick."[103]

Another effect of the militarization of schooling has been that students come to **expect** constant surveillance and a diminishment of their rights. This obviously has implications way beyond the confines of the school campus. Michel Foucault is perhaps the preeminent scholar on issues of discipline, punishment and power. Foucault argued that discipline is 'an art of the human body," and a method of mastering the body and making it obedient. According to Foucault, in the classical age the body became conceived as a target of power that could be controlled without violence. Some form of constant surveillance replaced violent tactics in controlling the body being disciplined. Not surprisingly, it was the army that first perfected such tactics, which quickly spread to classrooms, hospitals, and other institutions. The ultimate form of non-violent surveillance was to be Bentham's panopticon. It would render individuals constantly subject to the knowledge and power of authorities. Over time, this constant visibility and vulnerability allegedly induces self- control. In discussing the prison, Foucault commented that it's defects were known as early as the 1820s, yet it persists as an institution because it serves specific functions. Similarly, the defects in other non-violent, panoptic forms of surveillance and punishment such as those used in schools are well known, yet these too persist because they are useful to some. These forms of punishment essentially make delinquent classes by creating the conditions that lead to recidivism, as the labeling of students as "bad" and the surveillance of their every move often leads to a self-fulfilling prophecy. Delinquency is a useful political tool, as it divides the classes amongst themselves and to guarantee the power and authority of police.[104]

Ronnie Casella comments, "One comes to believe that students can be controlled if they are convinced of the nearly omnipresent power of the school to watch, to apprehend, and to quickly and severely respond."[105] Devine describes the interesting paradox in the school atmosphere; while student acts of violence are perceived as abnormal and as interrupting the pedagogical goals of the school, the militaristic responses have become normalized.[106] As Boire asks in regard to drug testing, "When a young person is told to urinate in a cup within earshot of a school authority listening intently, and then ordered to turn over his or her urine for chemical examination, what 'reasonable expectation of privacy' remains? When today's students graduate and walk out the schoolhouse gates, what will become of society's 'reasonable expectation of privacy'?"[107] The answer is that what we expect will become even further watered down.

Finally, there is a substantial amount of data indicating that people react differently when they think they are being monitored. Surveys about the effects of monitoring in the workplace, for instance, reveal that monitored workers experience higher levels of depression, tension, and anxiety, and lower levels of productivity than those who are not monitored. People who are unsure when they will be monitored will be more guarded and less spontaneous.[108] Is this really what we want for our future? Yet, again, in a militaristic society a lack of creativity is not considered a problem. So what if schools produce brainless automatons who lose all respect for the importance of civil liberties, at least they will excel when the military comes calling to round them up for the next war-on-whoever (or whatever).

QUESTIONS FOR REVIEW
AND CRITICAL THINKING

In what ways has militarism "invaded" schools?

What are some examples of militaristic language in schools provided by the authors? Can you think of others?

How might a peace-making model impact school search and punishment policies?

EXTENSION QUESTIONS AND ACTIVITIES

What are other institutions that have been militarized? What is the impact?

Do you agree that people **expect** less privacy today? Support your position.

Epilogue
A Five-Point Guide For Students

If you are a high school student, we recommend the following five actions. If not, read them anyways; perhaps you, too, can challenge the assault on teens in schools.

Know your rights.

> It is imperative that you understand exactly what type of searches are lawful in your state. You're a step ahead of many having read this book, but don't stop there. Read the other resources cited throughout this book. Question authorities at your school, as well as the police. Use the Internet, newspapers, journals, and magazines to keep updated on court cases.

Exercise your rights.

> Make sure you **use** your knowledge. If you see or hear of questionable searches occurring at your school, get involved. Contact organizations like the ACLU for help. If an administrator, teacher, or police officer asks you to submit to a search you feel is in violation of your rights, refuse consent.

Spread the word.

> Tell other students what you know. Tell your teachers, who may not have been exposed to this information. Tell your parents so they can advocate for you and for other teens' rights. Tell the local media; make this an issue in your community. If your school is conducting any of these problematic searches, awareness can make change. If they are not, perhaps you can prevent them from ever doing so.

Do what you can to create or maintain a positive school climate.

> School does not have to be like a prison. And students have power to make school a positive place by **demanding**

it. Get involved!

Learn about current events.

As we have outlined in this book, what is happening in schools does not occur in a vacuum; school policy tends to mirror social policy. The more you know about the culture of surveillance we live in the better prepared you are to question, and ultimately change, it.

Notes

Prologue

1   Kappeler V Blumberg M & Potter G. (2000). *The mythology of crime and criminal justice.* Prospect Heights, IL: Waveland.
2   Robinson M. (2002). *Justice blind?* Upper Saddle River, NJ: Prentice Hall.
3   Ibid.
4   Males M. (1996). *Scapegoat generation.* Monroe, Maine: Common Courage, p. 19.
5   Ibid., p. 119.
6   Astroth, K. (1994). "Beyond ephebiphobia: Problem adults or problem youths?" *Phi Delta Kappan 75*(5), pp. 411-414.
7   Ibid.
8   Ibid.
9   Schmalleger F.(2002). *Criminology today* (3rd. ed.). Upper Saddle River, NJ: Prentice Hall.
10 Males M. (1999). *Framing youth.* Monroe, Maine: Common Courage Press.
11 Sullum J. (2003). *Saying yes.* New York: Penguin.
12 DeGrandpre, R. (1999). *Ritalin Nation.* New York: W. W. Norton & Co., p. 180.
13 Males, (1996), op. cit., p. 275.
14 Ibid., p. 13.
15 Astroth K. (1994, January). "Beyond ephebiphobia: Problem adults or problem youths?" *Phi Delta Kappan, 75*(5), 411-414, p. 411.
16 Ibid.
17 Aronson E. (2000). *Nobody left to hate.* New York: W. H. Freeman & Co., p. 87-88.
18 Males, (1996), op. cit., p. 8.
19 Kappeler Blumberg & Potter, (2000), op. cit.
20 Moore M. (2003). *Dude, where's my country?* New York: Warner Books.
21 Redden J. (2000). *Snitch culture.* Los Angeles: Feral House, p. 95.
22 Males, (1999), op. cit.
23 Ibid.
24 Ibid., p. 54.
25 Ibid.
26 Males, (1996), op. cit.
27 "Addiction among seniors called 'hidden epidemic'." (2003, July 21). Retrieved July 23, 2003 from www.jointogether.org/sa/news/summaries/reader/0,1854,565371,00.html.
28 "More drug-related ER visits sparked by narcotic pain meds." (2003, August 27). Retrieved August 29, 2003 from www.jointogether.org/sa/news/summaries/reader/0,1854,566418,00.html.
29 Males, (1996), op. cit.
30 Moore, (2003), op. cit.
31   Males, (1996), op. cit.
32 Ibid., p. 74.
33 Ibid., p. 74.
34 Kappeler Blumberg & Potter, (2000), op. cit., p. 306.
35 Males, (1999), op. cit., p. 11.

36   Hall A. (2000, August 31). "Have we gone too far in policing the blackboard jungle?" *BusinessWeek Online*. Retrieved September 26, 200 from www.business-week.com/bwdaily/dnflash/aug2000/nf20000831_788.htm, p. 2.
37   Redden J. (2000), op. cit.
38   Ibid.
39   Ibid.
40   Hall, (2000), op. cit., p. 2.
41   Kohn, A. (April, 2004). "Test Today, Privatize Tomorrow." Retrieved June 5, 2004 from www.nochildleft.com
42   Ibid.
43   Ibid, p. 4.
44   Ibid, p. 5.
45   Ibid, p. 8.
46   Ibid.

Introduction

1   Cornfield v. Consolidated High School District No. 230, 991 F. 2d 1316 (7th Cir. 1993).
2   Bonilla D. (Ed.). (2000). *School Violence*. New York: H. W. Wilson.
3   Males M. (1999). *Framing Youth: 10 Myths About the Next Generation*. Monroe, Maine: Common Courage Press, pp 106.
4   www.speaker.house.gov/library/issues/drugs.asp
5   Males M. (1996). *Scapegoat Generation*. Monroe, Maine: Common Courage Press.
6   Males (1999), op cit.
7   National Institute on Drug Abuse. (19 December, 2003). "Teen drug abuse declines across wide fronts." Press release.
8   Siegel L., Welsh B., Senna J. (2003). *Juvenile Delinquency (Eighth Edition)*. Belmont, CA: Wadsworth.
9   Males (1999), op cit.
10   Males (1999); Males (1996), op cit.
11   Beckett K., Sasson T. (2000). *The Politics of Injustice*. Thousand Oaks, CA: Pine Forge Press.
12   Ibid, pp 92.
13   Huffington A. (February 7, 2002). *Common Dreams News Center*. www.common-dreams.org/views02/0209-02.html.
14   Males (1999), op cit, pp 137.
15   Dead Kennedys. (1980). "Drug Me." Fresh Fruit For Rotting Vegetables. San Francisco: Alternative Tentacles Records.
16   Males (1999), op cit.
17   Ibid.
18   Supreme court to weigh drug tests for after-school activities. (March 18, 2002). www.cnn.com/20…tus.school.drugtests.ap/index.html.
19   Males (1999),op cit, pp 8.
20   Kappeler V. Blumberg M., Potter B. (2000). *The Mythology of Crime and Criminal Justice. .* Prospecy Heights, Illinois: Waveland Press.

21 Males (1999), op cit, pp 27.
22 Daniel P. (1998). Violence and the Public Schools: Student Rights Have Been Weighed in the Balance and Found Wanting. *Journal of Law and Education*, 27(4), 573-614, pp 573.
23 Redden J. (2000). *Snitch Culture*. Los Angeles: Feral House, pp 95.
24 Kappeler, Blumberg, Potter, (2000), op cit, pp 2-3.
25 Ibid, pp
26 Dohrn B. (2001). Look out Kid, It's Something You Did. In Ayers, W., Dohrn, B., Ayers, R. *Zero tolerance*. New York: The New Press.
27 Kappeler, Blumberg, Potter (2000), op cit.
28 Jones, L. (2001). Students Report School Crime at Same Level as 1970s But the Use of Suspension Doubles. *Justice Policy Institute*. Retrieved 10/02/01 from the World Wide Web: www.cjcj.org/sss/.
29 Moore M. (2001). *Stupid White Men*. New York: Harper Collins, pp
30 Kappeler, Blumberg, Potter (2000), op cit.
31 Bonilla (2000), op cit.
32 Redden (2000), op cit, pp 138.
33 Aaronson E. (2000). *Nobody Left to Hate*. New York: W. H. Freeman and Co.
34 Redden (2000), op cit.
35 Jones (2001), op cit.
36 Daniel (1998), op cit.
37 Aaronson (2000), op cit.
38 Males (1999), op cit.
39 Ibid.
40 Males (1996), op cit.
41 Elikann P. (1999). *Superpredator: The Demonization of Our Children By the Law*. Reading, MA: Perseus, pp xi.
42 Siegel, Welsh, Senna (2003), op cit.
43 Kappeler, Blumberg, Potter (2000), op cit.
44 Ibid.
45 Elikann (1999), op cit.
46 Kappeler, Blumberg, Potter (2000), op cit.
47 Elikann (1999), op cit.
48 Kappeler, Blumberg, Potter (2000), op cit.
49 Males (1999), op cit.
50 Hyman I., Snook P. (1999). *Dangerous Schools*. San Francisco: Jossey-Bass.
51 Polakow-Suransky S. (1999). *Access Denied*. Ann Arbor, MI: Student Advocacy Center.
52 Elikann (1999), op cit.
53 Ball H. (2002). *The Supreme Court in the Intimate Lives of Americans*. New York: New York University Press, pp 23.
54 Rosen J. (2000). *The Unwanted Gaze: Destruction of Privacy in America*. New York: Random House, pp 62-3.
55 Baumgardner J. (February 10, 2003). *Roe* in Rough Waters. *The Nation*, 21-24, pp 23.
56 Redden (2000), op cit.
57 Maltby L. (1999). Drug Testing: A Bad Investment. www.aclu.org.
58 Ibid, pp 8.

59   www.aclu.org/library/pbr5.html.
60   Ibid.
61   "Blair: Schools can carry out random drug tests." (23 February, 2004). *Rocky Mountain News*, p. 32A.
62   Redden (2000), op cit.
63   Ibid.
64   Raines J. (1974). *Attack on Privacy*. Valley Forge: Judson Press, pp 36.
65   Redden (2000), op cit, pp 17.
66   Ibid.
67   Rosen (2000), op cit.
68   Ibid.
69   (www.aclu.org/pbr2.html).
70   www.aclu.org/issues/worker/gdfactsheets.html.
71   Goffman E. (1959). *The Presentation of Self In Everyday Life*. Norwell, MA: Anchor Press.
72   Rosen (2000), op cit, pp 25.
73   Pollitt K. (January 27, 2003). They Know When You Are Sleeping. *The Nation*, pp 9.
74   Beckett, Sasson (2000), op cit, pp 188.
75   Redden (2000), op cit.
76   Ibid.
77   Ibid.
78   Cole D. (September 5, 2002). Enemy Aliens and American Freedoms. *The Nation*, 20-24, pp 20.
79   Ibid.
80   Redden (2000), op cit, pp 2.
81   Goodman D (November/December, 2002). No Child Left Unrecruited.
82   Mills N. (1997). *The Triumph of Meanness*. Boston: Houghton Mifflin.
83   Ibid, pp 10.
84   Ayers W., Dohrn B., Ayers R. (2001). *Zero tolerance*. New York: The New Press, pp xii.
85   Males (1996), op cit.
86   Ferrarracio M. (April, 1999). Metal Detectors in the Public Schools: Fourth Amendment Concerns. *Journal of Law and Education*, 28(2), pp 209-229.

Chapter One

1   www.landmarkcases.org/newjersey/home.html.
2   Alexander K Alexander M D (1998). *American public school law, fourth edition*. Belmont, Ca: Wadsworth, pp 379.
3   Ibid.
4   Ibid, pp 380.
5   Ibid, pp 374.
6   www.landmarkcases.org/newjersey/home.html.
7   Alexander & Alexander (1998), op cit, pp 380.
8   Daniel P. (1998). Violence and the public schools: Students rights have been weighed in the balance and found wanting. *Journal of Law and Education*, 27(4),

pp 587.
9   Alexander & Alexander (1998), op cit, pp 381.
10   Ibid, pp 381.
11   Ibid, pp 374.
12   Ibid, pp 374.
13   Ibid, pp. 374.
14   Ibid, pp 374.
15   Daniel (1998), op cit.
16   Ibid, pp 588.
17   McCarthy M. (April 2001). Another high-stakes test. *Principal Leadership*, *1*(8), pp 14-19.
18   Alexander & Alexander, op cit, pp 381.
19   www.landmarkcases.org/newjersey/home.html.
20   Ibid.
21   Ibid.
22   Ibid.
23   Ibid.
24   Ibid.
25   Ibid.
26   Daniel (1998), op cit.
27   Zirkel P. (May 2000). Suspicionless searches. *NASSP Bulletin*, 84(616), pp 101.
28   Casella R. (2001). *'Being down': Challenging violence in urban schools.* New York: Teachers College, pp 3.
29   Ibid, pp 49.
30   Males M. (1999). *Framing youth: Ten myths about the next generation.* Monroe, Maine: Common Courage Press.
31   Ibid.
32   Elikann P. *Superpredators: The demonization of our children by the law.* Reading, Massachusetts: Perseus.
33   Tozer S Violas C Senese G. (2002). *School and society: Historical and contemporary perspectives, fourth edition.* Boston: McGraw-Hill.
34   www.landmarkcases.org/newjersey/home.html.
35   Casella R. (2001). *At zero tolerance.* New York: Peter Lang Publishers, pp 43.
36   Alderman E Kennedy C. (1997). *The right to privacy.* Santa Rosa, CA: Vintage.
37   Alexander & Alexander (1998), op cit.
38   http://archive.aclu.org/court/acton2.html.
39   Alderman & Kennedy (1997), op cit.
40   Alexander & Alexander (1998), op cit.
41   Alderman & Kennedy (1997), op cit.
42   Ibid, pp 48.
43   Alexander & Alexander (1998), op cit.
44   Ibid, pp 384.
45   Ibid, pp 384.
46   Ibid.
47   Ibid, pp 385.
48   http://archive.aclu.org/court/acton2.html.
49   Ibid.
50   Alderman & Kennedy (1997), op cit, pp 48.

51 Ibid, pp 48.
52 http://archive.aclu.org/court/acton2.html.
53 Ibid.
54 McCarthy M. (2001), op cit, pp 16.
55 Dowling-Sendor B. (October, 1999). The drug testing dilemma. *American School Board Journal*.
56 Alderman & Kennedy (1997), op cit, pp 49.
57 Ibid.
58 http://archive.aclu.org/court/acton2.html.
59 Ibid.
60 Roberts N Fossey R. (2002). Random drug testing of students: Where will the line be drawn? *Journal of Law and Education, 31*(2).
61 Males M (1999), op. cit, pp 104.
62 Naylor A Zaichkowsky L. (2001). Drug use patterns among high school athletes and nonathletes. *Adolescence, 36*.
63 Males (1999) op cit.
64 Meyer P. (May 19, 2003). Student drug testing not effective in reducing drug use." Retrieved June 12, 2003 from the World Wide Web: http://monitoringthe-future.org/pressreleases/03testingpr.pdf.
65 Taylor R. (December 30, 2002). Controversial drug testing study yields mixed results." Retrieved June 7, 2003 from the World Wide Web: www.dpf.org/news/12_30_02testing.cfm.
66 Ibid.
67 Supreme Court to weight drug tests for after-school activities. (March 18, 2002). *CNN.com*. Retrieved March 20, 2002 from the World Wide Web: www.cnn.com/20...tus.school.drugtests.ap/index.html.
68 Ibid.
69 Ibid.
70 Ibid, pp 2.
71 ACLU brings first federal challenge to drug testing of students in academic courses. (August 18, 1999). *American Civil Liberties Union Freedom Network*. Retrieved November 19, 2001 from the World Wide Web: http://www.aclu.org/features/f081899a.html, pp 2.
72 www.supremecourtus.gov/opinions/01pdf/01-332.pdf.
73 Greenhouse L. (March 20, 2002). Supreme Court seems ready to extend school drug tests. *The New York Times on the Web*. Retrieved March 21, 2002 from the World Wide Web: www.nytimes.com/2002/03/20/national/20SCOT.html, pp 2.
74 Ibid, pp 2.
75 Ibid, pp 2.
76 Dennisten L. (March 20, 2002). Justice Kennedy attacks student's views. *The Boston Globe Online*. Retrieved March 20, 2002 from the World Wide Web: www.boston.com/dailyglobe2/...edy_attacks_student_s_views+.shtml, pp 1.
77 www.supremecourtus.gov/opinions/01pdf/01-332.pdf.
78 Ibid.
79 Ibid.
80 Greenhouse L. (2002), op cit., pp 3.
81 www.supremecourtus.gov/opinions/01pdf/01-332.pdf.
82 Ibid.

83   Ibid.
84   Ibid.
85   Ibid.
86   Ibid.
87   Ibid.
88   Ibid.
89   Ibid.
90   Ibid.
91   Denniston L. (2002), op cit, pp 2.
92   Ibid.
93   www.supremecourtus.gov/opinions/01pdf/01-332.pdf.
94   Ibid.
95   Ibid.
96   Ibid.
97   Goldberg L et. al. (2003). Drug testing athletes to prevent substance abuse: Background and pilot study results of the SATURN (student athlete testing using random notification) study. *Journal of Adolescent Health, 32*, pp 16-25.
98   Ibid.

Chapter Two

1   Devine J. (1996). *Maximum security*. Chicago: University of Chicago Press.
2   Beger R. (2002). "Expansion of police power in public schools and the vanishing rights of students." *Social Justice, 29*(1-2), pps. 119-130.
3   Redden J. (2000). *Snitch culture*. Los Angeles: Feral House.
4   Beger, (2002), op. cit.
5   *In re Patrick Y.*, 124 Md. App. 604; 723 A. 2d 523; 1999 Md. App. LEXIS 14. Retrieved from Lexis Nexis Academic database.
6   *People v. William G.*, 221 Cal. Rptr. 118, 127 (1985). LEXIS 421. Retrieved from Lexis Nexis Academic database.
7   "Cars and the Fourth Amendment." June 28, 1999. Retrieved June 17, 2003 from the World Wide Web: http://civilliberty.about.com/library/weekly/aa062899.htm.
8   "Cops in the driver's seat." April 12, 1999. Retrieved June 17, 2003 from the World Wide Web: http://civilliberty.about.com/library/weekly/aa041299.htm, p. 3.
9   Ibid.
10   "Supreme Court Allows Broad 'Probable Cause' Drug Searches." (January 5, 2004). Available from www.jointogether.org/sa/news/summaries/reader/0%2C1854%
11   "Cars and the Fourth Amendment," op. cit.
12   Rossow L. & Stefkovich J. (1995). *Search and seizure in the public schools, second edition*. Topeka, Kansas: National Organization on Legal Problems in Education, p. 31.
13   "Institutional education." March 22, 1999. Retrieved June 17, 2003 from the World Wide Web: http://civilliberty.about.com/library/weekly/aa032299.html.
14   Dowling-Sendor B. (March 2000). "Zero Tolerance versus privacy." *American*

School Board Journal(Online). Retrieved June 17, 2003 from the World Wide Web: www.asbj.com/2000/03/0300schoollaw.html.

15 Rossow & Stefkovitch (1995), op. cit.

16 State v. Slattery, 56 Wn. App. 820; 787 P.2d 932; 1990 Wash. App. LEXIS 161. Retrieved from Lexis Nexis Academic database.

17 "State legislature to allow locker searches?" May 12, 2000. Michigan Education Report (online). Retrieved June 9, 2003 from the World Wide Web: www.educationreport.org/pubs/mer/article.asp710=2879.

18 In re Patrick., op. cit.

19 State v. Slattery, op. cit.

20 Ibid.

21 Rossow & Stefkovitch, (1995), op. cit.

22 Ibid.

23 Rossow & Stefkovich, (1995), op. cit., p. 11.

24 Redden, (2000), op. cit., p. 136.

25 Rossow & Stefkovitch, (1995), op. cit.

26 Ibid., p. 14.

27 Ibid., p. 15.

28 Ibid., p. 15.

29 Redden, (2000), op. cit., p. 132.

30 S.C. v. State, 583 So. 2d 188; 1991 Miss. LEXIS 387. Retrieved from Lexis Nexis Academic database.

31 Ibid., p. 4.

32 Ibid., p. 4.

33 Rossow & Stefkovitch, (1995), op. cit., p. 31.

34 State v. Slattery, op. cit.

35 Rossow & Stefkovitch, (1995), op. cit.

36 In re Patrick Y., op. cit., p. 2.

37 Ibid.

38 Ibid., p. 6.

39 Commonwealth v. Snyder, 413 Mass. 521; 597 N.E. 2d. 1363; 1992 Mass. LEXIS 465. Retrieved from Lexis Nexis Academic database.

40 Ibid.

41 Ibid., p. 3.

42 Ibid., p. 3.

43 Shamberg v. State, 762 P. 2d 488; 1988 Alas. App. LEXIS 101. Retrieved from Lexis Nexis Academic database.

44 Rossow & Stefkovitch, (1995), p. 53.

45 Ibid.

46 Ibid.

47 Ibid.

48 People v. Overton, 24 N.Y. 2d 522; 249 N.E. 2d 366; 301 N.Y.S. 2d 479; 1969 LEXIS 1339. Retrieved from Lexis Nexis Academic database.

49 Ibid.

50 Ibid, p. 2.

51 Ibid.

52 Ibid, p. 3.

53 Friedman D. "Privacy and Technology." Pps. 186-212. In Paul E. Miller F. &

        Paul J. (Eds.). (2000). *The right to privacy*. New York: Cambridge University
        Press, p. 200.
54   Cole D. (2000). *No equal justice*.New York: The New Press, p. 20.
55   Ibid, p. 22.
56   Brill A. (1990). *Nobody's business: The paradoxes of privacy*. Reading,
        Massachusetts: Addison-Wesley, p. xviii.
57   Zirkel P. (January 2002). "An unmitigated disaster." *Phi Delta Kappan*, 83(5),
        417-418, p. 417.
58   Ibid, p. 417.
59   Ibid.
60   Ibid, p. 418.
61   Ibid, p. 418.
62   Ibid, p. 418.
63   Ibid, p. 418.
64   *Milligan v. City of Slidell*, 226 F. 3d. 652; 2000 U.S. App. LEXIS 23836. Retrieved
        from Lexis Nexis Academic database.
65   Ibid.
66   Ibid.
67   Rossow & Stefkovitch, (1995), op. cit, p. 48.
68   Ibid.
69   *In re Frederick B.*, 192 Cal. App. 3d 79; 237 Cal. Rptr. 338; 1987 Cal. App.
        (1987). LEXIS 1758. Retrieved from Lexis Nexis Academic database.
70   "The People v. Randy G." (November 2001). *Security Management Online*.
        Retrieved June 17, 2003 from the World Wide Web:
        www.securitymanagement.com/library/People_Randy1101.html, p. 2.
71   Ibid, p. 2.
72   Ibid.
73   Ibid.
74   Ibid, p. 3.
75   Ibid, p. 4.
76   Ibid.
77   Ibid, p. 6.
78   Ibid, p. 6.
79   Ibid, p. 6.

Chapter Three

1   www.interquestk9.com.
2   Casella R. (2001). *At zero tolerance: Punishment, prevention and school violence*.
        New York: Peter Lang, p. 26.
3   Spina S. *Smoke and mirrors: The hidden context of violence in schools and society*.
        Lanham, Massachusetts: Rowman & Littlefield Publishers, Inc., p. 4.
4   Vanderpool T. (June 7, 1999). "Drug dogs: Deterrent or invasion of student
        rights?" *Christian Science Monitor*, 91(133), p. 2.
5   Pierson D. (April 21, 2003). "Dogs nose about school, seeking drugs." *Los
        Angeles Times*, Part 2, p. 3.
6   www.interquestk9.com.

7   www.supermetaldetectors.com.
8   www.garrett.com.
9   Johnson R. (April 2000). "Metal detector searches: An effective means to help keep weapons out of schools." *Journal of Law and Education, 29*(2), 197-203.
10 Beger R. (2002). "Expansion of police power in public schools and the vanishing rights of students." *Social Justice, 29*(102), 119-130.
11 Ibid.
12 Beger, (2002), op. cit.
13 Ibid.
14 Lausen w. January 17, 2002. "Hounding the public" Sniffing dogs at work and school." Retrieved June 29, 2003 from the World Wide Web: www.mapinc.org/drugnews/v02/n096/a01.html.
15 www.interquestk9.com.
16 Ferrarracio M. (1999). "Metal detectors in the public schools: Fourth Amendment concerns." *Journal of Law and Education, 28*(2), 209-229, p. 227.
17 www.bombdetectors.com/school_security.shtml.
18 Vanderpool T., (1999), op. cit., p. 2.
19 Pierson, (2003), op. cit.
20 "Drug sniffing dogs to aid in Logan High searches." (March 10, 2003). *Deseret News*, p. B04.
21 Pierson, (2003), op. cit., p. 3.
22 Rossow L & Stefkovitch J. (1995). *Search and seizure in the public schools, second edition.* Topeka, Kansas: National Organization on Legal Problems in Education.
23 Fleck T. (March 2000). "Narcotic canine legal update and opinions." Retrieved December 5, 2000 from the World Wide Web: www.policek9.com/Case_Law/Narcotics_Case_Law/body_narcotics_case_law.html.
24 Ibid.
25 www.interquestk9.com.
26 Rossow & Stefkovitch, (1995), op. cit.
27 Ibid.
28 Ferrarracio, (1999), op. cit., p. 219.
29 Ibid.
30 Ibid., p. 20.
31 Devine J. (1996). *Maximum security.* Chicago: The University of Chicago Press.
32 Ferrarracio, (1999), op. cit.
33 Ibid., p. 220.
34 Tanick M. (June 9, 2003). "Commentary: Court rules on three cases involving drug dogs." *The Minnesota Lawyer*. Retrieved from Lexis Nexis Academic database, p. 2.
35 Ibid.
36 Cited in Zirkel P. (2000). "Suspicionless searches." *NASSP Bulletin, 84*(616), 101-5.
37 Ferrarracio, (1999), op. cit., p.218.
38 www.channelonenews.com/articles/2003/04/15/ap_shooting/
39 Ferrarracio, (1999), op. cit., p. 219.
40 Devine, (1996), op. cit.
41 *Commonwealth of Pennsylvania v. Vincent Francis Cass*, 446 Pa. Super. 66; 666 A.

2d 313; 1995 Pa. Super. LEXIS 386. Retrieved from Lexis Nexis Academic database.

42 Department of Education and Department of Justice. (2000). 2000 Annual Report on School Safety. Retrieved from http://www.ed.gov/offices/OESE/SDFS/annrept00.pdf

43 Ibid.

44 U.S Department of Justice News Release. (March 14, 2003). Retrieved June 29, 2003 from the World Wide Web: www.usdoj.gov/usao/vae/ArchivePress/MarchPDFArchive/ebersole031403.pdf.

45 Cienski J. (June 10, 2003). "Sniffer dogs 'nose' nothing, officials charge." *CanWest News Service,* p. A12.

46 *Commonwealth of Pennsylvania v.Vincent Francis Cass,* op. cit., p. 5.

47 DeMarco T. (2001). "From the jailyard to the school yard." Pps. 42-50. In Ayers W. Dohrn B. & Ayers R. *Zero Tolerance: Resisting the drive for punishment in our schools.* New Yor5k: The New Press.

48 Hope-Cushey B. (February 26, 2003). "First drug search by canines net little." *Pittsburgh Post Gazette,* p. S-4.

49 www.kidserviceinc.com.

50 Keene S. (January 29, 2003). "L-S oks drug-detecting dogs at high school; Opinions differ as to when canines should be used." *Intelligencer Journal,* p. B-1.

51 Beger, (2002), op. cit.

52 Ibid.

53 Kozol J. (1992). *Savage inequalities: Children in America's schools.* New York: Perennial.

54 Kipnis A. (1999). *Angry young men.* San Francisco: Jossey-Bass.

55 Devine, (1996), op. cit.

56 Crews G & Tipton J. (2001). "A comparison of public school and prison security measures: Too much of a good thing?" *Koch Crime Institute.* Retrieved January 8, 2001 from the World Wide Web: www.kci.org/publication/articles/school_security_measures.html.

57 Diguilio R. (2001) *Educate, medicate, or litigate? What teachers, parents, and administrators must do about student behavior.* New York: Corwin, p. 15.

58 Webber J. (2003). *Failure to hold: The politics of school violence.* Lanham, Massachusetts: Rowman & Littlefield Publishers, Inc., p. 194.

59 Pierson, (2003), op. cit., p. 2.

60 Crews & Tipton, (2001), op. cit.

61 Casella, (2001), op. cit., p. 130.

62 Vanderpool, (1999), op. cit.

63 Sodders L. (April 21, 2003). "Students receiving canine intervention: Drug-sniffing dogs being used to search schools." *The Daily News of Los Angeles,* p. N6.

64 Vanderpool, (1999), op. cit.

65 Pierson, (2003), op. cit., p. 2.

66 Beger, (2002), op. cit., p. 127.

Chapter Four

1 *Widener v. Frye,* 809 F. Supp. 35; 1992 U.S. Dist. LEXIS 19934. Retrieved from

Lexis Nexis Academic database.

2   Alderman E & Kennedy C. (1997). *The right to privacy*. Santa Rosa, CA: Vintage, p 45.

3   *Martinez v. School District No. 60*, 852 P. 2d 1275; 1992 Colo. App. LEXIS 281. Retrieved from Lexis Nexis Academic database.

4   Redden J. (2000). *Snitch culture*. Los Angeles: Feral House.

5   Orwell G. (1949). *1984*. New York: New American Library.

6   Katz J. (2000). *Geeks*. New York: Villard, p. 148.

7   Ibid., p. 150.

8   Ibid.

9   "Officer entitled to immunity for clause arising from off-campus search." (April, 2003). *School Employment Legal Alert*, 2(6), p. 10.

10   Alderman & Kennedy, (1997), op. cit.

11   *Coronado v. State of Texas*, 835 S.W. 2d 636; 1992 Tex. Crim. App. LEXIS 164. Retrieved from Lexis Nexis Academic database.

12   Zirkel P. (May 2000). Suspicionless searches. *NASSP Bulletin*, 84(616).

13   "DesRoches v. Caprio." Retrieved December 5, 2000 from the World Wide Web: www.law.emory.edu/4circuit/sept98/972173.p.html.

14   Ibid.

15   Ibid., p. 14.

16   Ibid.

17   Ibid., p. 7.

18   Rossow L & Stefkovitch J. (1995). *Search and seizure in the public schools, second edition*. Topeka, Kansas: National Organization on Legal Problems of Education.

19   Ibid.

20   Ibid., p. 20.

21   Casella R. (2001). *At zero tolerance*. New York: Peter Lang Publishers, p. 43.

22   Gibbs, Nancy. (25 October, 1999). "A Week in the Life of a High School." *Time*, p. 75.

23   Hyman I & Snook P. (1999). *Dangerous schools*. San Francisco: Jossey-Bass, p. 101.

24   Ibid.

25   Ibid., p. 103.

26   Redden, (2000), op. cit.

27   Hyman & Snook, (1999), op. cit.

28   Gamble C. (2003). "Districts weight paying students for tips on crime." *Education Week*, 14(24), 8-11.

29   Redden, (2000), op. cit., p. 136.

30   Gamble, (2003), op. cit.

31   Redden, (2000), op. cit.

32   Schlosser E. (2003). *Reefer madness*. Boston: Houghton Mifflin.

33   Redden, (2000), op. cit.

34   DeMarco T. (2001). "From the jailyard to the school yard." Pps. 42-50. In Ayers W Dohrn B & Ayers R. *Zero tolerance*. New York: The New Press.

35   Redden, (2000), op. cit., p. 137.

36   See DeMarco (2001), op. cit.; Polakow-Suransky S. (1999). *Access denied*. Ann Arbor, MI: Student Advocacy Center.

37   Redden, (2000), op. cit., p. 132.

38   Ibid.
39   Dreyfuss R. (July/August 2003). "The watchful and the wary." *Mother Jones*, p. 60.
40   Redden, (2000), op. cit., p. 20.
41   Orwell, (1949), op. cit.
42   Redden, (2000), op. cit., p. 20.
43   Ibid.
44   Ibid.
45   Orwell, (1949), op. cit., p. 24.
46   Ibid., p. 24.
47   Rossow & Stefkovich, (1995), op. cit.
48   *Martens v. District No. 220 Board of Education*, 620 F. Supp. 29; 1985 U.S. Dist. LEXIS 15796. Retrieved from Lexis Nexis Academic database.
49   Rossow & Stefkovich, (1995), op. cit.
50   Hyman & Snook, (1999), op. cit.
51   www.plegroup.com/undercover/main.html.
52   Males M. (1999). *Framing youth*. Monroe, Maine: Common Courage Press.
53   Hyman & Snook, (1999), op. cit., p. 93.
54   Ibid.
55   Ibid.
56   Ibid., p. 100.
57   Ibid.
58   Ibid., p. 100.
59   Ibid., p. 94.
60   Beger R. (2002). "Expansion of police power in public schools and the vanishing rights of students." *Social Justice*, 29(102), 119-130.
61   Crowder C. (February 9, 2003). "Teenager busted for marijuana gets 26-year sentence." *The Birmingham News*.
62   Ibid., p. 1.
63   Ibid.
64   Ibid., p. 3.
65   Ibid., p. 4.
66   Ibid., p. 4.
67   Crowder C. (June 12, 2003). "Teen's drug sentence cut from 26 years to 2." *The Birmingham News*.
68   Raines J. (1974). *Attack on privacy*. Valley Forge, CA: Judson Press, p. 12.
69   Hyman & Snook, (1995), op. cit.
70   Cockburn A. (April 10, 2000). "Hold that nun-killer!" *The Nation*, p. 8.
71   See Kappeler V Blumberg M and Potter G. (2000). *The mythology of crime and criminal justice*. Prospect Heights, Illinois: Waveland Press; Perlmutter D. (2000). *Policing the media*. Thousand Oaks, CA: Sage.; and Surette R. (1992). *Media, crime, and criminal justice*. Pacific Grove, California: Brooks/Cole.
72   Cockburn, (2000), op. cit.
73   Ibid., p. 8.
74   Ibid., p. 8.
75   Webber J. (2003). *Failure to hold: The politics of school violence*. Lanham, Massachusetts: Rowman & Littlefield Publishers, Inc., p. 13.
76   Raines, (1974), op. cit., p. 58.

77   Rosen J. (2000). *The unwanted gaze: Destruction of privacy in America.* New York: Random House, p. 216-7.
78   Redden, (2000), op. cit., p. 54.
79   Postman N. (1996). *The end of education.* New York: Vintage, p. 13

Chapter Five

1   Ross C. (2003, June 24). "County settles inmate strip search suit; 700 women claim inspections violated their civil rights." *The Patriot Ledger*, p. 17.
2   Ibid.
3   Ibid.
4   "New York Judge OKs $50 million illegal strip search settlement." (2001, July 2). *Jet*, *100*(3), p. 38.
5   Zahniser D. (2003, March 24). "Proposed settlement shines light on Sheriff's Department strip-search policy." *Copley News Service.* Retrieved from Lexis Nexis Academic database.
6   Ibid.
7   Ibid.
8   "Connecticut strip-searches truants, runaways." (2001, July 21). *Women's e-news.* Retrieved July 28, 2003 from www.womensenews.org/article.cfm/dyn/aid/619/context/outrage.
9   Ibid., p. 1.
10   Walsh D. "Jail strip-searches recorded on video." (2003, March 1). *The Sacramento Bee.* Retrieved July 28, 2003 from www.geocities.com/CapitolHill/Parliament/2398/strip_searches.htm, p. 3.
11   Rossow L and Stefkovich J. (1995). *Search and Seizure in the public schools.* (2nd ed.). Topeka, Kansas: National Organization on Legal Problems of Education.
12   Ibid.
13   Ibid., p. 37-8.
14   Ibid.
15   Ibid.
16   Ibid.
17   Alexander K & Alexander M D. (1998). *American public school law.* (4th ed.). Belmont, CA: Wadsworth.
18   Hyman I & Snook P. (1999). *Dangerous schools.* San Francisco: Jossey-Bass.
19   Ibid., p. 86.
20   *Singleton v. Board of Education*, 894 F. Supp. 386; 1995 U.S. Dist. LEXIS 9507. Retrieved from Lexis Nexis Academic database.
21   Ibid.
22   *Jenkins v. Talladega City Board of Education*, 115 F. 3d 821; 1997 U.S. App. LEXIS 12658. Retrieved from Lexis Nexis Academic database.
23   Ibid., p. 4.
24   Ibid., p. 7.
25   Ibid., p. 8.
26   Ibid., p. 8.
27   Ibid., p. 13.
28   Ibid., p. 15.

29 Ibid., p. 15.
30 *Oliver v. McClung*, 919 F. Supp. 1206; 1995 U.S. Dist. LEXIS 20517. Retrieved from Lexis Nexis Academic database.
31 Ibid., p. 3.
32 Ibid.
33 Ibid.
34 Ibid., p. 10.
35 *Potts v. Wright*, 357 F. Supp. 215; 1973 U.S. Dist. LEXIS 12658. Retrieved from Lexis Nexis Academic database.
36 Ibid.
37 "Medal's disappearance leads to unfortunate strip search." (September 2001). *Curriculum Review*, *4*(1), p. 54.
38 "Black Arkansas teen's mother sues school district charging her daughter was strip searched." (1996, July 8). *Jet*, *90*(8), p. 26.
39 Hyman & Snook, (1999), op. cit., p. 88.
40 Ibid.
41 Ibid., p. 89.
42 Ibid., p. 89.
43 Ibid.
44 Ibid.
45 *Konop v. Northwestern School District*, 26 F. Supp. 2d 1189; 1998 U.S. Dist. LEXIS 18459. Retrieved from Lexis Nexis Academic database.
46 "Connecticut strip-searches truants, runaways," (2001), op. cit.
47 Alderman E & Kennedy C. (1997). *The right to privacy*. New York: Vintage.
48 Ibid.
49 Alexander & Alexander, (1998), op. cit., p. 376.
50 *Picha v. Wielgos*, 410 F. Supp. 1214; 1976 U.S. Dist. LEXIS 16320. Retrieved from Lexis Nexis Academic database.
51 "*Rudolph et al. v. Lowndes County Board of Education.*" (2003, February 26). *Your School and the Law*, *33*(4).
52 *Rone v.Daviess County Board of Education* , 655 S. W. 2d 28; 1983 Ky. App. LEXIS 332. Retrieved from Lexis Nexis Academic database, p. 4.
53 Hyman & Snook, (1999), op. cit.
54 Ibid.
55 Raskin J. (2000). *We the students*. Washington D.C: CQ Press.
56 Ibid., p. 146.
57 Ibid., p. 145-6.
58 *State of West Virginia ex rel. Galford v. Mark Anthony B.*, 189 W. Va. 538; 433 S. E. 2d 41; 1993 W. Va. LEXIS 53. Retrieved from Lexis Nexis Academic database.
59 Ibid., p. 10.
60 Ibid., p. 11.
61 *Konop vNorthwestern School District.*, op. cit., p. 12.
62 Ibid.
63 Ibid.
64 Ibid., p. 5.
65 Ibid., p. 17.
66 Ibid., p. 7.

67   *Kennedy v. Dexter Consolidated Schools*, 124 N. M. 764, 955 P. 2d 693. Retrieved from
     www.attygen.state.ut.us/Searchschoolmanual/Kennedy%20v%20Dexter%20Scho
     ols.html.
68   Ibid.
69   Ibid.
70   Ibid.
71   Coursey J. (2001, June 8). "Students strip-searched on D.C. jail tour." *Socialist Worker Online*. Retreived from
     www.socialistworker.org/2001/370/370_04_StripSearched.shtml.
72   Ibid., p. 4.
73   Raspberry W. (2001, June 12). "Teachers wanted kids to get 'scared strainght'." *Kalamazoo Gazette*.
74   Dowling-Sendor B. (September, 2000). "Is this search necessary?" *American School Board Journal* [online version]. Retrieved June 17, 2003 from
     www.asbj.com/2000/09/0900schoollaw.html.
75   Ibid.
76   Ibid., p. 3.
77   Ibid.
78   Ibid., p. 5-6.
79   *Bellnier v. Lund*, 438 F. Supp. 47; 1977 U.S. Dist. LEXIS 15032. Retrieved from Lexis Nexis Academic database.
80   Ibid., p. 6.
81   Hyman & Snook, (1999), op. cit.
82   Alderman & Kennedy, (1997), op. cit.
83   Ibid.

Chapter Six

1   Coakley J. (1998). *Sport in society: Issues & controversies*. (6th ed.). Boston: Irwin McGraw-Hill.
2   Ibid.
3   Ibid.
4   Reid S, Heisel W, Saavedra T. (2003, May 11). "U.S. Olympic athletes reportedly tested less frequently than other competitors." *The Orange County Register*. Retrieved from Lexis Nexis Academic database.
5   Ibid.
6   Ibid.
7   Ibid.
8   Ibid.
9   Ibid., p. 4.
10   Ibid.
11   Maltby L. (1999). Drug testing: A bad investment. [online version]. New York: American Civil Liberties Union.
12   Greenwood M. (2003, April 1). "False positives." PRIMEDIA Business Magazines & Media, Inc. Retrieved from Lexis Nexis Academic database.
13   Sullum J. (2003). *Saying no*. New York: Penguin.

14 Schlosser E. (2003). *Reefer madness*. Boston: Houghton Mifflin

15 Ibid.

16 Ibid.

17 Ibid.

18 "From wife-beaters to drunk drivers, Congress is a crime wave." (1999, September 2). *The Libertarian Party*. Retrieved October 23, 2003 from http://archive.lp.org/rel/19990902-Congress.html.

19 Maltby, (1999), op. cit.

20 Ibid.

21 Ibid.

22 Greenwood, (2003), op. cit.

23 www.4cleanp.com.

24 Maltby, (1999), op. cit.

25 Ibid.

26 Ibid.

27 Ibid.

28 Schlosser, (2003), op. cit.

29 Greenwood, (2003), op. cit.

30 Maltby, (1999), op. cit.

31 Greenwood, (2003), op. cit.

32 Ibid.

33 Ibid.

34 Maltby, (1999), op. cit.

35 Hawkins D. (1997, June 23). "A Bloody mess at one federal lab." *U.S. News and World Report*, pp. 26-27.

36 Orr G. (2000, October). "The *Knox v. Knox* decision and drug testing for public school employees: Why educators do not shed their rights at the schoolhouse gate." *Journal of Law and Education*, 29(4), p. 548.

37 Ibid.

38 Ibid.

39 Ibid., p. 551.

40 Ibid., p. 551.

41 Meyer P. (2003, May 19). "Student drug testing not effective in reducing drug use." The University of Michigan News and Information Services.

42 Ibid.

43 Lorenz, B. (2004, June 4). "'Drug Czar' backs random testing at Pawaukee High School." *GMToday Online*. Retrieved from www.gmtoay.com/news/local_stories/2004/June_04/06042004_03.asp

44 Office of National Drug Control Policy. (2003). "What you need to know about drug testing in schools." Available from www.sportsafe.com, p. i.

45 "National leadership supporters of drug testing." Retrieved April 9, 2003 from www.studentdrugtesting.org/National%20Leadership%20Support%20of%20SDT.htm.

46 Meyer, (2003), op. cit.

47 Ibid.

48 Winter G. (2003, May 17). "Study finds no sign that testing deters students' drug use." *The New York Times*, Section A, p. 1.

49   Ibid., p. 1.
50   Goldberg L et al. (2003). "Drug testing athletes to prevent substance abuse:
     Background and pilot study results of the SATURN (student athletes testing
     using random notification) study." *Journal of Adolescent Health, 32,* pp. 16-25.
51   Winter, (2003), op. cit., p. 1.
52   Denniston L. (2002, March 20). "Justice Kennedy attacks student's views." *The
     Boston Globe* [online version]. Retrieved March 20, 2002 from
     www.boston.com/dailyglobe2/...kennedy_attacks_student_s_views.html.
53   "ACLU sues Michigan community schools over drug testing policy." (2000,
     March 28). *American Civil Liberties Union Freedom Network* [online version].
     Retrieved November 19, 2000 from www.aclu.org/news/2000/n032800c.html.
54   Naylor A Gardner D & Zaichowsky L. (Winter, 2001). "Drug use patterns
     among high school athletes and nonathletes." *Adolescence, 36,* pp. 627-39.
55   Ibid., p. 5.
56   Hawkins D. (1999, May 31). "Trial by vial." *U.S. News and World Report,
     126*(21), pp. 70-3.
57   Greenhouse L. (2002, March 20). "Supreme court seems ready to extend school
     drug tests." *The New York Times* [online version]. Retrieved March 21, 2002 from
     www.nytimes.com/2002/03/20/national/20SCOT.html.
58   Hawkins, (1999), op. cit.
59   Ibid., p. 70.
60   Ibid.
61   www.passkit.com.
62   www.4cleanp.com.
63   Hawkins, (1999), op. cit., p. 72.
64   Hyman I & Snook P. (1999). *Dangerous schools.* San Francisco: Jossey Bass.
65   Ibid.
66   Hawkins, (1999), op. cit.
67   Ibid.
68   Ibid.
69   Ibid.
70   Ibid.
71   "Suspicionless drug testing in schools."(1997, July 19). Retrieved April 19, 2002
     from www.drugs.indiana.edu/issues/suspicionless.html.
72   Hawkins, (1999), op. cit.
73   Hyman & Snook, (1999), op. cit.
74   www.psychemedics.com.
75   "Drug wipes can prove guilt...or innocence." Retrieved July 29, 2003 from
     www.channelcincinnati.com/news/2319076/detail.html.
76   www.datia.org.
77   Hawkins, (1999), op. cit.
78   Ibid.
79   Office of National Drug Control Policy, (2003), op. cit.
80   www.studentdrugtesting.org.
81   W.M Todd, et al. v. Rush County schools, et al. Retrieved October 22, 2001
     from http://caselaw.lp.fi...arch&case=/uscircs/7th/972548.html.
82   Ibid.
83   Ibid.

84 Ibid.

85 Ibid.

86 Roberts N & Fossey R. (2002, April). "Random drug testing of students: Where will the line be drawn?" *Journal of Law and Education*, pp. 191-208.

87 Ibid.

88 "Students and parents challenge 'rumor mill' drug testing at Maryland High School." (2000, May 2). *American Civil Liberties Union Freedom Network* [online version]. Retrieved November 19, 2001 from www.aclu.org/news/2000/n050200b.html.

89 Hyman & Snook, (1999), op. cit, p. 126.

90 Ibid., p. 126.

91 "Some schools testing students for tobacco use." (2002, October 8). Retrieved July 20, 2003 from www.jointogether.org/sa/news/summaries/reader/0,1854,554674,00.html.

92 Ibid.

93 "Indiana school curtails nicotine testing." (2003, July 16). Retrieved July 20, 2003 from
    www.jointogether.org/sa/news/summaries/reader/0,1854,565121,00.html.

94 Roberts & Fossey, (2002), op. cit., p. 200.

95 Ibid.

96 Ibid.

97 James Randall Willis II, etc. v. Anderson Community School Corporation. Retrieved October 22, 2001 from http://laws.lp.findlaw.com/7th/981227.html, p. 2.

98 Ibid.

99 Ibid., p. 3.

100 Ibid., p. 3.

101 Ibid., p. 6

102 Ibid., p. 6.

103 Roberts & Fossey (2002), op. cit., p. 204.

104 "Privacy in America: Workplace drug testing." (1997). *American Civil Liberties Union Freedom Network* [online version]. Retrieved December 4, 2000 from www.aclu.org/library/pbr5.html.

105 Hawkins, (1999), op. cit.

106 Ibid.

107 Fields-Meyer T. (2000, August 21). "He just said no." *People Weekly*, *54*(8), pp. 77-8.

108 Ibid.

109 Boire R. (2002, November/December). "Dangerous lessons." *The Humanist*, pp.39-40.

110 Ibid., p. 39.

111 Taras H. (2003, May 22). "Drug testing in schools: Can it cause harm?" *The San Diego Union-Tribune*, p. B-11.

112 Casella R. (2001). *At zero tolerance: Punishment, preventions, and school violence*. New York: Peter Lang, p. 54.

113 Chambers R, Taylor J & Potenza M. (2003). "Developmental neurocircuitry of motivation in adolescence: A critical period of addiction vulnerability." *American Journal of Psychiatry*, *160*(6), pp. 1041-1052.

114   Boire, (2002), op. cit., p. 40.
115   Hood J. (2003, July 21). "Bret Harte High officials consider controversial plan to
      test student-athletes for recreational drugs." *The Modesto Bee* [online version], p.
      3.
116   Greenwood, (2003), op. cit., p. 3.

Chapter Seven

1   "National Leadership Supporters of Student Drug Testing." Accessed April 9,
      2003 from
      www.studentdrugtesting.org/National%20Leadership%20Support%20of%20SDT.
      html.
2   Ibid.
3   Hawkins D. (1999). Trial by vial. *U.S. News and World Report, 126*(21), pp. 70-
      3, p. 70.
4   Pfohl S. (1994). *Images of deviance and social control.* New York: McGraw-Hill.
5   Ibid.
6   Garland D. (1990). *Punishment and modern society.* Chicago: The University of
      Chicago Press.
7   Pfohl, (1994), op.cit.
8   Ibid.
9   Ibid., p. 88.
10   Fass S & Pi C. (2002). Getting tough on juvenile crime: An analysis of costs
      and benefits. *Journal of Research in Crime and Delinquency, 39*(4), pp. 363-99.
11   Pfohl, (1994), op. cit.
12   Pogarsky G & Piquero A.(2003). Can punishment encourage offending?
      Investigating the 'resetting' effect. *Journal of Research in Crime and Delinquency,
      40*(1), pp. 95-120.
13   Ibid.
14   Ibid.
15   Pfohl, (1994), op. cit.
16   Schwartz R & Rieser L. (2001). Zero tolerance and mandatory sentencing. Pp. .
      p. 31.
17   Nagin D & Pogarsky G. (2003). An experimental investigation of deterrence:
      Cheating, self-serving bias, and impulsivity. *Criminology, 41*(1), pp. 167-191.
18   Ibid.
19   Ibid.
20   Sughrue J (2003). Zero tolerance for children: Two wrongs do not make a right.
      Educational Administration Quarterly, 39(2), pp. 238-58, p. 239.
21   Braithwaite J. (1989). *Crime, shame and reintegration.* Cambridge: Cambridge
      University Press.
22   Ibid., p. 69.
23   Ibid., p. 72.
24   Males M. (1999). *Framing youth.* Monroe, Maine: Common Courage.
25   Ibid.
26   Ibid.
27   Ibid.

28   Dohrn B. (2001). "Look out kid, it's something you did": Zero tolerance for children. Pp. 89-113. In Ayers W Dohrn B & Ayers R. *Zero tolerance.* New York: The New Press.

29   Akom A. (2001). Racial profiling at school: The politics of race and discipline at Berkeley High. Pp. 51-63. In Ayers W Dohrn B & Ayers R. *Zero tolerance.* New York: The New Press.

30   Dohrn, (2001), op. cit.

31   Landis B. (June 1, 2003). Minorities more likely to be searched in traffic stops. *Providence Journal-Bulletin,* p. A-01.

32   Ibid.

33   Ibid., p. A-01.

34   www.gsparish.org/Handbook/Handbook/Rules% 20and%20Regulations/search_policies.htm.

35   Rolison M. (2002). Factors influencing adolescents' decisions to engage in risk-taking behavior. *Adolescence, 37*(147), pp. 585-597.

36   Post, T. (2003, October 9). "Cold Spring discusses tighter school security." *Minnesota Public Radio.* Retrieved June 5, 2004 from http://news.minnesota.publicradio.org/features/2003/10/09_postt_coldspgsecurity/

37   Males, (1999), op. cit.

38   Zero tolerance raises equity concerns across nation. *Mobilization for Equity Newsletter, Issue 5.* Available from www.ncas1.org/mfenews5.html.

39   Harris, Duncan, & Boisjoly, (2002), op. cit.

40   Bonilla D (Ed.). (2000). *School violence.* New York: W.H Freeman and Company, p. 196.

41   Braithwaite, (1989), op. cit.

42   Casella R. (2001). *At zero tolerance: Punishment, prevention and school violence.* New York: Peter Lang.

43   "Study: Teens not pressured to use drugs." (July 8, 2003). *Join together online.* Available from www.jointogether.org/sa/news/summaries/reader/0%2C1854%.

44   Aaronson E. (2000). *Nobody left to hate: Teaching compassion after Columbine.* New York: W.H Freeman and Company, p. 70.

45   DiGuilio C. (2001).*Educate, medicate or litigate?* Thousand Oaks: Corwin.

46   "Columbine jocks safely resume bullying." *The Onion, 35*(32). Available from www.theonion.com/onion3532/columbine-jocks.html.

47   Katz J. (2000). *Geeks* New York: Villard..

48   Hawkins, (1999), op. cit.

49   Greenhouse L. (March 20, 2002). Supreme Court seems ready to extend school drug testing. *New York Times on the web.* Available from www.nytimes.com/00.03/20/national/20SCOT.htnl.

50   Carpico M. (February 19, 2003). Boards considers revising drug-testing proposal. *Pittsburgh Post-Gazette,* p. N-6.

51   Ibid.

52   Bonilla, (2000), op. cit.

53   Post, (2003), op. cit.

54   See www.supermetaldetectors.com an www.garrett.com.

55   www.interquestk9.org.

56   "Six strip-searched students receive $30,000 in Virginia." (November 19, 1997). *ACLU Freedom Network* [online edition]. Retrieved November 7, 2000 from

        www.aclu.org/news/n111997a.html.
57   Wood D. (January 10, 2002). Recession snaps school budgets. *Christian Science Monitor* [online edition]. Available from www.csmonitor.com/2002/0110/p1s1-ussm.html.
58   Ibid.
59   Ydstie J. (April 22, 2003). Tough choices in state budgeting on education. *Talk of the Nation-National Public Radio*. Available from Lexis Nexis Academic database.
60   Ibid.
61   Ydstie, (2003), op. cit.
62   Ibid.
63   McKenzie, J. (June 2003). "Not One Dime!" *No Child Left.Com*. Retrieved June 5, 2004 from http://nochildleft.com/2003/jun03dime.html
64   Gamble C. (March 8, 1995). Districts weigh paying students for tips on crime. *Education Week, 14*(24), pp. 8-10.
65   Garland, (1990), op. cit., p. 73.
66   Ibid.
67   Akom, (2001), op. cit., p. 59.
68   Redden J. (2000). *Snitch culture*. Los Angeles: Feral House, p. 54.
69   Garland, (1990), op. cit., p. 187.

Chapter Eight

1   Jonsson P. (March 4, 2003). "Before you suspend me, can I call a lawyer?" *Christian Science Monitor*, p. 21.
2   Hyman I & Snook P. (1999). *Dangerous schools* .San Francisco: Jossey-Bass, p. 127.
3   *In re Patrick* 124 Md. App. 604; 723 A. 2d 523; 1999 Md. App. LEXIS 14. Retrieved from Lexis Nexis Academic database.
4   Beger R. (2002). "Expansion of police power in public schools and the vanishing rights of students." *Social Justice, 29*(1-2), 119-130, pp. 119-20.
5   Doctor D (July 22, 1999). "Student fights expulsion and 'zero tolerance' drug policy." *Libertarian Rock*. Retrieved September 10, 2003 from www.libertarian-rock.com/topics/school/zero_tolerance_car_seeds.html.
6   Beger, (2002), op. cit.
7   Holloway J. (December 2001/January 2002). "The dilemma of zero tolerance." *Educational Leadership*, pp. 84-85.
8   Burkett E. (2002). *Another planet*. New York: Perennial.
9   Holloway, (2001-02), op. cit.
10   Reno J Smalley S & Figueroa A (March 19, 2001). "Using students as metal detectors." *Newsweek, 137*(12), 28-30, p. 28.
11   www.landmarkcases.org/newjersey.html.
12   Dohrn B. (2001). "Look out kid, it's something you did: Zero tolerance for children." Pp. 89-113. In Ayers W Dohrn B & Ayers R. *Zero tolerance*. New York: The New Press., p. 97.
13   Ibid., p. 97.
14   Ibid., p. 98.

15   "Chicago teacher loses job for firing cap gun in class." (September 16, 2003).
     Available from www.jointogether.org/gv/news/summaries/read-
     er/0,2061,566780,00.html
16   Stefkovich J and Miller J. (Winter 1999). "Law enforcement officers in public
     schools: Student citizens in safe havens?" *Brigham Young University Education and
     Law Journal*, 25-60.
17   Beger, (2002), op. cit.
18   Ibid.
19   Ibid.
20   Ibid.
21   Lawrence R. (1998). *School crime and juvenile justice.* New York: Oxford.
22   Redden J. (2000). *Snitch culture.* Los Angeles: Feral House, p. 35.
23   Stefkovich & Miller, (1999), op. cit.
24   *People v. Overton* 24 N.Y. 2d 522; 249 N.E. 2d 366; 301 N.Y.S. 2d 479; 1969.
     LEXIS 1339. Retrieved from Lexis Nexis Academic database.
25   Cooke M. "Evaluation of the exclusionary rule." Available from http://sc.essort-
     ment.com/exclusionaryrul_rmlx.html.
26   Lynch T. (October 1, 1998). "In defense of the exclusionary rule." *Cato Policy
     Analysis No. 319.* Available from www.cato.org/pubs/pas/pa-319es.html
27   "Mugging the court: Exclusionary rule change would gut Americans' protections
     against abuses of power." (February 17, 1995). *ACLU Freedom Network Online.*
     Available from http://archive.aclu.org/news/n021795.html.
28   Ibid.
29   Stefkovich & Miller, (1999), op. cit.
30   Ibid.
31   Ibid.
32   Ibid.
33   Ibid.
34   Ibid., p. 52.
35   Beger, (2002), op. cit., p. 123.
36   Menacker J & Mertz R. (1994). "State legislative responses to school crime."
     West's Education Law Quarterly, 3(1), 57-65, p. 64.
37   Beger, (2002), op. cit.
38   Crowder C. (June 12, 2003). "Teen's drug sentence cut from 26 years to 2." *The
     Birmingham News.*
39   Alexander K & Alexander M. (1998). *American public school law, fourth edition.*
     Belmont, CA: Wadsworth.
40   Ibid.
41   Ibid.
42   Lawrence, (1999), op. cit.
43   *Goss v. Lopez* 419 U.S. 565. LEXIS 23. Retrieced from Lexis Nexis Academic
     database.
44   Ibid.
45   Sughrue, J. (April 2003). "Zero tolerance for children: Two wrongs do not make
     a right." *Educational Administration Quarterly*, 39(2), 238-58, p. 250.
46   Ibid., p. 250.
47   Alexander & Alexander, (1998), op. cit.
48   Ibid.

49   Collins M & Dowell M. (November/December 1998). "Discipline and due process." *Thrust for Educational Leadership, 28*(2).

50   Johnson V. (2001). "Decatur: A story of intolerance." Pp. 64-76. In Ayers W Dohrn B & Ayers R. *Zero tolerance*. New York: The New Press.

51   Bowman D. (April 10, 2002). "Interpretations of 'zero tolerance" vary." *Education Week, 21*(30).

52   Johnson, (2001), op. cit.

53   Sughrue, (2003), op. cit. p. 251.

54   "ABA recommends ending 'zero tolerance' policies in schools." (February 21, 2001). *Jefferson City News Tribune* [online edition]. Available from www.newstribune.com/stories/022101/wor_0221010033.asp

55   Schwartz R & Rieser L. (2001). "Zero tolerance as mandatory sentencing." Pp. 126-135. . In Ayers W Dohrn B & Ayers R. *Zero tolerance*. New York: The New Press., p. 132.

56   Doctor, (1999), op. cit., p. 1.

57   "Bill of Rights pared down to a manageable six." (December 18, 2002). *The Onion, 38*(47). Available from www.theonion.com/onion3847/bill_of_rights.html

58   Sherman L. (2002). "Learning police ethics." Pp. 145-157. In *Crime and justice in America, second edition*. Upper Saddle River, New Jersey: Prentice Hall, p. 150.

59   Dohrn, (2001), op. cit.

60   Tiggre D. (December 12, 1999). "Mosaic 2000: Weeding out troublemakers." *Spintech*. Retrieved August 13, 2003 from www.spintechmag.com/9912/dt1299.htm, p. 1.

61   Ibid.

62   Ibid., p. 2.

63   Ibid., p. 2.

64   Ibid.

65   Bowman, (2002), op. cit.

66   Sarvate S. (May 28, 2002). "Due process suspended for school kids." *Alternet.org*. Available from www.alternet.org/story.html.

67   Mitchie G (2001). "Ground zero." Pp. 3-14. In Ayers W Dohrn B & Ayers R. *Zero tolerance*. New York: The New Press.

68   "Students and parents challenge 'rumor mill' drug testing at Maryland High School." (May 2, 2000). *ACLU Freedom Network*[online]. Available from www.aclu.org/news/2000/n050200b.html, p. 2.

69   Webber J. (2001). *Failure to hold: The politics of school violence*. Lanham, Maryland: Rowman & Littlefield.

70   Burkett (2002), op. cit., p. 59.

71   Ibid.

72   Spina S. (Ed.). (2000). *Smoke and mirrors: The hidden context of violence in schools and society*. Lanham, Maryland: Rowman & Littlefield.

73   Hyman & Snook, (1999), op. cit., p. 87.

74   Ibid.

75   Alexander & Alexander, (1999), op. cit.

76   Ibid.

77   Neal M. (1999). "Does the fifth circuit diss qualified immunity." Available from www.schoollawsection.org/qualifiedimmunity.html

78 Ibid., p. 5.

79 *Jenkins v. Talladega* 115 F. 3d 821; 1997 U. S. App. LEXDIS 12658. Retrieved from Lexis Nexis Academic database.

80 Hyman & Snook, (1999), op. cit., p. 80.

Chapter Nine

1 McDaniel T. (1989). "Demilitarizing public education: School reform in the era of George Bush." *Phi Delta Kappan*, 15-19, p. 15.

2 Ibid.

3 Fogarty B. (2000). *War, peace, and the social order*. Boulder, CO: Westview, p. 83

4 Kraska P. (2001). *Militarizing the American criminal justice system*. Boston: Northeastern University Press.

5 Elikann P. (1999). *Superpredators: The demonization of our children by the law*. New York: Insight books.

6 Best J. (1999). *Random violence: How we talk about new crimes and new victims*. Berkeley, CA: University of California Press.

7 Kraska, (2001), op. cit.

8 Cooke D. (1998). Nuclear issues. In Hicks D. (Ed.). *Education for peace: Issues, principles, and practices in the classroom*. London: Routledge.

9 Reardon B. (1988). *Comprehensivepeaceeducation*. NewYork: Teachers College.

10 Eisler R. (2000). *Tomorrow's children*. Boulder, CO: Westview, p. xvi.

11 Merryfinch L. (1981). Militarization/Civilization. In Chapkis W. (Ed.). *Loaded questions: Women in the military*. Amsterdam: Transnational Institute.

12 Caulfield S. (2001). Militarism, feminism, and criminal justice: Challenging institutionalized ideologies. In Kraska P. (Ed.). *Militarizing the American criminal justice system*. Boston: Northeastern University Press.

13 Marullo S. (1993. *Ending the cold war at home*. New York: Lexington.

14 Sherry M.(1995). *In the shadow of war: The United States since the 1930s*. New Haven, Connecticut: Yale University Press.

15 Kraska P. (1999). Militarizing criminal justice: Exploring the possibilities. *Journal of Political and Military Sociology*, 27, 205-215, p. 206.

16 Caulfield S. (1999). Transforming the criminological dialogue: A feminist perspective on the impact of militarism. *Journal of Political and Military Sociology*, 27, 291-306, p. 299.

17 Ibid., p. 297.

18 Hooks b. (1995). "Feminism and militarism: A comment." *Women's Studies Quarterly*, 3 & 4, 58-64, p. 63.

19 Reardon, (1988, op. cit.

20 Caulfield (1999), op. cit.

21 Kraska (1999), op. cit.

22 Redden (2000), op. cit, p. 101.

23 Kappeler V Blumberg M and Potter G. (2000). *The mythology of crime and criminal justice*. Prospect Heights, Illinois: Waveland, p. 9.

24 Kraska (1999), op. cit., p. 219.

25 Ibid., p. 210.

26   Ibid., p. 210.
27   Retrieved October 19, 2003 from www.costofwar.com.
28   "Ashcroft wants reports on lenient sentencing." (2003, August 14). Retrieved
     August 19, 2003 from www.jointogether.org/sa/news/summaries/read-
     er/0,1854,56625,00.html.
29   Kraska (1999), op. cit., pp. 208-9.
30   Simon J. (2001). "Sacrificing Private Ryan: The military model and the new
     penology. In Kraska P. *Militarizing criminal justice*. Boston: Northeastern
     University Press, p. 107.
31   Smith D. (1997). De-militarizing language." *The Peace Magazine* [online ver-
     sion]. Retrieved January 8, 2001 from
     www.peacemagazine.org/9707/language.htm.
32   Orwell G. (1949). *1984*. New York: Harcourt Brace Jovanovich.
33   Beger R. (2002). "Expansion of police power in public schools and the vanishing
     rights of students." *Social Justice*, 29(1-2), p. 124.
34   Devine J. (1996). *Maximum security*. London: University of Chicago Press, p. 95.
35   Kraska (1999), op. cit.
36   Hersch P. (1998). *A tribe apart*. New York: Ballantine, p.73.
37   Finley L. (2003). "Militarism goes to school." *Essays in Education*,p. 4.
38   Crews G & Tipton J. (2001). "A comparison of public schools and prison securi-
     ty measures: Too much of a good thing?" Retrieved January 8, 2001 from
     www.kci.org/publication/articles/school_security_measures.html., p. 2.
39   Eisler (2000), op. cit., p. 12.
40   Ibid.
41   Ibid., p. 205.
42   Sizer T & Sizer N. (1999). *The students are watching*. Boston: Beacon Press, p.
     105.
43   ackson P. (1983). The daily grind. In Giroux H & Purpel D. (Eds.). *The hidden
     curriculum and moral education*. Berkeley: McCutchan Publishing Corporation.
44   Smith (1997),op. cit., p. 2.
45   Skiba R & Peterson R. (1999, January). The dark side of zero tolerance. *Phi
     Delta Kappan*, 372-382.
46   Casella R (2001). *"Being down": Challenging violence in urban schools*. New York:
     Teachers College, p. 35.
47   Ibid., p. 167.
48   Finley, (2003), op. cit.
49   Holtzman L. (2000). *Media messages*. Armonk, New York: M. E. Sharpe, p. 26.
50   Loewen J. (1994). *Lies my teacher told me*. New York: Touchstone, p. 307.
51   Killingbeck D. (2001). "The role of television news in the construction of school
     violence as a 'moral panic'." *Journal of Criminal Justice and Popular Culture*, 8(3),
     186-202, p. 189.
52   Thompson K. (1998). *Moral panics*. London: Routledge.
53   Goode E & Ben-Yehuda N. (1994). *Moral panics: The social construction of
     deviance*. Oxford: Blackwell.
54   bid.
55   Thompson, (1998), op. cit.
56   Ibid.
57   Goode & Ben-Yehuda, (1994), op. cit.

58   Kappeler Blumberg & Potter, (2000), op. cit.

59   Males M. (1999). *Framing youth*. Monroe, Maine: Common Courage Press, p. 14.

60   Ibid., pp.

61   Ibid.

62   Males (1999), op. cit.

63   Giroux H. (2000). "Representations of violence, popular culture, and the demonization of youth." In Spina S. (Ed.). *Smoke and mirrors: The hidden context of violence in schools*. (Pp.93-105). Lanham, Massachusetts: Rowman & Littlefield.

64   Glassner B. (1999). *The culture of fear: Why Americans are afraid of the wrong things*. New York: Basic Books.

65   Males, (1999), op. cit.

66   Ibid., p. 65.

67   Ibid., p. 59.

68   Killingbeck, (2001), op. cit., p. 195.

69   Brooks K Schiraldi V & Zeidenberg J. (1998, July). "Schoolhouse hype: Two years later." *Justice Policy Institute/Children's Law Center*. Retrieved January 8, 2001 from www.cjcj.org/schoolhousehype/shh2.html.

70   Kappeler Blumberg & Potter, (2000), op. cit.

71   Killingbeck, (2001), op. cit.

72   Robinson M. (2002). *Justice blind?* Upper Saddle River, New Jersey: Prentice Hall.

73   Males, (1999), op. cit., pp. 122 & 118.

74   Ibid., p. 105.

75   Males M. (1996). *Scapegoat generation*. Monroe, Maine: Common Courage Press, p. 22.

76   Ibid., p. 106.

77   Ibid., p. 23.

78   Ibid.

79   Glassner, (1999), op. cit.

80   Killingbeck, (2001), op. cit., p. 186.

81   DeGrandpre, R. (1999). *Ritalin Nation*. New York: W. W. Norton & Co., p. 180.

82   "Numerous factors contribute to school violence." (2003, October 1). Retrieved October 3, 2003 from www.jointogether.org/gv/news/summaries/readwer/0,2061,5670.html.

83   Kappeler Blumberg & Potter, (2000), op. cit., p. 305.

84   Rosenbaum M. (2003, September 30). "False drug information harms kids." *Seattle Post-Intelligencer*, p.2.

85   Ibid., p. 2.

86   Devine J. (1996), op. cit.,.p. 107.

87   Casella R. (2001), op. cit., p. 121.

88   Devine, (1996), op. cit.

89   Ibid.

90   Boire R. (2002, November/December). "Dangerous lessons." *The Humanist*, 39-40, p. 40.

91   Devine, (1996), op. cit.

92   Garland D. (1990). *Punishment and modern society*. Chicago: University of Chicago Press.

93 Ibid., p. 183.
94 Ibid.
95 Memmi A. (1965). *The colonizer and the colonized.* Boston: Beacon.
96 Kohn A. (1999, September). "Constant frustration and occasional violence." *American School Board Journal,* 20-24, p. 21.
97 Ibid., p. 21.
98 Ibid., p. 22.
99 Ibid., p. 22.
100 Memmi (1965), op. cit., p. 17.
101 Ibid., p. 85.
102 Kohn, (1999), op. cit., p. 22.
103 Ibid., p. 23.
104 Garland, (1990), op. cit.
105 Casella, (1999), *Being down,* op. cit., p. 44.
106 Devine, (1996), op. cit.
107 Boire, (2002), op. cit., p. 39.
108 Rosen J. (2000). *The unwanted gaze.* New York: Random House.

About the Authors

Laura L. Finley, Ph.D.

Laura holds a Ph.D. in Sociology from Western Michigan University. Her primary areas of study include juvenile and school violence. She has been published in numerous journals about such topics as privacy rights, crime and race in the media, perceptions of school violence, and peace education. Prior to working in higher education Laura was a high school social studies teacher for six years.

Peter S. Finley

A former high school teacher and track and field coach, Peter Finley received an Excellence in Education Significant Educator award in 1998. Peter is currently a doctoral candidate in Sport Administration at the University of Northern Colorado and works with the Sport Marketing Research Institute. He was elected to the student board of the North American Society for Sport Management in 2004.